P9-CBC-128

Praise for Pamela Paul's

The Starter Marriage
and the Future of Matrimony

"Well-written and intelligent. . . . The real strength of this book lies in its very thoughtful and original analysis of how the social revolutions of the 1960s and early 1970s—and the radical upswing in divorce in particular—played out in the hearts and minds of the children who witnessed them." —*The Washington Post*

"Paul knows her territory. . . . The author calls her book turning 'lemons into lemonade.' . . . A young reader thinking about marriage would be smart to buy a glass." —Cleveland *Plain Dealer*

"The starter marriage, which lasts only a short time and ends before children begin, is, Ms. Paul concludes, a new demographic phenomenon. . . . One strength of Ms. Paul's book is that she does not see the problem as one of over-arching expectations matched by lack of fibre or simple immaturity. Another great virtue is her refusal to be pigeonholed into any simple political agenda. Her book will be a lesson to those contemplating marriage and a comfort to those who falter."

—*The Economist*

"There are no easy answers, of course, but Paul's willingness to pose [provocative questions] makes *Starter Marriage* a worthy read."

—*Austin American-Statesman*

"Paul is good at the 'we' voice—she's been there, done that. Her book is perfect for a heterosexual college student or a parent of one." —*Publishers Weekly*

"The child generation that grew up with divorce is becoming an adult generation that is rediscovering commitment, as America transits from the nineties to the Oh-Ohs. In this useful book, Pamela Paul helps us understand how and why, on the brink of midlife, this previously hard-to-pin-down generation is at long last getting pinned down."

—William Strauss, coauthor of *Generations*, *13th Gen*, *The Fourth Turning*, and *Millennials Rising*

"I have a 17-year-old daughter and a 22-year-old son. I intend to have both of them read this book."

—*The Providence Journal*

"A thorough and insightful look at our ongoing 'matrimania,' and the pressures and self-deceits it engenders." —*Seattle Weekly*

PAMELA PAUL is currently an editor at *American Demographics* magazine, where she reports on social, political, and media trends. She is also a frequent New York correspondent for *The Economist*. In addition, her work has appeared in magazines such as *Elle*, *Redbook*, and *Time Out New York*. Her own starter marriage ended in 1999.

The Starter Marriage

and the

Future of Matrimony

Random House Trade Paperbacks
New York

The Starter Marriage

and the

Future of Matrimony

Pamela Paul

To my parents

2003 Random House Trade Paperback Edition

Copyright © 2002 by Pamela Paul

All rights reserved under International and Pan-American Copyright
Conventions. Published in the United States by Random House Trade
Paperbacks, a division of Random House, Inc., New York, and
simultaneously in Canada by Random House of Canada Limited, Toronto.

RANDOM HOUSE TRADE PAPERBACKS and colophon are trademarks
of Random House, Inc.

This work was originally published in hardcover by Villard Books in 2002.

Library of Congress Cataloging-in-Publication Data
Paul, Pamela.
The starter marriage and the future of matrimony /
Pamela Paul.
p.   cm.
Originally published: New York: Villard Books, c2002.
Includes bibliographical references and index.
ISBN 0-8129-6676-7 (pbk.)
1. Marriage—United States. 2. Divorce—United States. 3. Remarriage—
United States. 4. Young adults—United States. 4. Generation X—
United States. I. Title.
HQ536 .P378 2003
306.81—dc21   2002026588

Random House website address: www.atrandom.com

Printed in the United States of America

2 4 6 8 9 7 5 3 1

Book design by Meryl Sussman Levavi/Digitext

Contents

Introduction

Saying "I Do" Is Easy to Do

BEFORE I GOT DIVORCED, I GOT MARRIED FOREVER. I was twenty-seven and in love. I'd been engaged for longer than a year and had planned my wedding over the course of eleven blissful, intoxicating months. The September ceremony took place outdoors in a reverential setting in Upstate New York, attended by supportive family and friends. Wearing flowers in my hair and a flowing white wedding gown with train, I exchanged traditional vows with my betrothed. Including the rehearsal dinner, reception, and Sunday brunch, the affair consumed an extended weekend, thousands of dollars, and a lifetime of dreams, hopes, and anticipation.

I "believed in" marriage, and I certainly did *not* believe in divorce. I was pleased to settle into my new marriage, my new life, my new me.

Three weeks shy of our first anniversary, my husband and I decided to divorce.

No one goes into a marriage expecting divorce, though as prenuptial agreements become mainstream and the failure rate hovers between 40 and 50 percent, it's clear few of us go into a marriage with what one could call realistic expectations. Yet popular culture and the attitudes of today's marrying generation belie these facts. The virtues of marriage are extolled in the public sphere and reflected in public opinion. Young people today hold marriage in unusually high regard. In a 1997 poll, nine out of ten 18- to 29-year-olds said that a happy marriage is part of their idea of "the good life"—14 percentage points higher than only six years before. (This compared with their more jaded elders: roughly 80 percent—and falling—of adults aged thirty to fifty-nine agreed.[1]) Opinion surveys show that in the minds of most twenty- and thirtysomethings, marriage ranks higher in importance than career; Gen X* considers "being a good wife/mother or husband/father" to be *the* most important sign of success—ahead of money, fame, power, religion, and being true to oneself.[2] A recent *Redbook* report, "Why Marriage Is Hot Again," gushes, "Today, for the first time since the mid-1960s, smart women in their 20s—in some cases their early 20s—are not only unafraid but *eager* to become brides." As *The New Republic* pointed out in 1996, "In the last few years, there's been a yuppie stampede to America's altars: a 1993 University of Pennsylvania study found female college graduates were marrying younger than they did in the '70s. We've always been the most marriage-happy Western country, and lately we've started to celebrate it with a vengeance."[3]

This stands in striking contrast to the behavior and attitudes of Baby Boomers and the sixties generation. The widespread introduction of the Pill and the sexual revolution, the advent of feminism and "consciousness-raising groups," and the freedoms extolled by the "Me Generation" demonstrated to women in their twenties that they didn't *have* to marry, that marriage was unnecessary. A pop-psychological shift taught men and women in their thirties that if their marriage wasn't serving them well, it was

---

* In this book, "Generation X" refers to those born between 1965 and 1978; Generation Y, sometimes called "Echo Boomers," are those born between 1979 and 1994; Boomers were born between 1946 and 1964, Matures between 1909 and 1945. Matures are further subdivided into the GI Generation (pre-1930) and the Silent Generation, 1930–45. Currently, Baby Boomers constitute 29 percent of the American population; Gen X is a mere 16 percent; and Generation Y closely follows Boomers at 26 percent.

"okay" to divorce—even better for them in the end. The underlying core value, enthusiastically embraced, was *independence.*

Be free. Listen to your heart. Do what you need to do for the sake of your own happiness. *You deserve it.* In the suburbs of the seventies, unsettling waves of divorce passed over entire communities. In my parents' circle of tennis-club members and nursery school friends, only one marriage survived past 1976, and it wasn't in my family. By the time I was four, I was spending Divorced Dad Thursdays with half my nuclear family at the local diner.

Then in the 1980s a fundamental shift began to take place. AIDS, unwed motherhood, nuclear-arms buildup, homelessness, and other signs of instability left Americans grasping for a sense of security. With Ronald Reagan and his devoted Nancy ensconced in the White House, beaming at each other on the cover of *Vanity Fair,* the country had an icon of marital stability toward which to aspire (never minding the president's early divorce). And thus the birth of "family values," promoting the virtues of matrimony and personal responsibility, was greeted with welcome relief by social conservatives, lonely *Ice Storm* divorcés, and confused recovering hippies awakening from their sixties hangovers.

If the eighties marked a rebirth of moraliticking, the nineties saw "family values" flowing freely from the ranks of the religious right to the mainstream mind-sets of the average American youth. Today few people say they *don't* believe in the ideas behind the banner of family values, even if they scoff at the political baggage surrounding the term. What's more, that once amorphous phrase is now being replaced with policy specifics—most specifically, matrimony. In 1999, when the Senate Task Force on Culture, whose function it would be to "discuss pressing societal issues such as marriage," was created by Congress, Maggie Gallagher, director of the Marriage Project at the Institute for American Values, remarked, "Hold on! Did I read that right? Yes, there it is in cold print: the M-word, marriage. This is something new. Ten years ago, marriage was seldom mentioned in political discourse. In the late 80s and early 90s, when conservatives and other concerned Americans wanted to discuss disturbing cultural trends, they usually spoke not about marriage per se, but about family breakdown, or unwed childbearing, or (more often) just welfare reform."[4] But with Americans today agreeing to ideas such as covenant marriages (new "undivorceable" unions offered in several states), marriage-training high school classes, and calls to repeal no-fault divorce laws and the so-called marriage penalty tax, the idea that Congress would create a special committee on marriage should come as no surprise.

The ideal American lifestyle has become inextricably linked to matrimony. The CEO icons of the new millennium, both male and female, contrast themselves favorably with the power-hungry bankers and single-minded career women of the eighties by proudly brandishing their wedding rings, family-friendly SUVs, and well-rounded lifestyles. They boast of achieving "balance" in their lives. When they discuss their goals and their values, they point out their overriding desire to get home to the kids at the end of the day. They express their political beliefs by paying tribute to family and "the next generation."

One wonders why the voices of traditionalism continue to drone on censoriously at a generation that only nods in assent. Today's youth certainly doesn't need to hear these lectures. On the television show *Once and Again,* it's the parents who talk about the need to take care of themselves and pursue their own happiness, while the children lament their elders' sexuality and selfishness. In a 1999 poll more Boomers than Gen Xers agreed with the following statement: "People should live for themselves rather than their children."5 Perhaps Gen X is exercising a resentful revenge.

Gen X rebellions have turned out to be quite different from the brazen revolutions that came before them. After all, rebellion must acquire a new definition for a generation whose predecessors were the ultimate rebels. Today's twentysomethings show their parents that they are *not like them* by sidling up to the very institutions their parents neglected or debunked. And then they go one step further and prove they're better at the good life than their parents ever were.

Young Americans certainly continue to revere marriage, with the percentage of twentysomethings who value marriage as a personal goal having steadily increased since the 1980s. In a 1995 poll, Gen Xers overwhelmingly favored family over career. Over

half said they respect women who devote themselves wholeheartedly to their families (53 percent) compared with only one third
(33 percent) who respect those who devote themselves to career.[6]
Peggy Orenstein found in her book *Flux* that women "hadn't lost
faith in the idea of good marriages, and they fully expected their
own unions to last."[7] And in a March 2000 poll, 86 percent of
Americans responded yes when asked, "If you got married today,
would you expect to stay married for the rest of your life?"[8]

In its 1998 report, "Time to Repaint the Gen X Portrait," the
Yankelovich research firm warns, "Expect Gen Xers to place para-
mount importance on family togetherness."[9] Clearly Xers want to
build their own happy families. They aspire to more children than
their predecessors; 63 percent believe that "the good life" means
having two or more kids.[10] Over half claim that they get most or all
of their satisfaction from home and family, rather than from away-
from-home activities like work or friends.[11] Gen X's family ideals
remain traditional in several ways. Of those surveyed, 92 percent
believed that "it's critical for children today to have activities that
anchor them to their families, like regular sit-down family meals
or weekly religious services." Eighty-five percent believe "people
should pass on to their children a sense of belonging to a particular religion or racial or national tradition," and 83 percent felt that
"even though men have changed a lot, women are still the main
nurturers."

Today's twentysomethings look down on the radical lifestyles
of a rebellious yesteryear. Despite the commotion of the sexual
revolution, nobody is rushing into open marriages. According to a
1998 NBC/*Wall Street Journal* poll, 90 percent of Americans believe that extramarital affairs are "always wrong" or "almost always
wrong," up from the 1970s and 1980s,[12] and Gen X disapproves of
adultery to the same extent that their parents and grandparents
did.[13] In 1972, 10 percent of eighteen-to-twenty-four-year-olds considered premarital sex wrong; by 1998, the number had more than
doubled to 23 percent.[14] They may be criticized for their casual sex
lifestyles, but Gen Xers are very romantically inclined, believing in
"love at first sight" to a greater degree than their elders.[15]

It seems the pundits who badmouth today's supposed slackers
fail to recognize that if Gen Xers were to rebel, they would rebel

against the "loose morals" and free habits of Baby Boomers. Yet pundits continue to express astonishment when, in a highly publicized 1999 Gallup poll, the supposedly spoiled and dissipated Generation Y (the sons and daughters of those crazy Boomers) overwhelmingly told pollsters that they believe in God, marriage, and the institution of family.[16] *American Demographics* magazine notes that the typical Gen Yer is "in many ways more idealistic than his Baby Boomer parents ever were, at least when it comes to matters of the heart—and more conservative too."[17] In fact, in many respects, Gen X and Gen Y values tend to echo those of their parents' parents. In a poll taken in 1977, when Boomers were in their twenties, 56 percent desired a "return to traditional family life"; contrast that with the 74 percent of Generation X respondents who agreed with that statement in 1999.[18] And compare their responses to the following questions:

	Boomers Then	Gen X Today
Would you like a return to traditional parental responsibility?	47%	68%[19]
Would you like a return to traditional homemaking?	16%	39%
Having a child is an experience everyone should have	45%	68%

Source: Yankelovich.

According to the Census Bureau, about half of Gen X was married as of 1999, and by 2001, two thirds will have walked down the aisle. The bureau predicts a continued upswing through 2010, when 85 percent will have gotten married. Gen X is embracing matrimony, and it looks like Gen Y will join them in their cheerful march down the aisle. The 1997 issue of the *Cassandra Report,* an influential youth-trend-tracking publication, calls marriage for women aged nineteen to twenty-four one of the newest "things to do."

While the average age of women entering marriage has not significantly altered over the past one hundred years (it dipped sharply midcentury to 20.1 years and has now risen to age twenty-five, compared with twenty-two in 1890),[20] what *has* changed are the attitudes surrounding marriage. In 1890 women had little choice but to enter into marriage in their twenties; today, with the benefits wrought by the women's movement and economic advancement, women have the choice not to marry but do so nonetheless.

In recent books and magazine articles, marriage is hailed and divorce decried; one is plainly good, while the other is bad. Nuance, exceptions, and questioning are all firmly discouraged. "Angry," "outdated" feminists have been replaced by new, media-friendly "mavericks," many of whom have spoken out full force in favor of modesty, early marriage, "surrendering" to marriage, and restricted divorce while arguing fervently against the sexual freedoms attained by the women's movement. Their formulaic dictums and oversimplified moralizations are replete with dire warnings that women aren't getting married fast enough; by delaying vows until our thirties we're waiting too long and may lose out altogether. There's a kind of circular logic to their entreaties: panic now or you'll panic later.

Yet the basis and tenor of such arguments fail to resonate with most women today, even as they obsess over finding Mr. Right and enter wholeheartedly into early marriage. Such arguments ignore the fact that most young women, in fact, agree with their diagnoses of the difficulties of modern romance and with the desirability of their marital solutions, but often for very different reasons. Gen X women want what they want because it's their right to want it—not because they're "supposed" to. Both men and women today marry because they can—not because they must.

A 1997 *New York* magazine report, "Early to Wed," asks, "Why are so many women barely out of Barnard now becoming altar girls before they've earned their first promotion?"[21] Several theories float around to explain why young women and men today overwhelmingly believe in marriage—and in marrying relatively young. One popular hypothesis suggests that we are witnessing a search for stability in an era of instability. The "Free to Be You and Me" generation yearning for some ground rules, a measure of control, a way of grabbing on to something solid and secure amid the overwhelming range of options seemingly on offer.

Another possible motive, less discussed, focuses on the desire to create a safe launching pad from which to mount a career or pursue other goals—a sort of "one down, one to go" strategy of setting up shop before getting one's life into order. Check marriage off the list, and then full speed ahead. In a 1995 *Newsweek* column, "I'm Not Sick, I'm Just in Love," twenty-three-year-old Barnard grad Katherine Davis grumbled, "Marrying 'early' before a career has caused a furor among my friends." For Davis, getting married at twenty-three did not mean giving up her career. "My engagement has made me no less ambitious, hardworking—or a feminist," she explained. "Soon I'll be his blushing bride. And my rosy complexion will be from exuberance—not embarrassment."[22] A 1999 article in *Redbook,* entitled "Why Confidence Soars After Marriage," illustrates this phenomenon: "My friend Louise got married when she was 20—a decision that, most of us might predict, would put a serious damper on her professional ambitions. But we would be wrong. In fact, her career caught fire after her wedding."[23]

Another theory suggests that we harbor nostalgia for an era we never experienced, that the ideals of the *Leave It to Beaver* period propel Generation X toward the coveted icons of a bygone never-never land. We seem to have developed heightened expectations of marriage, which have flourished untempered by front-row seats to the realities of lifelong marital relationships. Compared with 18 percent of Boomers and 10 percent of Matures, one in three Gen Xers had parents who divorced before they hit age seventeen; 36 percent of these divorces took place by the time the child was five years old.[24] Perhaps, as the children of the first generation for whom divorce was accepted and common, we don't know just how bad marriage can get if you stay in an unhappy one long enough.

Certainly popular culture, in framing our unrealistic expectations of marriage, plays a role in generating the ideals to which we aspire. A 1999 issue of *Cosmopolitan* riles up anxious readers in an article called "When Should You Marry": "In the United States, the 20s are the picture-perfect decade for saying I do. The farther you stray from that magic era, the more freakish you start to feel. An article in a 1998 issue of the Journal of Family Issues confirms that being unmarried in your 30s can be bad for your state of mind because you feel like an outcast."[25]

Could we be succumbing to this type of scare tactic, and doing so in spite of statistics that overwhelmingly show the younger you marry, the more likely you are to divorce?

Because we seem to be divorcing as quickly as we marry. Divorce is occurring progressively earlier in marriage, often within five years of the wedding day, with 25 percent after only two years.[26] A 2001 survey by the Centers for Disease Control and Prevention found that one in five first-marriage divorces occur within the first five years.[27] Americans are diving in and out of matrimony with a seeming ease that belies the premise of the institution. Is this, one wonders, how the tensions between our optimistic yearning for marriage and our darker, childhood experiences with divorce are meant to play out? We may be witnessing the inevitable clash between our false expectations and an unforgiving reality.

Perhaps today's generation, accustomed to the instantaneous results of a one-click culture, fails to recognize that the act of marriage doesn't mean a money-back guarantee of marital happiness. Studies also show that satisfaction with married life decreases significantly after the first five years; in our accelerated society, it follows that this bliss period will shorten. We may have neither the patience nor the willpower to wait it out. We who are so accustomed to and enamored with speed may not understand that marriage is a series of developments, a never-ending process that is meant to last—*gasp*—longer than college or our last job. We could be coveting something that we're simply not equipped to sustain.

Whatever the case, today's twentysomethings continue to want marriage—persist in believing in it as a personal state worth striving for—even after they divorce. The turnaround among divorcés is remarkable: people who were once married overwhelmingly remarry. In 1999, only 10 percent of Americans described themselves as divorced "last year"—because though almost half get divorced at some point, many had since remarried.[28] Divorced status is decidedly not a permanent one.

In response to this recent proliferation of brief marriages, a new term, "starter marriage," has begun to circulate. A starter marriage, one that lasts five years or less and ends before children begin, may be part of a new marital pattern, as many trend forecasters and demographers predict. If they're correct, the average number of marriages per American will increase along the lines of today's high job-turnover rate. People will slide wedding bands on and off with the same ease with which they whip out updated résumés. One might shudder at the type of future this would bring. What does this mean about the way today's marrying generation—my generation—thinks about themselves as individuals, as half of a relationship, and as members of a family?

I began thinking about these issues because I was having so much trouble processing my own marriage and divorce. I debated whether I was now a "bad" person, and if I deserved to be divorced. I wondered if I should never have gotten married and what it said about me that I had. In addition to the typical detritus of divorce— the sudden absence of a supposedly enduring love, the sense of betrayal, the rupture of trust—I was troubled by what my experience said about me as a person.

Although marriage is supposedly a personal experience, I couldn't help thinking about what other people would think. My friends, my colleagues, and especially my parents. I felt like I was supposed to prove their worries unfounded. I was haunted by the idea that I had somehow let them down.

I couldn't help placing my own experience within the larger frame of what marriage and divorce means for my generation and for society. Because though I hadn't noticed that other young people were divorced while I was married (on the contrary, it seemed like *everyone* was married or engaged at the time), once I got divorced, young ex-marrieds seemed to surface everywhere. I spot on the Open Letters website a posting that begins, "Dear L., I keep thinking of you recently. You're the only one I know roughly my age who got married and divorced all within a pretty short period of time."[29] I learn that one of my bosses had been married and divorced by thirty. A new colleague is recently divorced. A woman I meet at a cocktail party, the type who seems to have everything going her way, reveals over a subsequent dinner that she had gotten divorced at twenty-seven. "You had a starter marriage too?" she asks. I bristle at the term; it seems derogatory, dismissive, superficial. It makes my marriage sound flighty and somehow featherweight. It also has the unpleasant ring of truth.

Who were all these divorcées—and what did it mean that I was now part of their clan? Unable to come up with my own immediate answer, I tried to analyze my experience from a range of perspectives. I wondered what lessons contemporary feminists like Naomi Wolf would have to impart. Would Gloria Steinem say, "I told you so"? (Or, in light of her own recent nuptials, "Honey, you should have waited"?) Maybe I was supposed to be "free" now—maybe I was "done" with marriage.

On the flip side of the ideological divide, I tried to imagine what the "marriage police" would think about the messy follow-up to my picture-perfect wedding. My marriage didn't seem to me to be what conservatives advocate when they champion "family values." The marriage police argue that divorce should be harder to come by; I wonder what they'd think if they could have witnessed the nasty underbelly of marriage that preceded our rupture.

Was I now a fallen woman, or did everyone else just think I was? Perhaps my divorce wasn't a failure at all but a success in certain ways. If the marriage had been wrong, we may have nipped something bad in the bud. "Good thing it ended now," friends consoled as I wept on their shoulders. "Thank God you two didn't have kids," my family said, sighing with relief while offering their condolences.

When you get married or divorced, every bureaucracy in America wants to systematically retool and recategorize you. Name changes, new membership cards, and endless documents require you to reassess yourself into neatly squared-off boxes. As I painstakingly rechanged my newly changed name back, I had to deal with the bright inquiries all over again: "Oh, did you just get married?" customer-service reps would bubble over the telephone. Only a year ago I was proudly and sweetly murmuring, "Yes"; now I was curtly saying no. I wanted to add, "That's really none of your business."

Part of my confusion was that I certainly didn't feel like a . . . *divorcée.* If I felt single, could I check that box? I wondered if it was against the law to check how I felt and not, perhaps, who I really was. If I didn't know how to treat the idea of my brief marriage, I certainly didn't know how I wanted the rest of the world to judge it.

Was I a lesson to be learned, or had I learned a lesson?

❧

There's a minefield of personal, psychological, and political booby traps awaiting any writer who sets out to document this type of phenomenon. On a personal level, there's the danger of relying too much on one's own experiences and prejudices to guide the way. The temptation to score a political point via one's personal experience is a facile enterprise and one I hope to avoid in this book. As Katha Pollitt astutely observed about much recent writing by women, " 'The personal is political' did not mean that personal testimony, impressions and feelings are all you need to make a political argument."[30]

In any case, the politicization of marriage in our culture has been overwrought, oversimplified, and overwhelmingly misused. Those who put forth arguments about marriage often confuse the real issues of personal relationships in the interest of promoting a broader agenda. Anyone who listened to Newt Gingrich's exhortations on family values or witnessed Jesse Jackson solemnly deliver Bill Clinton of his extramarital sins need only examine their respective personal affairs to know they didn't swallow their own prescriptions. When people use marriage to teach a political lesson, they are often really talking about something else entirely.

In exploring and understanding the significance of this starter-marriage trend within a broader social and cultural context, I tried to avoid the pitfall of attaching too broad an agenda to my stated purpose. It seems many recent books purporting to illustrate and explain a social or cultural phenomenon have sacrificed an accurate portrayal in favor of a political platform. (This is particularly true for books geared toward women, although since marriage affects both men and women equally, a book about marriage needn't be considered "a woman's book.")

My aim has been to stick to the issues at hand because they are compelling enough in and of themselves. People want to make sense of their own lives and of the lives of the people around them, to understand how their lifestyles are shaped by the social and cultural forces of the times—and how they in turn will affect our future. The ways in which we marry reflect who we are as individuals, what kind of families we form, and the manner in which we raise our children. Our marriage patterns bear a major social and cultural impact on America. And on a much more fundamental level, the types of marriages we have significantly shape our own personal happiness. Having happy marriages tends to make us much happier people. Certainly that's an ideal to which we can all commit.

In this book, I try to explore the issue of starter marriages beyond the strictures of my own story. My experience is only *my personal experience;* I wish neither to exploit the particularities of my marriage nor expose my personal life or that of my ex-husband to examination. Rather than rely on my own, limited experience, I've gone to the source of the phenomenon and interviewed nearly sixty men and women from around the country who had starter marriages. My hope is that my own story provides me with a dose of humility. That it simmers in the background as an informing principle, a guiding perspective, and a respect for the people who opened themselves up to my questions, often about very personal issues and emotions. Let it explain my decision to use pseudonyms for everyone I interviewed, to protect both their privacy and the privacy of those with whom they once shared a life, for better or worse.

At best, my personal experience will have allowed me to know which questions to ask; to understand many of the answers on a gut level and know how to respond; and to avoid some of the easy judgments of those whose primary purpose in discussing marriage is to cast a moral judgment or further a political cause. Just as a man can in many ways only speculate about what it's like to struggle over the decision to abort a pregnancy and most women can watch *Saving Private Ryan* with only a cinematically induced inkling of what it's like to advance under gunfire, only one who has married and divorced before thirty can know about the disappointment, shame, confusion, and self-doubt that such an experience entails.

Along similar lines, it's risky to draw sweeping conclusions from the particular circumstances of these individual marriages. I am not out to calculate what percentage of couples fight over cleaning the kitchen or investigate to what extent "fault" lies in either quarter. My aim is to better understand the kind of relationships that constitute starter marriages and to get a sense of the underlying attitudes and experiences of young marrieds. For this reason, I did not focus on the highly individualistic details and histories that characterized the marriages I learned about, fascinating though they were. Instead I honed in on what starter marriages have in common, and what distinguishes those who entered into and exited their marriages so quickly.

So what *was* this marriage of mine, and what are these quickie marriages to which so many of my generation seem to fall prey? Are we just taking marriage out for a test drive, giving it a go, getting our feet wet? Perhaps we see marriage as the romance equivalent of the first job, that horrible, "character-building" experience that left you feeling confused and undervalued yet in retrospect taught crucial lessons for your "real" career ahead.

Starter marriages may very well be the wave of the future. At a recent meeting of the World Future Society, one futurist predicted that within the next century Americans will marry four times over the course of their lifetimes; the first marriage will last no more than five years. It's time for all of us—single, engaged, married, divorced, remarried, widowed—to figure out what starter marriages are, why people jump into them and then jump out, and whether they're worth it.

With the writing of this book, I, like most other ex–young marrieds, continue to "believe in" marriage. But in a very different way.

The Starter Marriage

and the

Future of Matrimony

Chapter 1

Getting Started on
a Starter Marriage

ISABEL ALWAYS WANTED TO GET MARRIED. A TWENTY-NINE-year-old public relations executive from a New York suburb, she never lacked for male attention, though she says, "I mostly dated the wrong people. I just dated whoever liked me instead of trying to find the best person for who I am." Despite a steady stream of monogamous relationships, Isabel was afraid of ending up single. "That's why I married my husband," she explains with a wry laugh.

At twenty-five, she decided to marry a man she'd been dating for eight months. "My friends were starting to get married, and they had had their boyfriends for years before," she explains. "I felt like they were moving on with their lives, and I wanted to as well. I was pretty sure this was the right person, and I was tired of getting screwed over by men and at least he wasn't doing that. We were both sick of the New York dating life, so we were pretty relieved to be getting married." Marriage was something Isabel felt she was supposed to do. "You're expected to get married, buy a house, have two kids. I think everybody gets caught up in that, and I definitely did. When you're twenty-five suddenly you think you're old and the thought of being twenty-seven or twenty-eight and still being single is such a bad feeling. You think everyone is judging you."

After she got engaged, Isabel noticed several of her friends doing so quickly thereafter. "It's like this snowball effect. Once one person gets engaged, everybody has to get engaged. And then you get so wrapped up in whose ring is bigger and who's getting married where and how much everything costs."

Isabel expected her marriage to be "a nice life with nice things," but mostly she devoted her attention to the wedding. Over her year-and-a-half-long engagement, she and her fiancé planned the big day, which she now describes as "a three-hundred-person circus." During the engagement period, whenever she and her fiancé fought, which was often, Isabel wrote it off as prewedding jitters, assuming that once they were married, things would change. They didn't.

"Everything was a problem," she says. "I don't think we had any respect for each other. I didn't feel comfortable with him. I knew, pretty much right away, that something was definitely not right." Screaming matches and power struggles ensued. Isabel lost weight, grew depressed, and "didn't feel like myself." After only a year of marriage, they decided to divorce. "It was the one thing I hated to do because he came from a divorced family and I don't believe in divorce. But after a while you say, 'I'm too young. This is wrong. This is not what life's supposed to be like.' "

"I rushed to get married," Isabel explains. "My marriage was an unfortunate mistake, and it wasn't worth saving because we were not meant to be."

❦

Isabel describes a typical starter marriage.

Starter marriages, like all marriages, are meant to last forever. But they don't. Instead, they fizzle out within five years, always ending before children begin.

Starter marriages usually start young. While the age of Americans entering marriage has increased slightly over the past century (the average woman today marries at age twenty-five, the average man twenty-seven), many people still marry in their early and mid-twenties. Starter marriages end young too, with divorce papers often delivered before the thirtieth-birthday candles are blown out.

Divorce has long been common within the first five years of marriage, but today marriages are ending progressively earlier. And the new young divorcés are a bit different from their predecessors; rather than becoming single moms and alimony dads, we're divorcing before having children. Because while we still marry relatively young, we increasingly delay childbirth. The average age of first-time mothers has been steadily rising since 1972, and more couples are delaying children for three, four, five years into their marriages.[1] First marriages aren't exactly new, but starter marriages are more prevalent.

Pop culture is packed with new starter marriage icons. Drew Barrymore, Uma Thurman, and Angelina Jolie all jumped in and out of marriage and are already onto their seconds. Courtney Thorne-Smith, former *Ally McBeal* star, divorced her husband after seven short months of marriage—while still posing on the cover of *InStyle Weddings* magazine. Milla Jovovich was married for two months, alongside such temporarily committed people as Jennifer Lopez and Neve Campbell. Even Hollywood's reigning bride, Julia Roberts, had a starter marriage. Starter marriages have practically become trendy. *Self* magazine described the phenomenon with the snappy headline "Just Married, Just Split Up."[2] And in September 2000 *Entertainment Weekly* included "divorcing in your 20's" on its list of "in" things to do. In 2000 more than four million twenty-to-thirty-four-year-olds checked the "divorced" box.[3] *Jane* magazine heralded the trend in April 2001 with the headline, "Young, Hot, and Divorced."

But starter marriages are not to be glamorized or trivialized. To those who've had one, the very term "starter marriage" can sound dismissive and, frankly, demeaning. Some people still use the expressions "training marriage," "practice marriage," or "icebreaker marriage"; others prefer the generic umbrella "first marriage." This book will use the somewhat uncomfortable and imperfect term "starter marriage" when referring to this brief, twentysomething take on matrimony. Whatever they're called, these *are* marriages—in every sense except "till death do us part." A starter marriage isn't a whim or a fantasy or a misbegotten affair—it's a real marriage between a man and a woman, bound together by love, personal belief, state law, and, often, religious oath. A starter marriage doesn't *feel* like one when you're engaged or when you're inside it. It is charged with all the hope, expectations, and dreams that inspire almost all marriages. All starter marriagees truly believe they are getting married forever.*

A starter home is that first house you buy knowing full well that the bedroom is smaller than you'd like, the kitchen has no windows, and the insulation will have to be replaced. You accept these faults and make certain compromises knowing that you'll only be there temporarily or that you'll improve it. The difference between a starter marriage and a starter home is that virtually nobody who enters a starter marriage thinks he's in it for the short term and will eventually upgrade to a better marriage. "I had a firm belief in the fact that you only pick one partner for life," says James, thirty, a Seattle-based multimedia designer whose marriage dissolved after thirteen months. "I didn't have a thought in my mind about divorce. I had very strong values."

Indeed, today's young marrieds often think they'll *improve* on the institution of marriage, even when their relationships are less than ideal. Existing problems and doubts are submerged to the larger desire to marry and the overwhelming giddiness of love. All will be solved, everything will be fine, we will be happy, once we're married. Everyone who enters into a starter marriage, like most people who wend their way down the aisle, has dreams—and often fantasies—of what married life will bring.

Who's Who in a Starter Marriage

In order to figure out who gets into a starter marriage, I interviewed almost sixty starter marriage veterans. Because I wanted to focus on contemporary marriage and today's marrying generation, the interviewees were all between the ages of twenty-four and thirty-six (officially part of Generation X).

The participants shared a few general commonalities. The ma-

---

*For this reason, I did not include so-called green card marriages—marriages between an American and a foreigner aspiring to citizenship—in my interviews because they are at no point thought of as "real" marriages, entered into with the expectation that they will last forever.

jority married for the first time between the ages of twenty-two and twenty-seven. Most were college-educated and some had graduate or professional degrees, but several either bypassed college or left before earning a degree. They were predominantly white, mostly middle- to upper-middle-class. While these parameters necessarily limit the scope of this inquiry, both class and race add new dimensions that deserve a fuller treatment than this book can provide. The limitations imposed by these somewhat homogeneous characteristics will hopefully tighten and strengthen the discussion as it relates to this slice of American society and spark interest and research into others.

In other ways the group was quite diverse. The interviews were with people across the country—from more than thirty states including Arizona, California, Colorado, Florida, Idaho, Ohio, Minnesota, New York, North Carolina, Oregon, Pennsylvania, Texas, Vermont, Virginia, and Washington. At the time of the interview some had remarried, others were in long-term relationships, and some were single. Their jobs ranged from waiting tables to trading on Wall Street; they were photographers, marketers, sales executives, doctors, journalists, teachers, dot.comers, grad students, librarians, consultants, PR executives, editors, investment bankers, engineers, military personnel, government employees, lobbyists, and musicians. They described themselves as liberals, loyal Democrats, staunch Republicans, registered Independents, progressives, and conservatives. Among them were Southern Baptists, Methodists, Mormons, Episcopalians, Presbyterians, Reform and Conservative Jews, lapsed and practicing Catholics, atheists, agnostics, and a wide range of self-described "spiritual" but not formally religious individuals.

It's hard to pinpoint exactly what kind of person marries and divorces before many of his or her peers have shopped for engagement rings, because every marriage is as unique as the two people entering into it. Some suffered from drug and alcohol problems, family crises, insufferable in-laws, or adultery, though most were plagued by less dramatic conflicts. But while it's difficult to generalize about such a small group, some personality traits were common among the participants. Many were overachievers—socially, academically, and professionally successful. The women tended to describe themselves as "practical," "organized," "together," "strong," and "responsible." The men typically described themselves as "romantic," "traditional," "a good guy." In other words, not what one might deem "divorce types."

Overall, many starter-marriage pairs seemed to have been what from the outside looked like "power couples." These were men and women who appeared to have it all together. They were attractive, well-educated professionals with active social lives and promising careers—the kind of people one might envy for being on top of things. "I was into my job, I was into getting ahead," Olivia, a thirty-one-year-old graphic artist from Idaho, explains. "I wanted to get a head start on everything. I've always wanted to win, and my engagement made me feel like a winner." Having gone to the right schools, excelled at the competitive entry-level job, and marched onward up the ladder; and settled into the Upper West Side/Noe Valley/Adams-Morgan apartment, these couples saw marriage as the next challenge. "Getting married was like getting a big gold star," says Melissa, a thirty-year-old writer from Florida, who got married while in grad school. "You're okay. You're a person that somebody wants to spend his life with. People look at you differently. It's perceived as if your house is in order—you really know what you're doing. And I wanted to give off that perception, even though it couldn't possibly be true given my age and how little experience I had in the world."

One or both spouses tended to be at extremes. Either their lives were sailing merrily along and marriage was the last item to click into place ("When I got engaged I was on top of the world," Sophia, 35, recalls. "I had just gotten a promotion. Everything was falling into place. Time to get a dog!"), or everything appeared to be falling apart and marriage promised to tie it all together. The year she decided to marry, Lucy, a California-born thirty-one-year-old, saw her parents divorce, survived a car accident, had an abortion, and felt very unsure of what she wanted to do careerwise. The man she married was from her hometown, and she'd known him since she was a child. "Life felt very unstable," she says now. "I liked the thought of this person by my side. He felt very stable, and his love for me made me feel very stable."

Quite a few men and women were at a crossroads professionally or just starting out in their careers when they married, and a number were unhappy at work. Sam, a thirty-year-old self-described "dot.com droid" who married when he was a twenty-six-year-old teacher, says, "When I think back to the time when I got married, I realize I was miserable. I was really lonely. I wasn't doing what I wanted to be doing, and I didn't want to end up in some crummy job after grad school. I was very anxious about the fact that I wasn't heading in any particular direction." Charlotte, a twenty-nine-year-old school administrator from Minneapolis, was at the point of dropping out of college when she got married at age twenty-two. "I had hit a point where I was feeling a little lost. . . . The world was crumbling around me, and I needed to grab this one thing, marriage." She followed the only clear model she could find. "I think I was trying to emulate my parents, which is crazy because all my life I didn't want to be like them. Part of getting married wasn't so much how I felt about this person but because I felt like it was what I should be doing. I thought, I'm going to try to fit in with my family and kind of be like them."

From Trial Marriage to Starter Marriage

A number of starter marriages begin with cohabitation, which is no surprise considering the increasing popularity of living together before marrying, in what is sometimes called a "trial marriage." It's become almost de rigueur for couples to move in together before they even think about getting engaged. Today's marrying generation believes that "testing things out" will lead to stronger marriages and weed out potential mistakes. In a 2001 survey of twentysomethings, 62 percent agreed that "living together with someone before marriage is a good way to avoid an eventual divorce,"[4] and 43 percent would *only* marry after living together.

According to the Marriage Project at Rutgers University, over half of first marriages today are preceded by cohabitation—compared with about 10 percent in 1965.[5] Cohabitation has been steadily on the rise over the past four decades, increasing 864 percent since 1960.[6] If the number of trial marriages continues to increase at the rate of the past five years, by 2010 one in eight couples will cohabitate—8.7 million couples in all.[7] The Centers for Disease Control and Prevention note that "increasing rates of cohabitation have largely offset decreasing rates of marriage."[8] However, in the overall portrait of American society, trial marriages still figure rather small; estimates run between 4.8 and 7 percent of total households (compared with 30 percent of all households in Sweden, for example).[9]

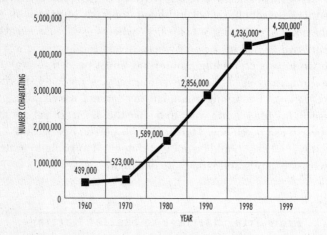

While cohabitation has its virtues, there may be a downside to trial marriage as a step toward real marriage. Recent studies show that couples who live together beforehand have rockier marriages and a significantly higher divorce rate—some studies claim up to 48 percent higher.[10] One report shows that first marriages beginning with cohabitation are almost twice as likely to end within ten years.[11] In *The Case for Marriage*, Maggie Gallagher and sociologist Linda Waite argue apocalyptically against cohabitation. According to Waite, live-in couples are less financially stable, less

---

*Matthew D. Bromlett and William D. Mosher, "First Marriage Dissolution, Divorce and Remarriage: United States," advance data, 31 May 2001, Centers for Disease Control and Prevention.

†Jay Tolson, "No Wedding? No Ring? No Problem," *U.S. News & World Report*, 13 March 2000, p.48 (cites 7%); Eric Nagourney, "Study Finds Families Bypassing Marriage," *New York Times*, 15 February 2000, Health and Fitness section (cites 4.8%).

faithful, and less happy than their lawfully wedded counterparts. They have a higher rate of domestic violence than married couples, and when they do marry they divorce more often.

However, such statistics must be put into context lest they sound unduly alarming. It may well be that those who cohabitated prior to marriage in past decades were less traditionally minded and less opposed to divorce—but this is changing. According to demographer Robert Schoen of Penn State University, those who lived together fifteen years ago tended to be different from those who cohabitate today. Back in the 1970s, living together was practically a political statement; those who did so were often viewed as radicals or free thinkers. They tended to be less religious and less faithful to traditional institutions overall. These were people more prone to divorce whether they lived with their partners beforehand or not. Nowadays, with cohabitation gone mainstream, its participants have as well. As a consequence, cohabitation cuts across all segments of society, and newer studies may well indicate little difference in outcome for couples who cohabitate prior to marriage.

Yet even if these statistics prove not to be prophetic for today's more marriage-minded cohabitators, trial marriage contains its own particular difficulties. The two individuals in a trial marriage often have very different conceptions of what cohabitation is and where they're heading. One person may see living together as a testing ground on the road to marriage, while her partner views it as a convenient form of serious dating: no need to commute to her home closet in the morning after yet another night at her boyfriend's apartment. A woman may be certain of her own desire to marry her live-in, while her unsuspecting mate thinks the situation is strictly on a trial basis. Or vice versa.

Cohabitation is predominantly seen as a means to an end—not an end in and of itself. As such, trial marriages are usually short-term arrangements; people either break up or, more likely (approximately 60 percent), get married—typically within a year and a half.[12]

Trial marriages tend not to exist long-term. Partly in order to hedge their bets, cohabitating couples often behave more like roommates than married partners. Their lives revolve around the day-to-day; they share occasional meals and split the rent, but their identities aren't intrinsically intertwined or their emotional lives fully interdependent. For the most part they keep their finances separate. They don't share insurance policies, bank accounts, tax forms, or investment portfolios. They often lead separate social lives; maintain separate groups of friends, and go out separately on social occasions. Their respective families are generally not integrated into their lives the same way they would were the couple married. Trial marriages place the Me above the Us, the If above the When, the Now above the Forever.

Love in a trial marriage is inherently conditional: "I'll love you for as long as this works out/makes me happy/fulfills me." It is an existence that is by its very definition unstable, and the transition from trial marriage to matrimony is often an uneasy one. Robert, a thirty-two-year-old musician, says that when he married at twenty-four, "the idea of marrying somebody just seemed like a long date. Like you're really, really, really going steady. Because divorce is so common and it's so easy to become unmarried, it seems like marriage gets turned into this boyfriend/girlfriend thing. You date, you go steady, you live together, you get married. But the stages are all so gray, and as a result, marriage has become less important and less valued. And more disposable."

Traditionally, marriage constituted a major life leap. You were either living at home or making a home. You were either economically dependent on your parents or banking with your spouse. You may or may not have been a virgin before marriage, but you certainly didn't spend every night and morning in bed with your partner. With cohabitation as a vague middle ground, the changes brought on by marriage are much less clearly defined. Marriage is no longer a formal rite of passage; it's merely a next step. It's hard to monitor exactly how the relationship is meant to change when one morphs from trial to reality; marriage seems to have a less definite beginning, fuzzier ground rules. Max, a thirty-one-year-old salesperson from Connecticut, regrets having lived with his girlfriend before getting married at twenty-six. "I think it was a bad idea," he says. "It took a lot of the mystery out of everything. Once we got married, it felt like nothing had changed. There was nothing of value that was different. We went on our honeymoon, we came back, and it was just the same thing."

Cosmopolitan magazine even offers tips for "Handling 'Already Shacked Up' Status" after getting engaged. "Deciding to get hitched is huge, but if you're cohabitating, your engagement might not seem as monumental as you'd imagined," the article warns, outlining ways to "realize that this *is* a big deal."[13]

A number of couples, particularly those who lived together before getting married, thought of marriage as a continuation of their previous relationship. "I figured nothing would change," says Melissa, who lived with her fiancé for four months before the wedding, "and everything changed. I imagined that it was this public confirmation of what we already had and that we would just go back to that."

The kinds of decisions our generation confronts, the choices we are asked—or demand the right—to make, and the ways in which we transition from our family homes to our marital beds are quite different from those of previous generations. The way in which we marry is very much a sign of the times.

Chapter 2

Generation We:
The Me Generation Rebellion

MICHAEL'S PARENTS GOT DIVORCED WHEN HE WAS THIR-teen years old. He describes their attitude toward marriage as "not very thoughtful" and says, "It didn't seem like my parents realized how they affected our lives. My father had affairs on my mother. My mother wasn't very available. . . . They didn't display a lot of affection for each other, and I saw them fight a lot." As he got older, Michael increasingly felt like "they were just cohabitating, they were that distant from each other."

Though his parents never gave him any specific guidance or advice about marriage, Michael, now a thirty-five-year-old preschool teacher and artist, picked up his own lessons. "I saw things that I thought they didn't do well. My father worked too much and wouldn't come home until eight at night." Michael describes their divorce as "the most anxious time of my life. I was in eighth grade, and I remember being just anxious all the time. . . . It left me feeling very insecure. I didn't feel safe in my relationships with friends or teachers. I didn't feel safe in my relations with anybody for a long time after that. I guess it made me realize that no relationship is secure. That you have to be careful. But it's funny because I didn't really keep that in mind at all when I got married."

When Michael married at twenty-eight he knew he wanted to avoid his parents' mistakes. "My ideas about marriage differed very much from theirs. But I guess since they didn't talk about their marriage, I didn't really know their ideas. I just knew that I wanted my marriage to be different. I knew that if I were with somebody, I wanted to really be with her, to spend time together. I wanted to have kids and be a big part of their lives, more than my father was in mine."

Michael's marriage lasted four years. "I really wanted to get married for the rest of my life," he says. "Even when it looked like we were going to get divorced, I thought we could work it out. I thought I was fully committed to the relationship until I died. . . . It was very sad for me that I loved this woman so much and we just couldn't work it out. When it broke up I felt like a total failure. It brought up this idea of 'First my parents' divorce—and now mine.' "

For many of today's marrying generation, notions of love and marriage were founded not on the experience of nuclear-family contentedness but on alimony disputes, visits to Divorced Daddy, Mommy's dates, and stepfamilies. We are the first real children-of-divorce generation, the product of a surge in the divorce rate during the seventies. For our parents, marriage often wasn't the pivotal decision in their lives—divorce was. And for their children, divorce became familiar; marriage remained the great unknown. Reared by the Me Generation, today's young adults find themselves searching for an elusive, ineffable sense of "we."

Most of us learned little about marriage growing up, even when our parents did stay together. Their marriages looked very different from what we imagined for ourselves. They were often the last "traditional marriages," split along rigid gender lines that strike most modern twentysomethings as both impossible and undesirable. "I absolutely did not want to re-create the marriage my parents had," says Yasmin, a thirty-four-year-old psychotherapist from the Bay Area. "My husband and I went into our marriage with the promise to stay conscious of doing everything we could to avoid the bleakness we came from. We thought we could redefine marriage."

But we don't really know what modern marriage is.

The result of our childhood experiences has been not, as one might expect, a wariness of matrimony. Instead, today's generation is reacting against divorce by romanticizing marriage—that supposedly problematic institution our predecessors so clearly rejected. "Somehow, despite a hippie childhood, divorced parents, feminist politics, and a preference for black above all other colors, I had developed a wealth of bridal dreams," writes Emily Jenkins in an essay entitled "Bridal Fantasies" on Salon.com.[1]

Welcome back, matrimony. Suburbia. Two to three children in the planning. Maternity fashion. Even *housewives*. We long for the marriages that Boomers grew up in and then renounced. According to the Yankelovich research firm, "Gen Xers are not likely to forget their Boomer parents' past. Career came first, marriage last and kids somewhere in between. In contrast, Matures' values about tradition and family remained steady throughout their lives. Matures, therefore, are poised to be a guiding force to Gen Xers as they enter family formation and strive to make 'better' choices than did their Boomer parents. . . . In many ways, Xers are embracing some of the values of Matures because they too have lived through uncertain formative years."[2]

Gen X is actually quite in line with these Matures—their parents' parents—who married in the 1930s and 1940s. Not only do we show a remarkable similarity in certain attitudes, particularly those that relate to family, we are also emulating their marriage patterns, trying to make marriage into what we want it to be.

The Multiplicity of Marriage

Contrary to popular opinion, marriage is not some kind of eternal truth or immutable institution. The way in which we conceive of our marriages is a fluid concept—one that we have vacillated back and forth from, deconstructed, argued against, rallied in favor of, hoped fervently for, examined and admired, reconstructed and rehabilitated, and promoted eagerly again. Cultures, classes, and generations define and redefine marriage over and over as they see fit.

Our immediate predecessors, the Baby Boomers, examined the institution of marriage obsessively. In the 1960s and 1970s, radicals, feminists, and academics went so far as to question the very validity of matrimony as a personal and social ideal. Yet despite these rancorous debates, the quiet majority of Americans continued to accept and even revere the institution of marriage. And the questioners eventually lost steam or faded from the media limelight. By the 1980s, while marriage continued to be a potent source of public discussion, it was clear that the institution would survive. Marriage itself was no longer at issue; it simply became a kind of litmus test or shorthand for a broader debate—a launching pad to other social, economic, and cultural issues like single motherhood, deadbeat dads, welfare policy, family values, and divorce law.

But while matrimony settled safely back into acceptability (if it ever really left its lily-white cocoon), many of the questions raised by feminists and others were left unanswered. What *is* this legal bond we're all so eager to get into—or more specifically, what is marriage today? Is it a phase or a lifelong commitment, a pleasure or a duty? Is it a chosen way of life, a vocation, or just another attribute?

Many argue that marriage is necessarily religious or spiritual in nature, that it requires oaths and sacrifice. Perhaps marriage represents a certain set of values. But if so, which and whose? Some claim that marriage is a moral institution; others see it as merely a social norm. Whether it is simply a legal contract, a binding agreement regulated by the state, a potential, or an ideal, it must be something wonderful for us to want it this badly.

Naturally, romantic love has always been a principal motive, but many pragmatic factors have also propelled couples down the aisle. Traditionally, men wanted to have a wife to care for them. Women wanted to get out of their parents' house. Men wanted to fulfill their role as provider. Women wanted financial stability. Men wanted to create a legacy. Women wanted to lose their virginity (or have access to officially sanctified sex). Both men and women wanted to legitimize unwanted pregnancies. Almost everyone wanted a family. At its most fundamental level, marriage was created for the purpose of raising children.

Today many of these pragmatic motivations no longer apply. A man no longer expects a wife to devote herself full-time to his care and upkeep, and a woman no longer needs a man to pay her way. With rare exception (mostly in certain religious and ethnic communities), sex has become almost entirely divorced from the notion of marriage. Rare is the woman who claims she's marrying in order to have intercourse. Even pregnancy doesn't lead to marriage in the way it used to. Today, only 23 percent of women pregnant and single marry before giving birth.[3]

Marriage has gone from being a necessity to being a choice.

A Short History of Long-Term Commitment

Matrimony has always meant different things to different people in different societies. In fundamentalist Islamic countries, marriage is practically a mandate. In modern Sweden, one third of couples forgo marriage altogether. Even when you restrict the perimeter to one country, marriage is perpetually in flux; the practice of marriage in America alone has changed tremendously according to social, cultural, and political circumstance.

Americans tend to have an overdeveloped short-term memory and an abysmal long-term one when it comes to their own history. Today college courses teach the events of the 1990s like relics of the distant past, ripe for deconstruction and dissemination. Come December, "history" is neatly summed up and analyzed by the editors of *Time* magazine's year-end issue.

With marriage, it seems our historical memory is particularly blunt-edged and myopic. Our beliefs and behavior seem rooted in the idea that in the 1950s marriage was suddenly created, achieved its ideal format, and set the standard by which all subsequent unions should be judged. Much of the comparative-trend data on marriage is culled from 1950 onward, as if that year were some kind of ground zero. Historian Michael Kammen remarks that the "traditional propensity of this society for being present-minded and having an unreliable attention span" leads to a "clear penchant for reconfiguring the past in order to make it comfortably congruent with contemporary needs and assumptions."[4] In other words, we use history to make certain points about marriage, and the usual marital history—depending on political persuasion—runs something like this:

RIGHT-WING VERSION: Back in the 1950s, marriage was the sacred ideal. Girls held on tightly to their virgin credentials until they eagerly entered connubial bliss. Once married, they devoted themselves with cheerful vigor to their domestic duties, ignoring such pesky diversions as career and independence and instead deriving feminine fulfillment from the bountiful challenges and rewards of motherhood and meatloaf assembly. Then along came the calamitous 1960s, when bitter frumps like Betty Friedan and spotlight seekers like Gloria Steinem bulldozed previously happy little girls into believing they'd been manipulated into their contentment by the "patriarchy." Man-hating, bra-burning femi-Nazis stampeded the political system, desecrating the traditional laws that sanctified the family and ensured societal stability. By the 1970s, serious destruction had set in: divorce spread, families broke apart, and once-pure women were copulating in a degenerate, drug-induced, venereal-disease-producing frenzy. In the 1980s, bereft of all tradition, women lived miserable career-driven lives full of empty sex, mannish big-shouldered suits, and a secret longing for children in a world where they were more likely to be hit by lightning than get married.* Those who did marry acted as if divorce were just another "life choice" or, worse, a form of "self-renewal." The current result is a morality-free mess. And after what women have wrought on the American family and the institution of marriage, this is exactly what they deserve.

RADICAL-LEFTY VERSION: Back in the benighted 1950s, women had no choice but to marry. Stifled by a society in which their sexuality was denied, confined into girdles and poodle skirts, and stymied by a Men Only economy, women were forced to wed in order to achieve some form of economic stability. They were marched

---

*This is based on a much disputed statistic from a notorious Harvard study that was heavily publicized and later firmly debunked. See Susan Faludi, *Backlash: The Undeclared War Against American Women* (New York: Crown, 1991).

down the aisle by their fathers, complicit partners in patriarchal oppression. In this pre-Pill world, once married, women became immediately and unhappily pregnant, embarking on a lifetime of subservient bondage. Relegated to the suburbs with their off-spring, women were hoodwinked by American advertisers into be-lieving that personal fulfillment could be attained through the acquisition of new household appliances. Meanwhile, their hus-bands expected them to serve their every whim, while at the end of their exciting corporate days they cavorted with their mis-tresses. Then, in the glory days of the 1960s, women began to free themselves from the shackles of tyranny, joining together in mu-tual outrage across economic, social, and racial divides to form a united gender front against the patriarchy. Women nationwide realized that marriage was nothing but an outdated institution created by men in order to keep their dominant position while en-suring that women remain trapped in a position of servile child-bearing. Yet despite limited gains, from the 1970s through the 1990s the forces of male reaction continued to battle against them, killing the ERA, dominating the antiabortion crusade, and forcing *Ms.* magazine into limited circulation. Even in the year 2001 the struggle for women's rights is stymied by a conspiracy of barriers. Forget worrying about marriage: until women can walk topless down Main Street, inculcate schoolgirls with masturbation guide-lines, and adopt children with their lesbian wives, they will never truly be free.

Obviously, both versions are exaggerations, but it's frightening just how slight these exaggerations are. An absurd amount of myth and distortion surrounds the history of the American family, which tends to go back, again, beyond a *mere fifty years.* Our coun-try may be young, but it nonetheless predates television. A more accurate portrait of marriage requires reaching backward a bit fur-ther and reassessing more recent decades within that broader con-text.

In colonial times marriage was an extremely stable institution in America. Though colonial settlers had much shorter life spans, their marriages lasted longer than the average marriage does today. Prior to the Civil War, only one married woman in a thou-sand was divorced each year.[5] Marriage was popular, as it served people well. Colonial men desperately needed wives to help them build homes, forge families, and create communities in the face of a chronic shortage of women. With the settlers' personal, social, and economic interests firmly intertwined, early marriages in America were definitely partnerships. Women took part in supporting the household by helping to manage the family farm or business, even if to a lesser extent than men.

Though divorce was hard to come by, the divorce rate began rising even in colonial times. The only traditionally acceptable grounds for divorce were bigamy, desertion, and adultery. Through the late nineteenth century, both men and women avoided divorce because in a precapitalist society it was often financially devastating for both; divorce could result in the loss of a job, a farm, a dowry, servants, and a home. A pervasive social stigma, in many ways created and enforced by our religious institutions, acted as an additional, powerful deterrant. As late as 1870, only 7 percent of first marriages ended in divorce.[6]

Marriage practice shifted during the nineteenth century, particularly following the industrial revolution. As more people gained the economic independence that enabled marriage, the marriage rate increased and the age of those marrying decreased. In many ways, marriage didn't achieve its modern incarnation until the twentieth century, when capitalism firmly took hold and people no longer had to marry to secure their financial future. It certainly didn't become "traditional" in the current sense of the word (breadwinning father, household mother) until economic advances created the right conditions.

Economic progress also meant divorce. Between 1870 and 1920 the divorce rate increased fifteenfold, and by 1924 one in seven marriages ended in divorce. Divorce rates largely rose alongside the rise of capitalism, as growth and opportunity afforded individuals the ability to survive financially outside the household economy. In other words, the more economic opportunity, the more marriage—but also the more divorce. Thus divorce rates spiked during war, when women joined the workplace (one in six marriages ended in divorce during World War I)[7] and fell during the Depression, when job opportunities for both sexes shrank. Not that divorce left everyone better off financially. Even after capitalism's triumph in the twentieth century, divorce continued to mean economic devastation for the many women who had spent much of their married lives at home. For a housewife, divorce also meant the loss of an entire way of life. She lost the very definition of herself, her job title; she could no longer be Mrs. John Doe or So-and-So's wife.

Perhaps the simplest way for today's marrying generation to understand contemporary marriage is to think of it in terms of three overlapping generations. The first is that of our grandparents, the "Matures," born in the first few decades of the twentieth century. The second, our parents', is composed of two groups: the Silent Generation, born between 1930 and 1945, and the Baby Boomers, born between 1946 and 1964. The third, Generation X, was born between 1965 and 1978. To really understand this third wave and today's marrying generation requires a look at the previous two.

Marital Status of Women Fifteen Years and Older: 1900–1998

Year	Percent Married
1900	57.1%
1910	59.0%
1920	60.7%
1930	61.2%
1940	61.0%
1950	67.0%
1960	67.4%
1970	61.9%
1980	58.9%
1990	56.9%
1998	54.9%

Source: U.S. Bureau of the Census, "Historical Statistics of the United States, Colonial Times to 1970"; "Marital Status and Living Arrangements," March 1998 Update.

Our Grandparents' Marriages

Our grandparents, the Matures, are on the early cusp of the so-called Greatest Generation. They lived through tough times—the

Great Depression and World War II—and became accustomed to hardship. As a consequence, their expectations were lower than those of subsequent generations, for whom peace and prosperity were more or less givens. On the whole, Matures turned out to be a hardworking, obedient, disciplined, and conservative lot. They believe in duty, obligation, teamwork, and self-sacrifice.

Married in the late 1920s through the early 1940s, our grandparents were on the forefront of the most marrying generation in America (of their peers, 96.4 percent of women and 94.1 percent of men tied the knot).[8] During the immediate postwar era people married earlier than they ever had; almost everyone was married by their mid-twenties. Women wed their high school sweethearts or came home from college proudly bearing "MRS degrees." In the postwar era, 86 percent of children grew up in two-parent homes; nearly 60 percent of children were born into male-breadwinner/female-homemaker families.[9]

There were few alternatives. Single women were disdained as spinsters and bachelors considered suspect—psychologically damaged by the war, immature, or ill-bred. Our grandparents stuck with their marriages, even when they were unhappy. Most of them didn't think they had any choice, and at the time they often didn't. Divorce was still both rare and looked down upon. Of the couples who married in 1950, it was twenty-five years before even 25 percent were divorced.[10]

The marriage boom and subsequent baby craze of the postwar era was partly the result of the psychological effects of having gone through childhood during the Depression, a time of uncertainty and unrest. As young adults, our grandparents finally lived in a peaceful era of opportunity, when people could afford to marry, buy homes, and start families. Marriage and the nuclear family were the twin prizes of prosperity. Ah, the 1950s. Giving birth to one baby after another, women stayed at home and worked while their husbands brought home the bacon. Nestled into their new suburban homesteads, these little nuclear units retreated into the bosom of hearth and home. Indeed, families were more stable in the 1950s than during any other period in American history.

Yet all was not Norman Rockwell. Sociologist Stephanie Coontz debunks many of the myths surrounding our ideas about families of the time in *The Way We Never Were: American Families and the Nostalgia Trap*. One overlooked factor contributing to the high marriage rate was the frequency of shotgun weddings. Many of the supposedly idyllic young love marriages were more like pre-Pill panics in an era when "illegitimacy" was a crime and single parents, pariahs. By some estimates, 60 percent of single white women in the fifties who got pregnant raced toward the altar.[11] People still had premarital sex, but the illegality and unavailability of safe abortions and the social stigma attached to unwed motherhood led many to wed under less-than-ideal circumstances.

Another reality that flies in the face of myth is that during the course of the 1950s married women increasingly began working outside the home. And while they were generally restricted to menial and secretarial work, by 1955 the average wife worked until her first child was born and returned to the workplace once her children started school.[12] Her extra income wasn't the only source of family stability. Much of the success of these families was due to wide-reaching federal-assistance programs and housing policies that supported young families. And in a booming economy, corporate-welfare programs provided workers with a relatively high standard of living and an unusual level of job security. All of which served to prop up the family unit. Coontz explains many of the governmental and economic factors underlying the transition from *Ozzie and Harriet* to *The Brady Bunch:*

> Ultimately . . . changes in values were not what brought the 1950s family experiment to an end. The postwar family compacts between husbands and wives, parents and children, young and old, were based on the postwar social compact between government, corporations, and workers. . . . In the 1970s, new economic trends began to clash with all the social expectations that 1950s families had instilled in their children. That clash, not the willful abandonment of responsibility and commitment, has been the primary cause of both family rearrangements and the growing social problems that are usually attributed to such family changes, but in fact have *separate* origins.[13]

Revisionist histories point to the era's strict social mores as enforcing and promoting family values. But why, then, did the children who were brought up in these bastions of June Cleaverhood become the "degenerates" of the late 1960s and 1970s? Clearly being raised in such an ideal family situation doesn't ensure the endorsement or continuity of family "virtue" for its progeny. As Coontz points out, "Ironically, it was the children of those stable, enduring, supposedly idyllic 1950s families, the recipients of so much maternal time and attention, that pioneered the sharp break with their parents' family form and gender roles in the 1970s. This was not because they were led astray by some youthful Murphy Brown in her student rebel days or inadvertently spoiled by parents who read too many of Dr. Spock's child-raising manuals."[14]

What *did* happen was that once the condensed period of child raising was complete, and given the economic demands these larger families imposed, more married women went to work. And after women had experienced both the imposed requirement of stay-at-home motherhood and the burgeoning opportunities of the workplace, they wanted to ensure that their daughters could make their own choices. These supposedly family-centric mothers were the very people who instilled in their daughters the notion that they should strive for careers, urging them to follow a very different path from the one they themselves had chosen—or had had chosen for them.

The Baby Boomers may not have been such rebels after all. In many ways, they were doing *exactly* what their mothers told them to do. They were doing what a changing society required of them. In fact, they may not have had as much choice as they would have liked to believe.

Our Parents' Marriages

The parents of Generation X lived through a kind of intermediary period, marrying in line with the mores of one generation and divorcing according to the practices of the next. As a woman born in 1934 who married at twenty explains, "In those days, if you were not married by twenty-five, you were an old maid. It was unheard of for a woman to say, 'I don't want to get married.' They would be ready to put you in a mental institution. . . . I started my adult life in the pattern of my mother's generation: get married, have a house, have four babies. The feminist movement, because of my age and energy, and maybe my divorce, let me have my cake and eat it too. I got to be traditional—cooking and gardening, volunteer leader—and then in mid-adult life the feminist movement came along, and I'm able to read all the material and buy into the tenets. . . . After my divorce, I moved from volunteer work to paid work, became involved in politics, and married again. My generation was transitional."[15]

Our parents are mostly members of this so-called Silent Generation, the often overlooked group hovering between what's become known as the Greatest Generation and the Baby Boomers, and some are part of the earliest wave of Baby Boomers. Either way, many began their lives mirroring the more conservative ethos of their parents and rebelled at some point in the 1960s or 1970s. To best understand our parents and our parents' marriages, it makes sense to discuss them in terms of these two different generations.

The relatively small Silent Generation was born during the lean years of the Depression and World War II (partially accounting for the small size of their offspring generation, Gen X). The Silents fell in between some of the twentieth century's major events, gaining neither glory nor condemnation. Most absorbed images of hardship and war before coming of age during the postwar expansion, but they didn't help overcome them. They didn't serve in World War II, and they slipped by Vietnam.

Silents started their own families in the mid-1960s through the late 1970s. They tended to marry young; in 1956, the average age entering marriage hit an all-time low, with women marrying at 20.1 years.[16] Many of our mothers were part of the last wave of virginal brides. Indeed 90 percent of women born between 1933 and 1942 were either virgins when they married or had premarital intercourse with only the men they wed.[17] One woman born in 1940 explains her reasons for marrying this way: "My husband was the first man I ever had sex with, and that's why I married."[18] Lucy, a thirty-one-year-old Californian, says, "My parents got married because my mother told my father she was pregnant. The day she told him, he was going to tell her that he wanted to see other people, but that ended that."

Following the Silents were the infamous Baby Boomers, at 78 million strong the largest generation in America. Baby Boomers are generally considered the most influential generation of the twentieth century. Born between 1946 and 1964 (the peak of the Baby Boom was in 1957, when 4.3 million American babies were born, compared with only 2.4 million in 1937),[19] Baby Boomers were raised in a cold-war era of happy, prosperous nuclear families cozying up at home against the dangers of the world outside. Growing up in a family-focused society and an era of prosperity, Boomers got used to being the center of attention and demanding what they wanted. They became the marchers, the protesters, the hippies, the feminists, and eventually the yuppies.

After years of unconscientious conformity, in the 1960s and the 1970s everything changed for our transitional parents. They may not have skinny-dipped in the Age of Aquarius, but they latched on to the tail end of the sixties revolutions along with the Boomer crowd. Concepts like courtship, dating, and marriage were replaced with coupling, relationships, and being together. New buzzwords like "freedom," "individualism," and "swinging" were casually uttered at suburban cocktail parties. People were encouraged to go with the flow, avoid hang-ups, be loose, laid-back, and mellow. Those who stuck with marriage made new demands. A 1975 article in *The New York Times* explained, "Marriage has been caught up in a revolution of rising expectations. People want more out of their marriages than their parents ever did, and in the words of one counselor, 'They're not willing to make do, or slide by anymore.' "[20] And that could mean any number of things, including open marriage, group marriage, communal living, or divorce liberation.

Our Parents' Divorces

In the 1970s, divorce, once defined as the death of a marriage, was hailed as a fresh alternative for financially dependent and trapped wives, for battered women, for bachelor-minded men, for loveless couples. Divorce was sometimes even considered a healthy, rejuvenating response to marriages that were often viewed as sick, lifeless, or dead. People were told that divorce would make them free, fulfilled, and finally happy.

Our parents, who had often unquestioningly married according to their parents' model, had also seen the unhappiness that afflicted many of those marriages. They witnessed the problems through which older couples clung together because they didn't have a choice. What few people realize is that many of the divorces blamed on the 1960s youth generation (most whom were still single and swinging free), were actually the breakups of those sugar-coated 1950s marriages. It seems Donna Reed wasn't so happy after all. What the newly favorable divorce laws and the rising social acceptability of divorce in the 1970s did was enable people to get out of unhappy marriages and still survive socially and financially. A fundamental shift in public opinion took place, producing a new truism: "People should not stay married if they're not happy."

The divorce epidemic hit. And it hit our families. Armed with the new acceptability of both divorce and the single lifestyle, our parents rebelled. Beginning in 1965, the divorce rate surged, peaking in 1979 at a rate of 23 divorces per 1,000 couples.[21] By 1974, the number of marriages ending in divorce surpassed those ending in death.[22] Of the couples married in 1970, 25 percent were already divorced by 1977. People also started divorcing more readily. By 1975, according to the Census Bureau, half of all divorces took place within seven years of marriage. (Today marriages are ending in divorce even earlier; the average marriage that ends in divorce lasts 6.3 years,[23] and most marriages end within two to five years, with the chance of divorce highest during the third year.)[24]

Marriage rates waned. Cohabitation rose, people started marrying later, remarriages became increasingly acceptable, and single-parent households and stepfamilies multiplied across the nation. New, complicated family structures arose in divorce's wake. By 1975, 5.2 million women and 5.7 million men were in a postdivorce remarriage.[25] In 1979 there were 3.8 million separated or divorced mothers heading families that included children under eighteen, an increase of 86 percent since 1970.[26] Eight in ten of postwar-generation children had grown up in the traditional, two-parent nuclear family; by the end of the 1970s, that percentage had dropped to half.[27]

What Our Parents Taught Us About Marriage

If our grandparents inadvertently taught our parents that it could be hell to live in a loveless marriage, then our parents showed us that it could be hell to be divorced. For those growing up in the 1970s, marriage often seemed either absent or irrelevant. Parents didn't discuss matrimony with their children even if they stayed married; if they divorced, they avoided the topic entirely. The underlying sentiment against parents giving advice to their children about marriage seems to have been, *Who am I to talk?*

With rare exception, the people interviewed for this book said their parents gave them no lessons about marriage, no guidance, no warnings, no encouragement, no words of wisdom. Just silence. At most they might have mentioned, "It would be nice if you got married in the Catholic church," or "I hope he's Jewish," or the new standby, "As long as you're happy." Laurel, a thirty-two-year-old Philadelphian, had parents who divorced when she was one year old. "My own parents didn't give me a lot by way of reasons or explanations for their divorce," she says. "They just said it was incompatibility. I kind of had a sense that my mother would have tried to work things out had my father been more behind the idea, but I definitely wasn't exposed to the practicalities of a working relationship. I never saw how hard it would be to stay together or what kind of work it would be."

We received no lessons, and given the prevalence of divorce, we couldn't very well learn on our own, if only by observation. More than 40 percent of today's marrying generation spent time growing up in a single-parent home by the time they were sixteen.[28] But the effects of divorce on children in our generation are not limited to those who experienced it in their own families. Divorce destabilized all children in the 1970s, even those who didn't grow up in a "broken home." Friends' parents split up, people relocated, suddenly everyone had visitation schedules. "The winds of divorce that blew so famously skipped my house but then swept through the entire neighborhood," George, thirty-two, recalls. George's parents remained married until his mother's death. "Before my mom died, nobody got divorced. Afterwards, the deluge. Eight years later, it was half the people on my street." An atmosphere of anxiety and instability prevailed among almost all children of the seventies, family intact or not. Charlotte, whose parents are happily married, recalls, "When I was a child, this one boy's parents got divorced and he transferred to another school, so I thought, 'Wow. Divorce must be really bad because you can't even come back to school afterwards.' "

One of the lessons the divorce epidemic taught was that marriage is disposable. In a Salon.com column, Larissa Phillips describes how her parents encourage her to marry, despite their own multiple divorces. "But the fact that my parents divorced well—and they really did—doesn't grant them immunity from their actions," Phillips argues. "The fact that my uncles and aunts and grandparents and family friends felt they had absolutely no choice other than to divorce doesn't change the outcome. They still got divorced, all of them. They still showed my generation, by example and by forcing us to go along with their example, that marriage was something easily and amicably exited from."[29] Children of divorce learn the hard way that marriage is not a sure thing. One twenty-nine-year-old divorced man from Texas, whose parents split up when he was "eight or nine," remarked, "My belief is that you marry for love and the long haul, but if things don't go right, it's better to be divorced than in a bad marriage. I believe in marriage, but if it's not meant to be, better to get out sooner rather than later."

The current received wisdom is that divorce breeds divorce. Statistics have shown that for children of divorced parents, the risk of divorce is two to three times higher than it is for children from married-parent families.[30] Yet one 1999 study found that the trend may be abating. According to *American Demographics,* "Children of divorced parents are less likely to end their own marriages today than their predecessors were back in the early 1970s. Before 1975, new research finds, people from divorced families were 2.5 times more likely to have dissolved their marriages than their counterparts from intact families (though they are also slightly less likely to marry). By 1996, the likelihood had slipped to just 1.4."[31]

Some claim that this is due to diminishing negative effects of divorce on children as divorce became more acceptable. Another possible reason is once again the backlash of current twentysome-things against their parents' generation. *You guys screwed up, but I won't. I won't hurt my children the way you hurt me.* As Larissa Phillips writes, "When my parents divorced in the late '70s, we children went along with it like troupers. When they started bring-ing home boyfriends and girlfriends in the '80s, we ultimately ac-cepted . . . and we dealt with the divorces and separations all over again. . . . But as for myself, the scattered, patchwork concept of family I grew up with has only increased my quest for commit-ment."[32] Or as Ben, a thirty-one-year-old, Ohio-based training man-ager, says of his failed marriage, "I thought we would establish a good foundation for having kids and that I would become the fa-ther that I never had because of my parents' divorce."

Another common observation is that children of divorce are more wary of marriage than their counterparts from intact fami-lies. To some extent this is true. One typical behavior pattern of children of divorce is to cohabitate before marriage. Research has shown that children of divorce are disproportionately likely to live with a partner and less likely to ever marry that live-in partner.[33] Divorced parents are often the first to tell their children to "live to-gether first" in an effort to prevent the same mistakes from being made.

But this story hides another children-of-divorce trend. Many children of divorce are all the more eager to seek out the very fami-lies they feel they lacked growing up. In *The Love They Lost: Liv-ing with the Legacy of Our Parents' Divorce,* Stephanie Staal identifies three types of romantic behaviors among adult children of divorce, one of which is the "nester"—children of divorce who "eagerly enter relationships with the highest hopes, often looking to find the attention and security they didn't receive as a child."[34] In a 1997 profile of Gen X, *Time* magazine quoted one woman whose parents divorced when she was three: "If I marry I will never get divorced," she said. "For me, the American Dream is a sta-ble family."[35] "I was definitely looking for a family member when

I got married, and so was my ex-husband," Laurel, first married at twenty-four, recalls. "He had been through a lot of ups and downs in his family—there were affairs and terrible fights between his parents, who got divorced and then remarried each other."

Children of divorce easily idealize marriage. "I was only there for four years of it," Sam says of his parents' marriage. "It was impossible for me to envision them together. I never really heard about their marriage. It happened when I was so young, it just became normal. Growing up, I didn't really think about marriage, but I suppose once I did, I had a pretty romantic view of it." Michael, also a child of divorce, admits, "I really wanted to be loved. That was a big part of my decision to get married. . . . And I thought that after the wedding, it would all be happily ever after and the marriage would last forever." Elizabeth, an Ohio-born consultant who married at twenty-three, explains her husband's desire to get married: "He desperately wanted security. He came from four failed marriages between his parents and a crazy, unpredictable life. I came from this secure, predictable, Midwestern family. I was steady and solid, this notion of the kind of wife you want and would be crazy to let get away."

Because they see the happy family in a vague, romanticized way, children of divorce long for it terribly, seeking out figures that offer stability and the golden ring of unconditional, everlasting love. "The children of divorce are displaying a yearning for restabilization," William Galston, a former domestic-policy advisor to President Bill Clinton, explains. "Faced with the reality of divorce, Generation X is expressing the ardent hope that 'this won't happen to me.' "[36]

Marriage Makes a Comeback

In the 1980s the divorce rate quietly reversed its forward march and began to dribble back down. The country veered rightward, yuppies boomed forth in pin-striped suits, success became the 2.2-children-plus-Volvo lifestyle. The most popular television sitcoms were family-oriented; *The Cosby Show* and *Family Ties* lit up prime-time living rooms. There was other, less family-friendly fare, but it wasn't as well received—single mom Murphy Brown was publicly flogged by Dan Quayle. And while many may have scoffed at first, by the time the early 1990s rolled around, "family values" had gained mainstream acceptance. In 1994 the Contract with America crowd had their way in Congress, and by the mid-1990s "Dan Quayle was right" had become the new consensus.

The 1980s were also the decade of the infamous—and later famously debunked—study, published in *Newsweek,* "If You're a Single Woman, Here Are Your Chances of Getting Married."[37] At the time, the study was taken quite seriously; in the 1980s, American teenaged girls learned that they better marry early—or else end up miserable. Holding out for marriage meant you would miss the boat altogether, waiting out your days as a wretched spinster or career viper. We learned that men disliked powerful women and were annoyed by their incessant and impossible demands. In *Backlash: The Undeclared War Against American Women,* Susan Faludi remarked of the decade's magazines, "The headlines spoke bleakly of THE SAD PLIGHT OF SINGLE WOMEN, THE TERMINALLY SINGLE WOMAN, and SINGLE SHOCK. To be unwed and female was to succumb to an illness with only one known cure: marriage."[38]

Young women who grew up during the backlash 1980s inadvertently lashed back against the backlash itself—trying hard to prove all the statistics wrong. "*We* won't end up bitter and alone like those 1970s feminists," Gen X women told themselves. Buying into those messages, Gen X took a decidedly traditional turn. "I believe that being a feminist should mean that I'm not afraid of my desires," writes happily engaged Emily Jenkins on Salon.com. "Coming to terms with tradition, and finding a way to embrace the parts of it that feel good to me, is a step towards self-definition, even if it means doing things that seem rooted in an outdated set of values and conventions."[39]

A fear of singlehood, combined with the fear of AIDS, crime, and social instability, made young Americans yearn for security. In *Last Night in Paradise: Sex and Morals at the Century's End,* Katie Roiphe observes that by the mid-eighties, stability and safety were the new buzzwords, and family values the way to secure them. "The loss of control, the consumption of a few glasses of wine on a date, the introduction of any degree of 'instability,' any lack of 'commitment,' any departure from 'monogamy,' suddenly seemed, to the keepers of public health and to a certain segment of the public itself, to be tantamount to suicide."[40] Generation X, along with the rest of the country, was suddenly, desperately trying to get back some form of stability and commitment.

But what is it that we want back, really? Nostalgia distorts the past to the extent that most people don't even know what they're yearning for when they talk about "traditional marriage." We may think of the fifties as the peak of family functionality, but nobody really wants the rampant sexism and racism of that era. (After all, it wasn't until 1967 that the Supreme Court knocked down laws forbidding interracial marriage.) Conservatives who wax rhapsodic about 1950s families would shudder at a return to the expansive role government played in subsidizing the family boom. Yet we've absorbed the fantasy of the 1950s family, even as we reject some of the social conventions that supported it. In Stephanie Staal's *The Love They Lost,* one thirty-one-year-old man admits, "Between my parents they have had five marriages, and they have all sucked. The only role models I have are my grandparents who have been married for fifty-five years and are joined at the hip, in a healthy way . . . and I think, 'Why can't I learn from them?' I think I can't because I feel like they are from a different era and that kind of relationship doesn't exist anymore."[41] Noelle, thirty-four, a sales executive from New Jersey who is now in her second marriage, says, "I never looked toward my parents as role models for marriage. If I had, I probably would never have gotten married. I've always admired people who had good marriages, like my grandparents."

Gen X Marriage

Some say the radical ideas of the sixties and seventies have become the conventional wisdom of today. The reality is a bit different. Most young people are reacting against the divorce of that era, or the unhappy marriages they witnessed in their childhood homes, *not* against the institution of marriage itself. The Yankelovich research firm identifies the Boomer bible as the me-centric

I'm OK, You're OK; for Generation X, it's the relationship-centric *Men Are from Mars, Women Are from Venus.* Both Yankelovich and Youth Intelligence, another market research firm, use the word "nostalgic" to describe the Gen X view of hearth and home. The childhood that Boomers supposedly had has informed their model of the perfect, traditional marriage.[42] In a 1999 poll, 57 percent of Gen Xers said they "would like to see a return to more traditional standards of marriage."[43]

If, as Douglas Coupland posited in his book *Generation X,* there is such a thing as "clique maintenance"—the need for one generation to disparage the next—there also exists its corollary: the need for that next generation to flog its predecessors. Gen X is rebelling against the ultimate rebels by romanticizing marriage and many of the "traditional" virtues that Boomers (often inadvertently) left behind. "I'm not a big fan of the Baby Boomers," a thirty-three-year-old divorcé from Washington, D.C., admits. "They contributed so much to the destruction of how we treat one another. There's no acceptance of responsibility for anything anymore. The Boomers are all about pointing fingers and projecting. People should just face it when they're wrong. Because of the Boomer mentality, there's too much individualism emphasized in marriage. Too much of one partner demanding acceptance for who they are rather than working on their faults."

Today's twentysomethings aspire to the marriages and intact families that their predecessors rejected. If children of divorce are more wary of marriage, what they're really wary of is marriage as they saw their parents carry it out. Most young adults feel that they will approach matrimony in a very different way. In a 1999 poll, 71 percent of Gen Xers agreed with the statement "I will do a better job raising my kids than the generation before me"; interestingly, only 64 percent of Baby Boomers agreed.[44]

Our ideas of what marriage will be like are quite different from those of our parents. As Rosalind Miles writes in *Prospect,* "The marrying generation of today, disheartened and disgusted by their parents' divorces and degrading sexual degringolades, currently display in their conversation, in their behavior, in their music and culture, a fierce faith in monogamous, exclusive, lifelong love and mutually faithful partnership which is likely to make anyone over

35 think of tooth fairies and Tinkerbell." And Gen Xers are curiously optimistic about their ability to make marriage better. Ben, a native New Yorker now living in the Midwest, admits, "We tend to think of marriage as the white picket fence, the two kids, the dog, and the station wagon—like *My Three Sons* or *Leave It to Beaver.* It's the all-American institution. Ideally, that's what everyone still talks about and what everyone expects—perfection. And we all still think that our marriage is going to be the best. I'll make it work, I'll have all the answers, it will be different for me. . . . It's totally unrealistic."

Gen X is decidedly more conservative than the Me Generation in its approach to relationships and marriage. Many young women today are rejecting the freedom *not* to marry that the women's movement bequeathed upon them. As Katie Roiphe wrote in an *Esquire* essay, "It may be one of the bad jokes that history occasionally plays on us that the independence my mother's generation wanted so much for their daughters was something we could not entirely appreciate or want." Baby Boomer Marie Brenner contrasts today's female with her own generation of feminist pioneers: "They do not want to run their houses and children from a cell phone. They have learned from our stressed-out example that you cannot do it all. Marina Rust, a young novelist and great-dame-to-be, said, 'This is a reaction against choices our parents made.' . . . The cultural historian Ann Douglas calls this period of American life 'a serious retro time' in which there are obvious echoes from the 50's, the 20's, and even the gilded 1880's."45

For all the attention drawn to how diverse, multicultural, adventurous, technohappy, and body-pierced our generation is, it's pretty astounding just how traditional our weddings and, in certain ways, our conceptions of marriage have become. Often they're miles of white tulle behind of our parents' weddings. "I think I had a kind of old-fashioned, fairy-tale image of marriage," says Jodie, a thirty-year-old librarian and self-described "bleeding heart liberal" and feminist. Alexandra Jacobs notes in *The New York Observer,* "We seem to have passed into a new phase . . . the era of the 'I Do' feminist. Women are not only embracing marriage, which in theory could have been obsolete by now, but manicuring to hyperperfection the very domestic idyll their mothers rallied to escape."46

While couples may have wedding web pages and document the big day with digital video cameras, for the most part the current wedding culture is positively feudal. The 1997 book *The Future Ain't What It Used to Be* notes, "Indicative of the tenacity of traditional values is the return of 'Mrs.' as a title. A generation after feminists fought to claim their own identities, in part by not assuming their husbands' surnames, many twentysomething brides are now eagerly becoming 'Mrs.' when they get hitched." The authors lump this trend alongside a longing for the "mythic age of stability defined by prescribed gender roles" and the "growing number of men reclaiming their 'rightful' places in the families."[47] "I was thinking about not changing my name, but he said if I didn't, he wouldn't introduce me as his wife," Olivia, married at twenty-two, explains. "I definitely did *not* want that, so I did."

Women who once talked about getting married barefoot or in flowered sundresses find themselves hoisted into Cinderella skirts with sweeping trains and coy veils come wedding day. In an outraged essay on the new retroactivity, *New York Times* columnist Maureen Dowd grumbled, "Are we evolving backward?" noting that at three wedding showers a friend of hers had attended in 2000, "the presents were always very 50s—soup ladles and aprons were unwrapped with see-through nighties and push-up brassieres."[48]

Yet the retro rebound is more of a gloss coating than a core tenet of the Gen X marriage package. We're not looking for a *total* throwback to Dick and Jane. Those whose parents stayed together often didn't like what they saw—and are as determined as the children of divorce to do things differently. Many with parents who remained married through the 1970s divorce tidal wave emphasized the alternative ways in which they conceived marriage. Juliet, a thirty-two-year-old court reporter, considers her parents' marriage very dysfunctional. "I remember looking at them and thinking, 'That's *not* the marriage I want to have.' I knew that since I was in my teens. In my marriage, I wanted to get more respect. I didn't want to end up bitter or angry." Jodie's parents remain married despite several rocky periods. "When I got married, I would hear myself say things that my mother said to my father and I would automatically stop myself," Jodie says. "I did *not* want my marriage to be like theirs." Zoë, a thirty-two-year-old bookkeeper from California, also wanted to avoid her mother's marriage. "I thought that my marriage would be different from that of my parents in that I wasn't going to put up with some of the stuff my mom had to put up with."

The current marriage ideal reflects this strange hybrid of romanticized traditionalism and new-millennial modernity. "I thought that we'd be one of those rare marriages that would work out perfectly," says Jodie, who was divorced after two years of marriage. "I thought, 'We're such good friends. We both want to remain individuals. We're so equal. We'll have that one marriage that lasts—happily—forever.' "

When asked what marriage represents to them, Gen Xers use words like "family," "stability," "security," and "lifelong love." But they also say they want egalitarian marriages, in which they are peers, partners, best friends, part of a team. We want to have adventures, learn together, and be the kind of couples to challenge old stereotypes and succeed at a lifelong marriage of equals. We want the kind of marriages that we've always fantasized about but have never actually seen.

Let's Get Married!

Considering the changing world we live in, Gen X continues to marry at a remarkably high rate. In 1867 there were 9.6 marriages per 1,000 people; in 1967, the rate was 9.7. (In between, it dipped to 7.9 in 1932 and peaked at 16.4 in 1946.)[49] The 1998 rate seems low at 8.3, but Generation X, the current marrying group, is also one of the smallest generations in history. Furthermore, with the population in America aging and the chances of marriage thereby becoming less likely over time, the marriage rate is lowered for the overall population.

And although the rising age at marriage has garnered a lot of attention, the truth is, the figures aren't rising that much. Indeed, it's surprising that they haven't risen considerably higher. If we are getting married later, we're only getting married significantly later than we did fifty years ago, certainly a short period in historic terms. The current trend more accurately reflects a turn back toward the marital patterns of the early twentieth century. In 1870, only two out of every five Vassar graduates married by age twenty-seven; by 1960, four out of five did. Now, with the average woman marrying at twenty-five and more educated women marrying slightly later, we are mirroring this century-old practice.[50] And even though people are getting married "later" than they had in the previous two decades, they are not forgoing marriage altogether. The proportion of people who never marry is actually still *lower* than it was a hundred years ago.

But what does "later" mean anyway? Though many people are getting married at a relatively older age, they are also marrying at an *earlier* stage in life. In many ways, the life stage we're at is more relevant than actual age, particularly given the fact that we mature earlier and live longer, altering the nature of physical age itself. The pattern of life in one's twenties has changed tremendously. More people go to college today than ever before. With many men and women adding four years onto their education, the year they get married might be expected to rise four years as well. In addition, more young adults are staying at home after high school, extending the period of adolescence into early adulthood and lessening their chances of early marriage.

Furthermore, traditionally for men and today for women as well, marriage isn't considered until one can afford it. In recent years people have delayed their entry into the workforce, and one would imagine these delays would also delay marriage. Whereas our parents were economically self-sufficient and often were homeowners by the time they hit their mid-twenties, our generation is more likely to find themselves at age twenty-five struggling to find a career while living in a rented apartment. That we continue to marry under such precarious circumstances is in itself an extraordinary testament to the ongoing draw of marriage.

While some people look at the current statistics and bemoan the fact so many twenty-five-to-thirty-four-year-olds haven't married yet, the reality is that over 65 percent have (an additional 11 percent are currently divorced or separated.[51]) That's a lot of Gen X weddings, and it doesn't even include an additional 25 percent married of those ages twenty to twenty-four.[52]

Though we may be marrying later on the whole, a sizeable portion of Gen Xers marry relatively early. A "rebel" group of trend-setters, overlooked amid all the fears surrounding marriage, may be transforming into a quiet majority, setting the standard for an entire generation. *American Demographics* magazine noted in 1997, "Underneath the bravado of many in the so-called 'Generation X' beats the heart of an old-fashioned romantic. Indeed, adults aged 18–29 appear to be leading a revival of that most romantic of institutions—the happy marriage."[53] Marriage is back, indeed.

Chapter 3

Matrimania

AT LAUREL'S IVY LEAGUE COLLEGE, MARRIAGE SEEMED TO be the thing to do after graduation. Laurel didn't question that assumption. When she got engaged at twenty-three, she recalls, "No one said, 'Are you crazy?' In fact, a fair number seemed to want to follow precisely the same pattern. Half of them, I would say. I had another friend who got married right before I did, just before we graduated from college. There was a comfort to having another close friend who was getting married too." The idea of a wedding was exciting. "We were shopping for wedding rings before we even really thought about marriage," Laurel recalls. She spent the next year with a wedding planner preparing for what she called "a huge post-Diana wedding."

Laurel married her college sweetheart, a man with a similar background to hers. She assumed they had similar ideas about the kind of life they wanted to live. She saw her husband as "faithful, loyal, reliable, and consistent. He was the good citizen—a clean-cut, responsible type of guy," but "once he graduated, he had major problems as part of the postcollege, what-the-hell-do-I-do-with-my-life panic."

Laurel quickly realized that their ideas about money, lifestyle, and marriage didn't match at all. "At one point, my ex-husband took a commission-only job and then decided he couldn't deal with it. But he didn't even take the time to think it over. He just stopped going to work and started dicking around a lot. This was even before we were married. I should have seen a red flag. . . . I guess I'm tough about stuff like that. I needed a guy who would get up and hustle. "Once I was a year and a half into my marriage I started to get frustrated. I thought that being a wife meant you could choose to work or not to work and that a husband should be able to provide for you."

Laurel's husband had completely different expectations. "He knew when marrying me that my father had made a lot of money and that I would inherit it. As a result he didn't believe that we would have to take care of ourselves, which may have been true from a purely practical standpoint. But neither of us really anticipated that I would want him to make a living—as an example to our future children and even just psychologically, I'm more comfortable with that. I grew up with a man in the household who really worked hard to provide for us—and I wanted my husband to be the same way. I remember shouting at him, 'You've got to make a living. We couldn't have kids even if we wanted to,' and he just said, 'But you have plenty of money.' 'That's not the point!' I yelled back. I saw that our income was going to just go downhill, and that not only from a financial point of view, our marriage was a downhill movement."

Three years after their wedding, and many, many fights and disappointments later, Laurel and her husband got a divorce.

Getting married sends a strong signal: you've got it all together. You're in control, on top of things. Being married creates a powerful message about who you are and where you're going, because we assume that once you're wed, the rest falls into place—the beautiful home, the gourmet dinner parties attended by other witty, vivacious couples, the glorious pregnancy—with a trouble-free, healthy baby its proud result, the child-rearing years complete with nanny and perhaps some part-time work for Mom, comfortably carried out from her home office. The kids who always do their homework and get into prestigious schools, the fabulous family vacations to Tahoe and Paris and the Grand Canyon, and ultimately, home fires burning into the golden years, furnished with grinning grandchildren and oversized family portraits. All you need to do is marry; the attendant rewards are waiting.

We boost up marriage because marriage is important to society, and society in turn supports marriage. In *From This Day Forward* by married journalists Cokie and Steve Roberts, Steve Roberts notes, "Marriage is not only a ceremony between two people. It is a communal event, symbolizing a relationship between families and friends and relatives."[1] Sociologist Linda Waite explains, "Marriage connects people to other individuals, to their social groups (such as in-laws) and to other social institutions (such as churches and synagogues) which are themselves a source of benefits."[2] According to Sarah Willie, a sociologist at Swarthmore College, "Most people still want that formal recognition, and not just by the state. Culturally, it's quite meaningful to have one's friends and family and society at large recognize a lifelong partnership."[3] In some ways, marriage can be as much about other people as it is about ourselves. "I never thought about what marriage itself would actually be like," Amy, a twenty-five-year-old medical student from North Carolina, confesses. "In fact, I never thought past being able to say, 'Oh, how cool is it that I'm married!' I kept fantasizing about these high school reunions where I would come back and show people that I was married to this great guy now."

The Marriage Culture

The message in America these days is splashed across movie screens, squawks out of television sets, shrieks across newspaper headlines, bubbles forth from popular magazines, and fills countless self-help manuals and girly novels. *Get married.* Get married after receiving a proposal in Times Square on *Bride's* magazine–sponsored "Marry Me Day." Get married in El Paso at the annual "Mega-Marriage" ceremony, where more than a hundred couples exchange vows in a mass affair every Valentine's Day. Get married to a woman you just met at the Mall of America, as one man did in 1998 after a conducting a highly publicized wife search. Get married on live television as more than ten thousand viewers applied to do on *Live! With Regis & Kathie Lee*'s annual "Wedding Week." Get married for money on Fox television in front of 22.8 million viewers as Darva Conger did on *Who Wants to Marry a Multi-Millionaire?* Get married like fourteen couples choose to do every year on the eightieth floor of the Empire State Building.

Nowadays, marriage seems to be on everyone's minds—whether they admit it or not. "Love is in the air, but marriage must be in the water," notes a 1999 article in *American Demographics* in response to the cheery 1998 Marital Status and Living Arrangements report, which paints "a pretty rosy picture of family values."[4] In 2000 *The New York Times* reported, "It turns out, for better or for worse that 'I do's' are expected to reverberate more than usual this year."[5] *Redbook* magazine exclaimed in the late nineties, "Marriage Is Hot Again!"[6] There's even a holiday for it: June 27 has been designated the official "Decide to Be Married Day."

We live in a carefully woven web of wedded bliss. After a brief period of denigrating marriage during the 1960s and 1970s, America is harkening back to its marriage-happy state. In the nineties and noughties, there's no shame in declaring that you're looking for commitment. We once again openly believe in the long-cherished ideal of lifelong love, what Margaret Mead called "one of the most conspicuous examples of our insistence on hitching our wagons to a star."[7] As an article in *The New York Times* notes, "Indeed it's no coincidence that our interest in marriage's storybook representation grows just as fast as our practical evidence of its failures. For the American penchant for serial marriage is a perfect testament to the repeated triumph of hope over experience."[8] These days we're constructing our marriage mythology with a new sense of urgency—almost desperation.

In America today the good and the beautiful is all about fidelity and family. The triptych of "commitment," "children," and "the future" fills our public rhetoric, justifying, informing, and exalting everything we do or plan on doing in our personal lives right on through to our governmental policy. And if you don't get married, you just don't get to take part. Not only is it a lonely world out there on your own, but choosing to be there is downright un-

American. "American culture portrays marriage like it's the ulti-mate goal worth striving for," Helena, a thirty-one-year-old editor from Wisconsin, notes. "Your wedding is supposed to be the hap-piest day of your life. It's something that will not only make you forever happy, but on that day you will be admired by all others. You've done what everyone wants to do. You've won."

It seems marriage is for winners. On February 15, 2000, Fox debuted its infamous special, *Who Wants to Marry a Multi-Millionaire?* Creator Mike Darnell explained, "*Who Wants to Be a Millionaire?* inspired me. So I thought, 'What else do people wish for? They wish for relationships."[9] The show, which featured a pa-rade of fifty wanna-be brides (culled from a pool of one thousand applicants), drew a third of all female television viewers eighteen to thirty-four. The furor was later tempered by revelations that the groom once faced charges for domestic abuse and the bride's ad-mission that she had entered on a whim. When happily-ever-after failed to materialize, audiences went sour on the idea. In a follow-up survey, 64 percent believed the show was "harmful to the insti-tution of marriage."[10]

But that didn't halt the TV marriage lineup. MTV aired the game show *I Got Married at Spring Break.* Monday, May 8, 2000, was Wedding Night on ABC. First up, *InStyle*'s Fourth Annual Celebrities Weddings, an hourlong look at the latest Hollywood nuptials. In 2000 TheKnot.com and the *Today* show launched a "groundbreaking new summer wedding series," "*Today* Ties the Knot," featuring "live, on-air and online planning of one lucky cou-ple's wedding" culled from over one thousand entries. Each week the show aired events from the wedding-planning process—from bridesmaid-gown selection to the ring bearer's attire—culminat-ing in an "interactive event [that] allows the audience to vote on-line and choose every element of this wedding—down to where the newlyweds will travel on their honeymoon." Documentary filmmaker Nina Davenport's autobiographical *Always a Brides-maid* debuted on Cinemax at the height of wedding season in 2000. The film explores Davenport's career as a wedding photog-rapher, her long-term relationship with a commitment-phobic boyfriend, her desire to marry, and her underlying fear of being alone. Even the Learning Channel offers a wedding special, *A Wed-*

ding Story (part of a series that also includes *A Dating Story* and *A Baby Story*), which features *Bridal Guide* magazine's "Bride of the Year." In November 2000 Fox debuted *Surprise Wedding,* a two-hour program featuring five women proposing to their boyfriends on-air.

The wedding formula has proven so successful that more shows are in development. In the works from Fox is *I Do, I Don't,* in which couples about to marry in Las Vegas take a battery of compatibility tests and then audiences and analysts vote on whether the couple should go through with it. Green-light ceremonies are aired at the end of the show. Another potential program from Universal, *Wed at First Sight,* shows couples taking their vows on air after having just met for the first time. Filming of the pilot program attracted fifteen hundred applications from willing participants.

The Cinderella story expands on the big screen. *The Wedding Singer* with Drew Barrymore, *Runaway Bride* and *My Best Friend's Wedding* with Julia Roberts, *The Wedding Planner* with Jennifer Lopez—incidentally, all three actresses had their own starter marriages—the trailers go on. Destined couple meets, falls in love, and, the grand finale, weds in a blissful blur of cake and flowers. The on-screen marriage culture is dedicated to finding love, falling in love, ring shopping, blustering but heartfelt toasts, and silly wedding dances. *Committed* stars Heather Graham as an extremely enthusiastic newlywed determined to hold her marriage together. "Let's face it," says the film's writer and director, Lisa Krueger, "marriage is dramatic. You're saying, 'This is it for life.' People can't resist that—they crave that drama and that kind of gravity, that intensity. People want to see that people will join themselves for life in this one singular moment." Joel, a Brooklyn-born photo editor who married at twenty-three because "it was the romantic thing to do," complains, "Movies and advertisements still show this Norman Rockwell, nuclear family. They always have the guy proposing, the girl crying, the grand wedding, everyone's happy."

These movies rarely show us what follows the wedding. The state of marriage itself is considered an afterthought. As writer Kathryn Harrison notes, "The romance is a form that, like the fairy tale, tends to draw a 'happily ever after' curtain of privacy at the altar."[11] We cleave close to the opening verses of champagne and roses or its polar opposite, the perils of ill-fated love, adultery, and husband-assassination plots. We want drama. We want passion. We would rather show spouses being cheated on, maimed, and divorced into oblivion than observe the ins and outs of tussles over toilet-bowl cleaning and the balancing of checkbooks. For sheer entertainment value, courtship and wedding rings far outshine the humdrum state of daily matrimony. Michael, a thirty-five-year-old New Yorker, acknowledges that he bought into the dream. "I think our culture portrays marriage completely idealistically. . . . It's as if you should just be happy that you're married and destined to live happily ever after that. Which of course was nothing but a big fantasy."

We are mesmerized by the romantic idea of marriage, and blinded to the reality. Zoë confesses that, when she married at twenty-three, "I had this knight-on-a-white-horse vision that this man would come and always take care of me. . . . I thought getting married meant that there would always be someone there to make everything okay." We are sold on Cinderella, not on how uncomfortable wearing glass slippers for the next fifty years might be.

In our marriage-happy culture, marriage is positioned as the end goal for the attractive and successful. Eat right, look good, work hard, make money, meet your mate, get married.

So Long, Single

At a certain point, being single simply becomes acceptable. Part of the reason people want to marry so much is that *they just do not want to be single anymore.* "I've been dating since I was fifteen years old, and I'm exhausted," Charlotte complains on television's *Sex and the City.* "Where *is* he?" A 1999 *Self* magazine headline asks, "Is It True Love or Marriage Panic?"[12] Often it's a bit of both.

Social commentators like to protest that America glorifies the single set. "Nothing could be more antimarriage than much of popular culture," claims David Popenoe of the National Marriage Project.[13] Critics point to TV shows like *Sex and the City, Friends,* and *Seinfeld.* They flip through books like *Bridget Jones's Diary* by

Helen Fielding and *The Girls' Guide to Hunting and Fishing* by
Melissa Bank. There's too much pro-single culture going around,
they argue, discouraging people from choosing marriage and even
stigmatizing those who do.

Total patent nonsense, as the audience actually targeted by
such fare will attest. The corollary to the pro-marriage culture is
the culture of antisingledom. Pop culture portrays the single life as
either unrealistically entertaining or downright miserable—and it
depicts single people accordingly. The supposedly liberated singletons on HBO's *Sex and the City* voraciously read "the women's
sports pages," openly, if defensively, admitting that what they're
really looking for is Mr. Right. *Friends*'s main attraction is to each
other (witness the two intrafriend weddings to date), and dating
woes are cushioned by a fantasy system of friends-as-family that
bears little resemblance to real single lives.

Popular culture shouts loud and clear that normal people want
marriage and their own neuroses are what prevent them from getting it. The irony-resistant members of the moraliticking brigade
fail to notice that *Seinfeld* is *mocking* the neuroses of its permanently single characters. Compulsive, harried Bridget Jones just
wants to get married; jittery, fleshless Ally McBeal dreams of dancing babies; and Melissa Bank's tales of singlehood were aptly described by one reviewer as "a glorified version of the matrimonial
how-to manual."[14] None of these singletons is single for the sake of
it; they're alone because they screwed up or are screwed-up in
some way. Women learn that they are too independent, too neu-
rotic, too needy, too immature, too ugly, too careless, too ambitious,
too selfish, too plain not-good-enough for the glorious state of matrimony. Men are taught that they're too stupid, too insecure, too
self-absorbed, too clueless, too out-of-sync, and too repressed to
know that marriage is good for them.

Most fictional plots centered on single women trace their woe-
ful attempts to meet Prince Charming. And in addition to the back-
handed entreaties of the hip, novelized versions, plenty of more
straightforward manuals do the job. Countless volumes extol the
glories of marital bliss. *Will You Marry Me? The World's Most Romantic Proposals; Why Men Marry: What Every Single Woman
Should Know;* and a host of other books carefully explain why we

should get married, why married people are happier, and that marriage is the end goal of existence. Bookstore shelves stagger under reams of get-wed guides for those presumed to be unhappily alone. Titles like *Single No More: How and Where to Meet Your Perfect Mate* and *Marry Me! Three Professional Men Reveal How to Get Mr. Right to Pop the Question* are ready to explain what you're doing wrong, what you did wrong, why you did it, and how you can "fix" yourself in order to achieve a marriageable state. You're needy. You're trying too hard. You're not trying hard enough. You need to be smarter/thinner/sexier/more giving/more interesting. You need to stop beating yourself up, take charge, take control, give up control, stop waiting around, and stop worrying. You need to make different choices, better choices, smarter choices, the choices nobody told you to make. You've got to put yourself out there, make the effort, put your best face forward, be a better person altogether.

You need to change, because if you're still single, something is wrong with you.

Single books come equipped with defensive titles like *Even God Is Single (So Stop Giving Me a Hard Time)* and *With or Without a Man: Single Women Taking Control of Their Lives.* One self-help book goes by the honest title *Being Single in a Couples' World,* providing guidelines to bypass the "cultural scripts" that insist that you need a spouse to be fulfilled. An Amazon.com review explains, "Sometimes when you look around, it seems as if the entire world is coupled up. Family, friends, that cute twosome holding hands walking down the street, everyone is either married or in a serious, committed relationship." A grateful reader responds, "Finally a book that eliminates the guilt of singlehood. Helps you get over the feeling that if you're single, you're a freak."

Marriage Panic

"Look Out, Singletons. Marriage Is Back. Back, Back, Back," shouts *The Washington Post.*[15] The infamous biological clock that's supposed to toll "Baby" begins with an even earlier alarm: "Wed." Once you're in your mid-twenties, it's high time to get hustling. *Cos-*

mopolitan warns, "Older brides often have to fight off fears that people will think there is something wrong with them for having waited so long or that they had to rope their men into marrying at all. It seems that for an 'I'm normal' peace of mind, the 20something brides have the edge."[16]

For women, the first jangle of nerves triggers at twenty-three, when a flurry of precocious weddings portends the coming onslaught. By the time they hit thirty, still-single women are in a panic. In *The Atlantic Monthly* Barbara Dafoe Whitehead issues a bleak warning to the aging single female: "Men may be able to pursue their careers singlemindedly during their twenties and postpone marriage until their thirties without compromising their fertility or opportunities to find a suitable mate, but women cannot."[17] It's not surprising that the most common time for women to enter into therapy is around their thirtieth birthdays. Therapists attest that the fear of never finding a lifelong love often sends them there. "If you're the last member of your posse to get a proposal, don't panic," soothes *Cosmopolitan* in an article entitled "Help! Everyone's Hitched."[18] Helena, thirty-one, observes, "My single friends all feel miserable. They see that a number of our friends are already married and having babies and that's supposed to be the ideal. They feel like they have to get married and they simply won't be happy until they do."

Not only do women express a strong personal desire to marry in their twenties, society exerts a none-too-subtle pressure. "Today marriage has practically become chic," notes *Newsday,* "a fashion statement for conservative and liberal spouses alike."[19] In *Glamour* magazine a quiz asks, "Are you caught up in convention or unusually unorthodox?" Considered "conventional" (i.e., normal) is a yes to the question "Does your life plan involve work, marriage by 25 and kids by 30?"[20] The assumption is that women marry, and if they don't, something has gone wrong. At best, they're "offbeat," "funky," "weird." Unmarried women are made to feel like they're not quite legitimate as women, not quite *there* yet. "Sure, it is more socially acceptable to stay single longer," Ilene Rosenzweig writes in *The New York Times.* "But the assumption remains that women who do so are either obsessive 'career gals,' as my grandmother would say, or unable to throw an effective lasso."[21]

One glance at women's magazines confirms the continuing dominance of marriage messages targeted to women. While these magazines aren't realistic so much as aspirational, it's interesting to examine what we wish for. The ideals these magazines promote, the ideas they encourage, and the fantasies they project reveal a lot about their readers. And boy, do these magazines project and promote. In *Cosmopolitan*—the supposed bible of the liberated singleton—a headline suggests that readers "Meet the New Housewife Wanna-bes." According to the article, "They're young, they're hip—and they want to hang out at home. (Can you relate?) Find out why more and more 20something women dream of quitting the daily grind."[22] It goes on to celebrate Erica, who "couldn't wait to get out of college and start my brilliant career" but then found "a new goal: marry that cute associate two cubicles down and embark on a full-time stint as his housefrau." Not there yet? "*Cosmo's* Guide to Getting Engaged" offers readers "the world's best advice on everything from getting your guy to pop the question to handling friends who freak out to finding the most romantic ring."[23] In October 2000, *Elle* handily declared marriage to be "in" (and cohabitation "out").

Young marriage is seen as a sign of affluence and social achievement. *Redbook* notes, "Today, for the first time since the mid-1960s, smart women in their twenties—in some cases in their early twenties—are not only unafraid but eager to become brides. . . . Among well-educated, career-minded women, becoming a wife at around age twenty-five has grown not only socially acceptable but enviable."[24] According to a *New York* magazine report on young brides, "The circle of women who seem to be skipping their Mary Tyler Moore, Murphy-bed phase altogether is bigger than just the 'Waspy, preppy circuit' but not much: It's the college-educated, cosmopolitan young women of privilege who seem to be choosing early marriage—at least marriage under 25—as an accessory to their post-graduation life and beyond."[25]

The pro-marriage inducements emanate from all corners—left-wing, right-wing, bohemian, yuppie, African-American, immigrant cultures—everywhere. Even the fearless feminist editors of *Bust* magazine lament, "When we were in our early twenties we thought that the biological clock and 'juggling career and family' stuff was yuppie bullshit for women who wore beige stockings or relaxed their hair. We knew better. We would figure it all out, in our own radical bohemian thrift-store ways. Surely it would happen to us in its own time. . . . And yet it hasn't. We haven't figured it out. And now here we are."[26] Unhappily single, reading books about marriage.

To a lesser degree than women, unmarried men are also criticized and ridiculed. They're deemed "afraid of commitment" and "immature." They're referred to as lads, dudes, and guys. Single males are told to just grow up already, face responsibility, be a man. "I am struck by the feeling . . . that everyone around me is getting married," begins an essay entitled "Marriage Mania" on the website Ironminds. The author, once engaged at twenty-one, goes on to lament, "It's just that there's a lot of marriage going around. I'm 24 years old, and I've got a bit of whiplash . . . the ex-fiancée is getting married, plenty more exes are on their way. And here I am, muddling through the muck, head in my ass, just trying to figure out if I have any matching socks. Am I supposed to be that grown up already?"[27]

The Married Man is the new male hero. Harrison Ford in *The Fugitive,* Russell Crowe in *Gladiator,* Tom Hanks in just about everything—all fight the good fight—*for their wives.* Marriage imbues him with honor, elicits courage, gives him a sense of duty. Advertisements celebrate the married man (particularly when he has an infant propped up in his muscular arms). In our confused era of redefined gender, men are struggling to define what "masculine" is, and often the only tried-and-true definition is the proud-husband model. To be a married man is to prove your manhood.

It's no wonder young men and women today are eager to escape the odious state of singlehood and leap into happy, socially sanctioned matrimony. We want to abandon the singlehood stigma as fast as humanly possible.

When Are You Getting Married?

By the time April rolls around, the complaints begin. "I have to go to six weddings starting in May," a twenty-six-year-old man groans. "I'm in three wedding parties this summer," a twenty-five-year-old boasts as she embarks on a presummer, must-fit-into-a-bridesmaid-dress diet. "We're spending so much money on wedding travel this summer, there's no way we can take a vacation. I won't even have any vacation time left with all the long-weekend weddings we have to go to," another woman despairs.

May to October is wedding season for the blissful bridal set.*

But no matter what time of year it is, the current marriage craze is apparent. Not only does our culture idealize and endorse marriage, society enforces it as well. Twentysomethings are under a tremendous amount of pressure to get married—from their friends, their peer groups, their families, even their colleagues. One by one, as friends, coworkers, and siblings begin to sport wedding bands, the pressure mounts. Friends get divided into two distinct groups: the Single Ones and the Married Pairs. At one point "single" meant utterly unattached; suddenly the word gains a new meaning. Even when you've got a significant other, if you're unwed, you're still "single" in the married world. You're not legit until you're legally bound. Helena remarks that in addition to the tremendous pressure she felt from "advertising and the media and her parents," she found that "people who are married pressure other people to get married. Both at work and in social circles, if you have a boyfriend, the question is always there: 'When are *you* getting married?' "

Max, a computer executive from Connecticut, felt that his girlfriend, two years older, pushed him toward marriage. "Her friends were all getting married, and I think she felt pressure from all sides," he explains. "From her friends, from her parents, from society. Nobody actually said anything to her, but she felt it. Other people were getting married who'd been together a shorter period of time than we had. And in the end, I felt pressure from her too."

The pressure isn't just on women. Wes, a New York City investment banker, says a subtle social pressure to marry pervades

---

* According to the Association of Bridal Consultants, 14 percent of American weddings take place in June, followed in popularity by September, which hosts 11.8 percent of all weddings.

the world of high finance. "I worked at a pretty conservative firm," he explains. "The senior people were all married, and there was a lot of expectation that you would be too. Socializing through work is almost always centered on spouses and kids." When his four-year marriage fell apart, almost all of his friends were married and he didn't want people in the office or friends through work to know. "I was ashamed and embarrassed. At the time, I didn't know anyone who was divorced at my age. And I was initially very reluctant to talk about it. I certainly wasn't going to talk about it at work because divorce is a real taboo there. I kept the whole thing quiet for about a year, during the entire separation period."

George was unhappy at his job when he got engaged. "In a way, I looked at getting engaged as a way to blow me out of where I was professionally and get me somewhere else," he says. "And the horrible thing is, it kind of worked." Being a married man carries a certain amount of cachet, especially in the office. "People dealt with me differently as an engaged man. When I got a new job, I was one of only two men in the office and they made a big fuss. They threw me a wedding shower at work, which was lovely. . . . It was very classy. And they all gave me these stereotypically male gifts. Very male, male, men's club type of things like a Tiffany decanter, that sort of stuff."

"Part of the attraction of marriage for some heterosexual males . . . is that it confers status," explains an article in *The New Republic*.[28] In *The New York Times* Rick Marin writes, "I'm a 'scorekeeper,' as a friend once labeled me. Children are one more measure of success to me, like an I.P.O. or a first novel. 'He's got two kids already,' I berate myself. 'Where am I on this?' A competitive-male thing, maybe."[29] Olivia's boyfriend asked her to marry him after several months. She attributes his eagerness to marry to his competitive nature. "He had just broken up with this other woman, and she got married to someone else almost right away. I think he was trying to one-up her, or at least stay even." One woman explained that the day her husband proposed, he forbade her to tell anyone. "I don't know what was going on with him. Or why I had to keep it a secret. But then later that day, his ex-girlfriend called and told him that she was engaged. When he got off the phone, he turned to me and said, 'Okay, you can call your parents and tell them.' And I was like, 'Wait. You need to decide what *you* want to do.' . . . Something happened to him that day. There was something going on, but I think I was kind of naïve at the time."

People feel pressured to get married by their social milieu, whether it's the world of East Coast debutantes or the small Midwestern town. Marriage often breaks out in clusters. At Clara's Ivy League school, a huge number of women got married shortly after graduating: "You're in such a bubble at college, so these things can happen easily among a group of friends." Clara wed when she was twenty-three. "We started dating our senior year in college. . . . We sort of became this Big Couple. So much of it was societal, all the pressure we were under. He was president of his fraternity, and I was president of my sorority. We were looked at as the kind of perfect-sweetheart couple that will inevitably end up together." It's as if we get married by consensus. Clara explains, "If you're not married, people are shocked and then they just feel sorry for you. I was at a conference last week with a female colleague who is forty and unmarried. This other woman looked at her and said condescendingly, in a very sad voice, 'You know, I used to be in your situation.' " Being unmarried becomes "a situation"—cause for concern, something to pity, a problem to be eradicated. The older one gets, the more fear of losing out in the marriage game. Charlotte grew up in rural Minnesota, where "everyone gets married at eighteen and if you're not married by twenty, you're a spinster." In her world, "marriage was just something you did. That was the climax of your life, what gave your life direction. . . . Everyone was getting married all around me. I was surrounded by newlyweds. There was definitely social pressure to get married." As she puts it, "In the Midwest, everyone decent is married. And all the other people move away." Charlotte married when she was twenty-two. "I thought it was kind of cool; it was like, 'We're all wives!' It was kind of a novel idea, kind of silly, not realistic at all. It was like, 'Oooh! I'm a wife! We *all* are!' "

Marriage loves company. George discovered a similar sense of camaraderie among his married friends. "There's this sort of group thing, this new kind of status. It's such a cute thing. This feeling like you're this young married person and you've got all your

young married friends." Friends want their friends to get married—
and stay married. Melissa, now thirty and single, explains, "There's
tremendous pressure to be in a couple as a lifestyle choice. People
don't like being single. It's a state of ambivalence that people don't
like to participate in and they don't like to be around. *I* don't like
it." She recalls getting engaged at twenty-two. "Once I had on
that engagement ring, I was in this total wedding zone where
everything was about marriage. It was always, 'Why aren't you
married? Are you going to get married? When are you guys getting
married?' "

People clearly have an investment not only in their own
unions but in other people's marriages as well. Couples often become competitive in a way. "There was a close group of about six
of us who got married at the same time," Charlotte recalls. "We
were constantly one-upping each other. We all bought our houses
at the same time, the whole thing. I couldn't stand it. The last person to get engaged ended up feeling pretty bad."

For other young marrieds, social pressure works in the opposite direction, particularly for people in their late teens and early
twenties, many of whom married precisely because their friends
and peers weren't. Marriage feels like a daring move, and some
couples like to see themselves as rebellious or as leaders of the
pack. "When he proposed marriage it was so different from what
everyone else was doing," says Amy, twenty-five, who was a freshman at a prestigious state university and a star athlete. "I wanted
to be so different from what everyone thought I was in high
school. I was a nerd with a capital *N*. I had never been the focus of
any gossip or anything like that, and half the people I went to high
school with were at my college. It was like this big rebellion against
everyone from my little high school. I guess I just wanted to say to
everybody, 'Screw you, I can have fun too! Look at me; I'm with
this really cool guy. I'm better than you. He loves me and I'm married.' " In retrospect, Amy thinks that for her getting married was
essentially about *other* people—not about who she really was or
what she wanted. "It's incredible looking back. I was very insecure,
very concerned about what other people thought. Everything I did
was done for appearances' sake."

Marriage gives you that sense of Us against Them. Lucy was

the first to go in her San Francisco crowd, wed at twenty-five. "None of our friends were getting married at the time, so there was this idea that we were doing something none of our peers were doing," she says. "It felt different and kind of exciting." At twenty-three, Joel was the first of his friends to get married. "They all thought we were crazy." In the face of his parents' disapproval, he and his wife decided to elope. "Not including our families was kind of exciting. I was in a high-pressure situation, because they were treating her really badly. So in a certain way it was an easy thing to do. It was us against them, or us against everybody."

As marriage becomes more the norm, jealousy surfaces among single friends. "One of my friendships ended when I got engaged," says Bethany, who married at twenty-three. "I had this girlfriend who had a fixation with this guy she wanted to marry. Then all of the sudden I was the one to get married. She no longer had her trusty sidekick. When I told her I was engaged, she just said, 'Oh, brother,' in this very chilly way. She was totally hateful. And that was that." Michael reports that two of his wife's friends stopped talking to her after they got engaged. "She knew it was because they were jealous." Helena said that though "some of my good friends seemed more excited about my marriage than I was," she also lost a good friend. "She kind of slipped away. I know that she really just wanted to get married herself, *and she was jealous.*"

Sibling rivalry can breed similar reactions. Juliet's sisters, both unmarried, gave her a hard time when she announced her engagement, refusing her request to serve as bridesmaids. "They were very jealous and extremely petty," she remembers unhappily. Another woman explains how in the middle of her wedding plans, her fiancé's brother also got engaged. "It became a bone of contention because they got very competitive throughout the whole wedding-planning process. His brother was older, and he was annoyed that the younger sibling was getting married first."

Parental expectations are also often a factor, though frequently not acknowledged by young men and women, in the desire to get married. Many twentysomethings feel that their parents looked to them as the absolution or correction of their own regrets and mistakes—or are excessively anxious about their children repeating their patterns. Parents may long for the wedding they never had or hope to eradicate the memory of the one they did. Many pressure their children to marry. Kate, a media planner from Chicago who married at twenty-six, explains, "My mother was in her sixties and single. Even after her own two divorces, she was by no means turned off by the idea of marriage; in fact, she wanted more than anything to marry again. I could always tell that, even though she didn't say it outright, she worried that I would become one of those women—thirty-five, lonely, careerist, with a cat and a studio apartment, contemplating in-vitro fertilization. Sometimes I think she projected her own loneliness onto me. When I got engaged, part of me didn't want to tell her because her overwhelming relief would turn me off. The other part couldn't wait to relieve her of the anxiety."

Parents are often heavily invested in their children's marital status, though they seldom admit it. Often they are indirectly involved in their children's decision to get married—whether out of emulation, admiration, rebellion, or consolation. They think their son is a good catch, and they want to make sure his wife measures up. A mother considers her daughter homely and wonders who will take her. A father doesn't want his daughter to marry and objects to anyone who does. Almost inevitably, parents project their own desires and their desires for their children onto the all-important decision. "Everyone always expected us to get married," Elizabeth says. "I reminded [my husband] of his mother, and he was very pleased to have this woman by his side that seemed like the type he should marry. I fit the image perfectly of who his wife should be. He even told me so."

The Marrying Kind

In former times, the wifely woman was an easy order. She simply needed to deliver the three Cs: cooking, cleaning, and children, and most women were amply prepared by the time engagement season rolled around. If Mother hadn't taught her how to properly tend to her husband, a bevy of women's magazines, home economics classes, and advertisements drummed the training in.

Today those qualifications are no longer enough to assure

marriageability. Men want a new breed of female companion—independent and dependent at the same time. They want a woman who can earn her keep, entertain herself, and stand on her own two feet under a variety of circumstances. She needs to be tolerant of his working hours, able to live her own life, and skilled at maintaining a balance between both partners' competing demands. However, when push comes to shove, women are still expected to encompass the traditional wifely virtues and perhaps make the necessary sacrifices "when the time comes." Most modern men want the perfect hybrid of traditional wife and modern woman, a complicated creation that most women haven't figured out how to become.

This new traditionalism is apparent in the way men currently conceive of their roles as husbands. "I was psyched about becoming a husband," says Max. "I always wanted to be the man, the provider, stuff like that. I liked the idea of being a husband. It felt good to be able to take care of a woman, to feel responsible for something important." Most men still talk about their husbandly responsibilities largely in economic terms. But they also hope to provide more; many marrying men think of themselves as being "the right kind of guy" for marriage: responsible, sensitive, decisive, affectionate. Growing up during the 1980s family-values backlash, these young men learned as teenagers that women were desperate to marry; they like to think of themselves as the best kind of "new male," ready to rescue women out of their precarious situation.

Women are equally demanding. The new husband-hunting formula is a similar version of tradition plus, with its contradictory expectations and demands. The prefeminist wifely request was very simple: food and shelter. Now that women are their own breadwinners, the stakes have changed—and gotten much higher. Women still look for someone who represents stability, constancy, and trustworthiness, but they also require a great deal more. Elizabeth describes the qualities that attracted her to her husband, placing him effectively above the pack. He was "handsome," "dressed nicely," "worldly," "interesting," and "well traveled"; he had "good taste," "neat hobbies," and "nice possessions"; he "showed character," "found things in life that were meaningful to him," and "cared for things." Barbara Ehrenreich calls the current ideal husband "the perfect, all-purpose Renaissance man."

> He should be a co-provider and a reliable financial partner; a co-conversationalist and sparkly dinner companion, fully briefed by CNN. In the event of children, we expect he will further develop into a skilled coparent with a repertoire of bedtime stories and remedies for runny noses. He should be prepared to jump into sweats and serve as a sturdy fitness partner, plus handling home repair; a husband who can't locate a fuse box is about as useful as one of those little plastic tool kits from Toys "R" Us. And since we are modern women, we have every right to think he will manage, in addition, to be a tireless and imaginative lover, supplying orgasms virtually on demand.[30]

Men are well aware of women's lofty aspirations, and it scares the hell of out of them. "I think the dating scene is a nightmare," says Robert, who married at twenty-four and is now engaged to a childhood friend at thirty-two. "It's so smarmy. It's all about your portfolio. Women have this whole checklist they run down. He's got to be good-looking, arty, have a good income, good clothes, impeccable taste, live in a good neighborhood. You have to have this, you have to do that."

Both men and women have become demanding—for good reason. After all, it's important to secure the right kind of mate. Showing off the proper husband and wife seems to say a lot about who you are as a person.

The Social Wedding

Sound the herald. Beat the wedding drums. Tell everyone you're getting married. For those who don't know how, *Cosmopolitan* offers tips on "Spreading the News: The Right Way to Tell the World—Including Jealous Friends and Evil Exes—That You're Getting Hitched." The article warns the betrothed to "call anyone who might be offended if he or she heard about it from someone else first (don't dawdle—you'll be shocked at how fast word spreads)."[31] "There's all this social pressure to show the world that you're worthy of getting married," says Helena. "It's like this public announcement of your worth as a human being. Someone loves you and wants to marry you, and you've reached a certain stage in your life."

Wedding announcements are placed as public advertisements for the all-important, pivotal transformation. Many couples file in their respective hometown papers as well as one or two metropolitan papers, which reflect a clear social hierarchy, featuring highly educated, upscale movers and shakers, or the sons and daughters thereof. They typically include the couples' parents' names, hometowns, and occupations as well as any distinctive family lineage; the couples' respective college degrees and occupations; their ages and marital histories; and a brief summary of the ceremony particulars including place and type of venue, time, and officiate. All the qualifications for becoming a deserving matrimonial mate. In February 2000 *The New York Times* decided to ratchet up its wedding coverage, presumably in response to public interest. Announcements were expanded to include commentary from the couples and their friends, stories revolving around their first meeting and courtship process, and decisions along the path of wedding preparation. One twenty-eight-year-old male confessed that the new format was intimidating: "I did very well with the straight credential thing, and now I would have to do well with this additional set of specs?" he complained. "You're going to have to come up with some little anecdote if you want to be in it? It's going to have to be witty? I feel like it sort of adds to the pressure."[32]

Getting married becomes another tick on the social register. As one L.A.-based wedding consultant proclaimed, "It's your chance to tell the world who you really are in terms of the big picture."[33] And the ad is no longer enough. On top of newspaper announcements and wedding invitations, people increasingly ship out a barrage of wedding-announcement cards to alert extended family, colleagues, and acquaintances of their new status. "Look at me, look at what I've done," such public-service announcements seem to claim.

Weddings not only tell the world who you are, they show the rest of the world how much everyone else cares about you. They have transformed from personal affairs into social events, akin to fund-raising balls and cotillions. If we have 150 or more invitees, we are socially adept and popular. We're terribly well connected. We had to invite all of our colleagues, our network, and our associates. Or we have large families, with dozens of doting uncles and close cousins. We're worthy.

Wedding parties are back and bigger than ever. Marie Brenner noted recently in *The New York Times,* "The new dames marry younger, with bridal parties that seem to echo Queen Elizabeth's."[34] The modern set includes best man, maid of honor, six to ten groomsmen, six to ten bridesmaids, attendants, honorees, ring bearers, flower children, toastmakers, and poetry readers. "Consensus of the month," *Harper's Bazaar* decides, launching into a photo spread of Beau (son of Ted) Turner's four-hundred-guest extravaganza: "Texas weddings are all about 'big.' "[35] In *Redbook,* a Texas-based photographer, noting the recent spate of ranch-based weddings complete with 500 to 750 guests, says she feels like she's stepped back thirty years in time: "Man, do I have a jillion twenty-something Texas weddings down here!"[36] "What's a wedding without the guests?" asks *Vogue* in a feature listing "identifiable invitees who are sure to make the big day memorable,"[37] including the jet-setter, the too cute cousin, the cool cousin, the dowager aunt, and the spotlight-stealing supermodel (doesn't *everyone* have at least one at their wedding?).

In February 2001 the editor of *Town & Country* concludes, "One thing is certain about Generation Xers. They like their weddings big, extravagant and in unusual locations."[38] The editor of *Bride's* explains, "Today marriage is a choice. And people are choosing to put their money into having an event that can't be replicated. Let's create a wonderful memory for all of us in this room tonight because we may not be together like this again."[39]

The Wedding Industry

That wonderful memory happens to have a price tag of about $20,000. Costs vary regionally, with the New York wedding coming in at an average of $75,000, according to one New York wedding planner, and 2 percent of American weddings weighing in with price tags of over $500,000.[40] Budgets skyrocket when you factor in all the costs—not only the reception-hall rental and the bridal gown, but every last detail down to the dipped shrimp hors d'oeuvres and those lovely printed place cards. The average wedding meal, including passed appetizers, salad, and entrée, costs $50, according to *Bride's*—not including wine or champagne. To finish it off, the average wedding cake is baked for a whopping $900.[41] "Wedding fairs," also called "bridal expos" or "planning fairs," have sprouted up across the nation, allowing vendors to display their wares.

The sheer consumerism of the American wedding is almost enough to convert one into a Marxist by wedding day. DeBeers starts the ball rolling with its beautifully photographed black-and-white commercials, which to the sound of soaring violin chords convince us that "a diamond is forever" and that any marriage meant to last begins with a sizeable engagement ring. These messages work wonders: today, after a long period out-of-fashion, diamond engagement rings are sported alongside wedding bands by almost 85 percent of new brides. The latest ring extravagance is the platinum band; according to Platinum Guild International, this tony metal now captures 40 percent of the market for first-time brides, up from just 25 percent a few years ago.[42]

Weddings have morphed into massive extravaganzas. In our consumer society, it's almost as if we think that by spending money on our weddings, we'll be able to buy ourselves happy marriages. People want so desperately to believe in marriage that an entire industry, the so-called wedding-industrial complex, has exploded around it. Hire an art director. Commission your own wedding wine vintage. Sell the event to sponsors, who place their brand name strategically around the wedding site. In the last five years, the wedding industry has bloated upward an additional $6 billion, with over $38 billion spent annually on the big day.[43] Another estimate holds the industry at between $40 and $100 billion a year.[44] With an average of 2.4 million weddings a year, weddings are big business in America. Moët & Chandon, the champagne company, has even created an economic index, the Matrimonial Matrix, to track the cost of twelve elements constituting the luxury

New York wedding, including engraved invitations, tuxedo rental, and birdseed with which to shower the newly married.[45] The editor of *Elegant Bride* justifies the hoopla by explaining, "There is a seriousness we're seeing that is new, which is why the money is being spent."[46] That's one way to view it.

"The whole focus on weddings makes marriage seem so materialistic," Max complains. "I support marriage, but they portray it like it's an advertisement or something. It's just about the diamond engagement ring, these enormous weddings. But you have this big wedding and then it's over. There's nothing about marriage itself. And there's nothing spiritual about it at all."

USA Today explains the recent surge in wedding extravaganzas by citing "the trickle-down effect of celebrity weddings, and the coverage of same in magazines such as *InStyle*."[47] Check out Jennifer Aniston, Catherine Zeta-Jones, and the next Hollywood starlet's bridal gown in *Us Weekly* magazine's "Weddings of the Year" issue. Readers not only gobble up, and base their own fantasies on, such celebrity wedding coverage, but they take it personally, attaching elaborate emotional meaning to it. As one convinced reader effused to *Us*, "I enjoyed your special package featuring famous newlyweds. . . . [One famous pair] really caught my attention—the couple looks so much in love. It's nice to know that love humbles even Hollywood stars!"[48]

The wedding ceremony has ballooned into a two-year ritual: agreeing to marry, throwing an engagement party (sometimes several) before the obligatory yearlong engagement, followed by endless wedding plans, bridal showers, and bachelor/bachelorette parties, all eventually culminating in the Event. The average time between engagement and wedding has stretched out to eighteen months, as couples either milk the process for all it's worth or suffer through the considerations and delays imposed by family, potential wedding-party members, and the overtaxed wedding industry.[49] Trying to book a popular reception hall less than a year ahead of time is an exercise in futility. No wonder the betrothed are extending their wedding days into weekendlong affairs; something needs to justify all that preparation. "This is *my* week," insists bridal Charlotte on *Sex and the City*. "It's your *day*," a frustrated bridesmaid retorts.

We've become convinced that our weddings symbolize who we are individually, what we believe in, what we stand for, what our hopes for the future are, and what kind of couples we plan to be. As one bubbly bride said of her reception, which featured a cigar bar, a giant ice sculpture, and a martini lounge, "Tom and I put thought into everything that goes into that room. When people walk in, I want them to say, 'Wow, *that's* Jennifer and Tom.' "⁵⁰ By May 2001, *The New York Times* documented a new offspring of wedding fever: "Attack of Bridezilla."⁵¹

"Everything in the culture pulls you towards marriage," George, a New Yorker who married at twenty-seven, notes. "We're set up to think that marriage is this profoundly transformative act, that we become new, better people once we're married. It's what keeps the entire wedding industry afloat, so it's in a lot of people's interests to foster that myth." Each aspect of the wedding is intended as a form of personal expression and achievement. "This is *your* moment," the bridal magazines coo at legions of brides eager to put their personal stamp on the affair. *Wedding Gowns* magazine asks brides to ogle hundreds of dresses before making the pivotal selection. Products like Lucky Chick's Blushing Bride box, filled with body lotion, massage oil, lip balm, and the like, ensure that a bride's inner conviction is outwardly displayed. Philosophy's "Here Comes the Bride" gift set, which includes shampoo, facial cleanser, exfoliating foot cream, and Eye Dew, a special cream for "pre-ceremonial crows' feet and puffiness," are there to convince the bride that on her wedding day she'll be, as the Estée Lauder perfume ad promises, "Beautiful." "Our culture tends to market marriage as a goal towards which to aspire regardless of whether or not it's appropriate for the person or the couple or the situation," says Zoë, who was divorced by age twenty-five. "If you're married, you get to have all these 'things'—just look at *Bride's* magazine. You get a house, a car, two or three kids, this whole package of stuff wrapped around an institution that's supposed to be acceptable for everyone."

Additional signs of wedding mania include a surge in "destination weddings," where friends and family jet off to an exotic locale for up to four days of wedding festivities. According to *Modern Bride* magazine, the number of such affairs has tripled in the

last three years, now comprising 11 percent of all weddings.⁵²
Though the average amount spent on wedding photography and
videography is $1,260,⁵³ the Professional Photographers of
America recently reported that due to high demand they have
been booking photographers who charge up to $15,000 a wed-
ding.⁵⁴ Planning has become so complex that more people are hir-
ing wedding coordinators to tie it all together. The Association of
Bridal Consultants has expanded from 27 members in 1980 to
today's swollen patrol of 2,350 professionals.⁵⁵

Bridal magazines boast more ad pages than ever. The February/
March 2001 issue of *Bride's* broke records for the fourth straight
year; the largest consumer magazine ever, it weighed in at 4.9
pounds, with 1,286 pages devoted primarily to advertisements for
wedding dresses, reception venues, bridal consultants, stationers,
caterers, wedding photographers, photo-album manufacturers,
travel agencies, makeup artists, wedding stylists, florists, and
bridesmaid-dress shops. New bridal magazines are popping up; in
January 2001 *InStyle* hatched a bridal spin-off. Envious fashion
and celebrity magazines now boost their own bridal coverage.
Martha Stewart Living sprouted *Martha Stewart Living's Weddings. Vogue* and *Glamour* now include special wedding sections,
their photo spreads teeming with marital glory. *Talk* magazine features a section called "Marriage Exchange." Even *Ms.* boasted a
cover package devoted to the marriage frenzy: "I Do! I Do?"

Once you've finished reading the bevy of magazines devoted
to the ins and outs of weddings, reams of wedding books await,
both newly published and old standbys reprinted every spring.
Some provide general advice (*The Best of Martha Stewart Weddings*), others are all-out "planners"—actual workbooks to assist
the betrothed in carrying out the necessary wedding prep. For
those who truly suffer through the prewedding jitters, self-help
books like *Tying the Knot: A Couple's Guide to Emotional Well-
Being from Engagement to the Wedding Day* ensure that you make
it intact to the Big Event.

Wedding madness can also be tended to on the Internet. Websites like TheKnot.com, WeddingChannel.com, and BlissBridal.com
have made bridal sites one of the hottest categories online. In
2000, Condé Nast invested $18 million in WeddingChannel.com

("Everything You Need to Plan the Perfect Wedding. Yours."), which provides content from *Bride's* magazine to its 1.5 million monthly visitors. Dreamweavers.com offers "virtual bridesmaids" and allows you to calculate whether or not you're astrologically fit for each other. And surprise! Nearly every wedding website offers an online gift registry, along with the major e-commerce sites from Target's Club Wedd to Williams-Sonoma. Business has gotten rather competitive. Weddinglist.com sends out e-mail notifications to guests alerting them to the couple's desires. Couples who register with TheKnot.com get a frequent-flier mile for every dollar purchased on their online registry. Even the government has gotten in on the game. At the Housing and Urban Development site, www.hud.gov, guests can register for mortgage payments. A guide to the entire process, *CyberBride,* recently hit bookstores.

The wedding-gift industry has expanded into a $19-billion-a-year business.[56] The days when a gift list was truly necessary to provide the essentials of a new home are long gone. The nature of bridal registries has become completely altered, blurred, and, to many minds, obsolete, as most people own the blender and toaster oven long before they wed. Better to register for an upgraded stereo system or a spa vacation in place of traditional china. According to a *Wall Street Journal* report, "I Do . . . Take MasterCard," the new trend among the betrothed is registering for stock or cash gifts, often through an online registration service. Today, registry URLs are printed plainly on the wedding invitation list, a far cry from the subdued behind-the-scenes whispering of wedding gifts past.

The Moneyed Marriage

Money and matrimony share a long history. In fact, marriage has more of a tradition as an economic arrangement than as a romantic ideal. Originally, the diamond ring was meant to signal to the bride's family that the groom could afford to keep her. And he got a dowry in return. Before the rise of capitalism, marriage was often the primary means of making a living. You married a woman for her dowry, and you married a man for his farm. Applying for a job was often one and the same as selecting a spouse. Thanks to capitalism, we can now make money individually, but the marriage bond still constitutes an economic exchange on many levels. As the National Marriage Project delicately puts it, "Marriage remains a vitally important economic institution and a source of economic advantage."[57]

The unspoken truth behind modern marriage is the prevalence of financial considerations. There's still the mentality that "Once this is settled, I'll have the security I need to get on with my career/make a change/make enough money so that I/my wife can take time off to have children." *New York Times* columnist Felicia R. Lee wrote a two-part series, "Looking for Mr. Goodbucks," about the supposedly passé search for a rich husband. After interviewing a dozen single career women, she found that "many admitted to a nagging little voice inside their heads that says they want a man to take care of them."[58] Feminists as likely as not, Lee concludes, these women nonetheless want "love and security in one cuddly package." Lee received a number of angry letters and e-mails from men who deplored "the rampant market culture" that runs with particular forcefulness in the New York marriage scene.[59] Apparently Lee struck a chord.

America should not have been so astonished by the success of *Who Wants to Marry a Multi-Millionaire?* Or so appalled. (Even *The Rules* girls trembled with outrage. "What's Love Got to Do with It?" they demanded. "We don't believe in the girl-asks-boy-how-much-money-he-makes so they can get married."[60]) Doth we protest too much? There's an unspoken taboo that thou shalt not mingle money and marriage. Yet with an institution that for centuries survived as essentially a business transaction and in today's capitalism-fueled culture, the intermingling of marriage and money should come as no surprise.

The link between money and matrimony is evident in many arguments about marriage's fate. Social critics blame the declining marriage rate in terms of women's earning power. What they mean is, marriage is financially motivated: women need to be fed, clothed, and housed—and in order to secure men's financial function, the system needs to stay that way. Americans bemoan the rise in prenuptial agreements because of the message it sends about divorce, but it also implies that people are really just after money when they marry. Men complain about "high-maintenance women"; what they mean is, not every man can afford to marry them. We talk about marrying up, marrying down, and "perfect mergers." It's all too often clearly about cash. At the height of the Internet boom, a flurry of articles appeared discussing the search for the Silicon Valley spouse. "Silicon Valley turns out 64 millionaires a day, most of them young, single men," *Harper's Bazaar* announced in an article about "dot.com gold diggers."[61] The dot.comers are apparently not unaware. In a recent *New York Times* report, "Marriage Insurance for the Young," a divorce lawyer notes, "I see lots of kids"; today, 70 percent of prenuptial agreements are for people under thirty-five.[62] One twenty-nine-year-old pro-prenup entrepreneur explained, "You look at the people who were in love and are now divorced and you realize that so many had hidden agendas."

Even if you don't hunt down a millionaire mate, marriage makes you richer. The wedding itself brings newlyweds hefty cash gifts, which they get to enjoy while their parents wrestle with wedding bills. Married couples pool resources, achieving economies of scale, decreasing expenses, and increasing income. Two individuals have only one household to take care of and only half the work to do at home (naturally this is in theory; in reality labor at home is often unevenly divided, but that's another story). They are freed to work harder or longer earning money outside the home. They save more, and they die with an average of nearly twice what never-marrieds end up with in the bank. As one twenty-four-year-old wife tells *Redbook,* "Price-wise, everything is split in half. When you're married, everything is 50 percent off."[63]

For men, there are other financial incentives to marry. In one survey, 95 percent of top-ranking male executives were married with children, and three quarters of them had stay-at-home wives.[64] Marriage is associated with upward mobility. Once you've made it, you can marry. Or vice versa: once you're married, you've made it. It turns out that married men make more money in the same jobs held by single men, though they also tend to work longer hours and save at faster rates.[65] While it's possible that men who are better off are more inclined to marry in the first place, marriage itself gives men an incentive to earn and save more money.

Despite feminism, despite a booming economy, despite our as-

sumptions that it's a new world out there, for many women marriage still means money. In a 1997 essay "The Independent
Woman (and Other Lies)," writer Katie Roiphe discusses the Gen X
woman's yearning for a male savior. She calls her own independence "an elaborately constructed façade that hides a more traditional feminine desire to be protected and provided for" and that
"somewhere deep in the irrational layers of my psyche" lies the desire to find a male breadwinner. This fantasy of what she calls "the
Man in a Gray Flannel Suit" is one that "independent strong-
minded women of the nineties are distinctly not supposed to
have," she says, "but I find myself having it all the same. And many
of the women I know are having it too."[66] As *Harper's Bazaar* puts
it, "the knight in a pin-striped suit is a potent fantasy for many
women," even in this day and age.[67]

For Gen Xers who grew up with feminist ideals as a given,
there's something seductive about being the damsel in distress. It
goes against the grain, feels rebellious. "The gold digger is alive
and well ... in a bottom-line, post-feminist culture, where marrying for money is no longer something that many women feel compelled to hide," writes Ruth La Ferla in a 2001 article entitled "They
Want to Marry a Millionaire."[68] An upswing in upscale singles
events, eligible bachelor lists, and continuing-ed classes encourage
willing wives-to-be in such financial pursuits.

Though not often admitted, it's not uncommon for a woman to
assume her husband will take care of her. It doesn't take a mathe-
matician to spot the high frequency of kindergarten-teacher/
investment-banker mergers in the wedding announcements.
Think of how often we read that the bride "until recently" worked
at Such and Such Company. What happened? They quit their jobs
to pursue full-time wedding plans and then assume housewife positions after marrying, devoting themselves to volunteerism, setting up their new homes, supporting their husbands' careers. On
Salon.com, Ann Marlowe asserts that many women take lower-
paying jobs because they still expect to be supported by higher-
income-earning husbands. Women still want to be rescued, she says,
and they do so by depending on marriage. "In middle- and upper-
class life, it's almost a rule," Marlowe argues. "The lower paid the
occupation, the more obvious it is that the woman in it expects to

attract a man to support her. Publishing? Auction houses? Private school teaching? Classic postdeb, waiting-to-be-wed jobs."[69]

For women, getting married can mean getting out of a job altogether. In 2000, in a Youth Intelligence poll, 68 percent of three thousand single and married young women said they'd rather not work if they could afford it. *The Wall Street Journal* recently concluded, "The New Economy has meant a return to the Old Family, with Dad as sole breadwinner."[70] As Maureen Dowd complained in *The New York Times,* "Five years ago, you would often hear high-powered women fantasize that they would love a Wife, someone to do the shopping, cooking, carpooling, so they could focus on work. Now the fantasy is more retro: They just want to be that Wife."[71]

There has long been a bubbling nesting movement of women choosing to stay home following childbirth; in the 1980s the so-called resurgent mommy track was extensively covered by the media.[72] In the 1990s the stay-at-home mom decision gained a new respect, and importantly, it did so in the mainstream. The elevation of this lifestyle was not dominated by a particular political viewpoint. Surveys show that young women, many the daughters of women who worked full-time, take more of an interest today in raising children full-time than did their counterparts of the previous two decades. In a 1995 poll, more women were likely to want to stay at home and care for their families than to work outside the home (31 percent versus 27 percent in 1989).[73] Though the numbers are small, more upscale marriages are opting for the solo-breadwinner format. According to a study conducted by the investment banking firm Donaldson, Lufkin & Jenrette, between 1990 and 1995 the number of American families with only one wage earner grew approximately 1.8 percent a year.[74] Of households earning between $250,000 and $499,999, almost 50 percent feature a stay-at-home spouse (usually the wife), up 38 percent from six years ago.[75]

The latest twist is that the new nesters want to take a permanent office hiatus immediately following, or even the year before, the wedding takes place. A 2000 *Cosmopolitan* poll shows that two out of three women would rather stay home than work after wedding. This can be a source of tension if the husband assumes the wife would hold on to her earlier declared intentions and continue working. Many men figure they no longer have to contemplate the potential scenario of being the family's sole financial supporter. Most assume that that burden will be shared, and if a woman chooses otherwise, many men see it as a form of betrayal—something they didn't plan on, don't want, and most important, rarely can afford. In a 2000 survey 70 percent of five hundred men polled claimed they would support their wives if they didn't work—but two thirds added that they would do so *only* after having children.[76]

After all, many of the rules have changed since the 1950s. Though 39 percent of Gen Xers say they'd like to see "a return to traditional standards" in homemaking,[77] technology has made full-time housewifery obsolete, at least until children enter the picture. Things can be done much more quickly and easily today. Obviously, the stay-at-home-wife phenomenon only affects only a small population of young marrieds—but the same underlying issues presage potential problems after couples have children, when women increasingly opt to stay home. If nothing else, these issues signal the difficult landscape of negotiating marital roles in a post-feminist, dual-income, multicareer world.

Though marriage has clearly changed with the times, it has remained a potent fantasy. We truly believe or want to believe in matrimony. We hope against hope that it will all work out, it will all be wonderful, and it will last forever. Marriage will bring us everything we've always wanted.

girlfriend I was already physically gone, but I guess on a symbolic level I was truly breaking away by getting married."

Being a husband also provided a clear role for Joel to play at a time when he was unsure of himself, of what he wanted and the kind of life he hoped to lead. "I was trying to create an identity for who I was going to be, and my marriage was fundamental to that," he explains. "I wanted to be the young married guy, to be able to walk around knowing I was married. It would create this new identity for myself: I have this job, I live in this place, and here's my wife. This is who I am."

Being a young husband seemed to provide an attractive way of life. "Living downtown I would see these young, handsome people married, walking around these cool downtown places, and they're married. I had always thought of married men as older, just sitting around the breakfast table, reading the newspaper. But at the time, I saw all these young people getting married and these hip young husbands, and that was very attractive.

"I never thought I would get divorced. That just wasn't part of the fantasy."

※

People who enter a starter marriage do so because they always wanted to get married or always assumed they would. They've planned on it—if only in the abstract—for a long time. Getting married is the fulfillment of a long-cherished dream or firmly held expectation.

In many ways, marriage is a coveted ideal because we've made it one. We've developed a new marriage formula, one that puts a huge amount of pressure on the institution. Because marriage is no longer primarily about creating a family, it's now about becoming two well-rounded, fulfilled individuals. Marriage is no longer about creating a new unit through procreation; it's about creating a new unit ("the marriage" itself) while maintaining two individual ones—both of whom are somehow meant to become better, stronger, happier, and more worthy in the process. Not only is there no longer one central goal to marriage, the multiple "goals" of marriage are so diverse and demanding that one may as well say, "What I want from my marriage is a happy life."

Chapter 4

The Search for Marriage

JOEL CONSIDERS HIMSELF A ROMANTIC. "I ALWAYS WANTED to get married really young. . . . I was just waiting for that right girl." His impulsive decision at age twenty-three to marry his girlfriend of only two months seemed natural. "We had such a strong connection," he says. "I'd never felt anything like that in my life, and I just thought, well, this has just got to be it." For Joel, the idea of being a husband was "really cool. I felt like it would elevate me. . . . I had a very romantic view where, with other women, I would just be like, 'Sorry, ladies, can't help you.' I liked the idea that I would just be there for this one other person." Besides, Joel had never liked the dating scene; he wanted to settle down.

And nothing else in his life was very settled at the time. Miserable at his job and still living at home with his parents, Joel saw marriage as a firm step toward adulthood. "My parents were really overprotective; they just didn't think of me as an adult. They had gotten used to having me around and were really clingy, and they saw [my wife] as taking me away. They disliked her before they met her." In the end, he and his wife decided to elope. "Getting married was an adult decision to make. Maybe I wanted to show them I was an adult. After I moved in with my

For today's marrying generation, marriage is almost the means to an end. Buoyed by a culture that esteems both idyllic romantic relationships and mutual self-actualization, many twentysomethings go into marriage with impossibly high expectations for the happiness and fulfillment they'll derive from the state of marriage itself. "I was so happy when I got engaged." "It was such a relief." "I was ecstatic." "I felt safe." "I could finally stop worrying." "It was so comforting." "This was the beginning of the rest of my life." One woman says that she and her husband used to giggle together in self-congratulation. "We were like, thank God we found each other. Thank God I found my person. How lucky we are to have gotten that out of the way. We were both pretty relieved."

In *Goin' to the Chapel: Dreams of Love, Realities of Marriage,* Charlotte Mayerson says that from childhood, people's marriage expectations divide them into two types: "sleepwalkers" are those whose romantic ideals propel their adult decisions, and "calculators" are those who make specific connections between their marriage decisions and the kinds of lives they want to lead.[1] People today tend to be both. Juliet demonstrated naïveté and idealism about the romantic possibilities of marriage, yet was simultaneously aware of the pragmatic benefits attributed to marriage itself. "I thought of being a wife along typical, storybook lines," she recalls. "I'm big into romance, and the idea of sharing my life with somebody was gloriously romantic. I wanted everything to be perfect, because that's how I am. But at the same time, I thought I was going to do marriage better than everybody else, and certainly better than my parents, who had a functioning but not very happy marriage. I was also very pragmatic."

We live in an era when anything is possible, where both men and women have many more choices. Yet a growing number of young people are overwhelmed by this wide-open field of opportunity. While few would wish for the rigidity of the more stagnant, nineteenth-century society, people long for some of the certainty that these established ways provided. *New York* magazine explains, "To twentysomethings faced with what seem like insurmountable obstacles . . . marriage looks like one aspect of adulthood they can actually control."[2] Laurel married her college boyfriend. "When I graduated from college, I thought, what now? I had no direction careerwise. I didn't know what the heck I wanted to do. I didn't have any guidance from my parents, and I had never focused on myself. At college, all I did was party and worry about other people. I hadn't done any preparation. Getting married was another occupation for me. I was, like, 'Get me out of here! I love this guy, let's get married; we'll go to Atlanta. I'll figure out what we'll do once we get there.' "

Nearly all young divorcés were in love when they married, and most wanted marriage for the usual reasons—love and companionship. But they also looked toward marriage for much, much more. Often when people get married, they're really after something else entirely.

The Search for Identity

We like to have roles to play. We think of ourselves as "a something"—an artist, an entrepreneur, a leader, a thinker, a software consultant. Our multiple roles fluctuate depending on circumstance—sometimes we act the part of "the boss," other times we're "a good friend" or a loner or a party girl. On a deeper level, we need to establish an identity in order to feel validated and accepted, included and desired.

In high school and college we could choose with ease one-size-fits-all roles that gave us a sense of personal identity. If you decided to be a Deadhead, in addition to knowing what music to listen to, you knew what kind of clothing to wear, which politics to embrace, and even what kind of language to speak so that other Deadheads would understand and respond to you. After graduation, finding a role for oneself becomes a lot less simple.

Transitioning from student to spouse was once a much swifter process. The postschool identity search was pretty rote, as students went from cheerleaders or nerds or class clowns to wives with families and husbands with entry-level jobs into permanent careers. According to Stephanie Coontz, in the 1950s "very few people spent any extended period of time in a nonfamily setting: They moved from their parents' family into their own family, after just a brief experience with independent living, and they started having children, soon after marriage."[3]

Today that definitive rite of passage no longer exists. In a society where most men and women move out of their family homes at age eighteen or after college to build their own single homes, the highly ritualized transition from childhood home into a new family has almost entirely disappeared. Most young people live on their own or with a rotating shuffle of roommates or live-in lovers long before they create their own new families.

Gen X has been saddled with a lot of the blame for this hazy transition. In the early nineties, Gen Xers were dubbed slackers because they seemed to lack a set of definite goals and their lives seemed without structure. Yet many rightly resented the label. They weren't lazy or undisciplined, they complained. It was the circumstances into which they'd been thrust. Social guidelines and pathways were no longer set out in front of them, leaving many in a state of confusion. As a result, the search for identity has become stretched out across one's twenties—delayed, prolonged, and complicated.

Many Gen Xers also started out in the early 1990s recession, a set of economic circumstances that may be replicated in the early new millennium; with jobs scarce, many people fled, flopped, or scattered around. "I was really unhappy at work at the time that I got married," says Bethany, now thirty-one. "I just couldn't figure out what I wanted to do. I was working at a hair salon where I felt like a glorified shampoo girl. Finally I got a real job, but I just couldn't make up my mind about where I wanted to go. I was so indecisive. I wanted to do everything, but I didn't know how to do anything."

Even when we do find ourselves immersed in our careers, they no longer supply the identifying markers they once did. One used to be considered an IBM man or a welder or a teacher. But many jobs today seem abstract, obscure, or undefined. We are associate product managers, Internet gurus, intelligence officers, customer-service technicians, and change-management consultants. Many people find themselves unable to explain to people outside their industries exactly what it is that they do. Sometimes they can't figure it out themselves. White-collar workers once viewed their jobs with a sense of smug superiority. Nowadays it's the blue collars who seem to be doing the "real" work, while many office employees complain that they seem to be shoving around papers, end-lessly loitering in meetings, sending out mass e-mails to employees and clients they've never met, and coordinating transactions without ever so much as glimpsing palpable results.

Changes in the modern office have made work more often destabilizing than not. Following the downsizing and consolidation of the nineties and early millennium, many young Americans feel more than ever like pawns on a large chessboard—one that might be knocked over by a careless player at any moment. Gone is the sense of order the workplace used to impose, one that could be very restrictive but was nonetheless secure. Ties between employer and employee and the resulting sense of corporate loyalty are lost. We don't feel as though our employer will take care of us; we feel we have to take care of ourselves. Barbara Dafoe White-head notes that after "the highly educated daughters of educated Baby Boomers" go through "a prolonged period of higher education and career apprenticeship in order to establish themselves in a demanding job market . . . they may be laid off, downsized, or fired at least once or twice. . . . Neither their love life nor their work life is settled or secure."[4]

The new work style provides some definite upsides. We don't feel as pigeonholed or regimented as the Organization Man of the 1950s, and in a new casual work atmosphere, where youth and risk taking are revered, opportunity and creativity abound. But at the same time there's a lack of clarity with regard to role. In the organization charts of old, lines between title boxes were clearly drawn; you knew who was above you, who was below, to whom you reported, and whose job you eventually would have. Today, org charts are more like org soups—fluid and constantly over-turned.

Even those who find a role for themselves in their professional lives discover that most jobs are so unstable that the roles they offer don't stick. A man who works for one year as a magazine editor and the next year as a content provider at a new Web startup would be hard-pressed to define himself as either a "content provider" or an "editor" or even an "Internet person." And he most likely has no idea what he'll be doing a year from now. Sometimes it feels like we're caught in a game of catch-up. Something new, someone younger, something different seems to pop up every day, threatening to leave us behind. High schoolers are transformed into Internet billionaires; day traders make a mint on the stock market; one year later, they're both broke. For people raised to believe that if they went to the right college, got the right job, and worked hard for their promotions, they'd be set for life, the new marketplace, particularly in today's newly resurgent recession, can be demoralizing. With real, bottom-line results increasingly harder to prove, advancement can seem arbitrary.

In a 1999 poll, 55 percent of Gen X women agreed that "having a career is not as rewarding as I thought it would be"—up from 41 percent only a year before.[5] If work doesn't work, these women need to find something else around which to build their identities, and their idea of what's important to them has become interwoven with the idea of marriage. Many long to think of themselves as wives first, widget marketers second or third. "I was really excited about becoming a wife," admitted one woman who married at twenty-seven. "And I was this hard-core feminist. But in spite of that, I was also really influenced by the media and the message sent about being a good wife and mother. I wanted to come home and make dinner. I saw that as my role—and I still do. I have to admit that I don't want to work that hard. I want to be a mother. I'd like to work part-time at most."

Being a wife is satisfying, important, feminine, reassuring. Most wives-to-be I interviewed were excited by the idea. A few had problems with the connotations of the word, saying, "It seemed too dependent," or "I was a bit nervous about what it meant." But the majority didn't question their desire to call themselves a wife. Marriage, rather than posing an identity crisis, was seen as an identity *opportunity.* At least they knew how these roles were supposed to work and felt confident that it was something at which they could succeed. One woman who married at twenty-two recalls, "I loved the idea of becoming a wife, of being the happy wife. It filled me with pleasure—and relief."

Similarly for men, when identity isn't found in the workplace, the possibility of calling oneself a husband is very attractive. Everyone knows how those "normal," common, straightforward, given roles work. "When I got engaged, I felt pretty damn good,"

Ben, married at twenty-eight, recalls. "It was like, 'Okay, here we go! Now it's time to start the rest of my life.' You've made it to the next level, you're finally grown up." Becoming a husband provides a sense of purpose. "My husband instantly settled into this husband role," Yasmin recalls. "It's like he sighed this huge sigh of relief. He was very identified in being married, in being one of two, and moving into this caretaker/provider role. He practically turned into his father right away." George, now thirty-two, explains, "I wanted to be a grown-up. . . . Once I was married, it really suited me. I've found this with a lot of my married friends—you just feel more solid. You have this definite position in the world."

Many people seem to believe that their self can be created through their spouse, whose talents and characteristics are somehow acquired in the marital contract. If your wife is decisive and ambitious, well then, congratulations, so are you. Need some confidence? Get a brash, successful lawyer for a husband. James says, "I saw my wife as stability because I was pursuing a risky career change at the time that would take time to evolve. I found in her the stability that I really wanted in myself. Because she was secure financially and had a stable career, I gained the freedom to pursue a new direction and make a transition in my own career." Zoë explains, "At the time, getting married meant that I was giving up my larger goals about what I wanted to do with my life and how I wanted to make an impact. By marrying, I was trading in my goals and aspirations for a more secure path."

The clarity that marriage provides can feel liberating. Getting married enables both men and women to define, enhance, and in some way free themselves as individuals. "I was always afraid of not finding the woman I wanted to marry," Robert, a thirty-two-year-old Californian, admits. "But I realize that that wasn't really what the fear was about. What I *really* was afraid of was what would happen to me after college. I had no idea what I was going to do with my degree. . . . I was terrified of the future. I had no money, no job, no prospects. I wasn't really trained to do anything. I wanted to be a sax player, but it was vague to me how to do that. And all of a sudden, here's this hot girl who was like, 'Let's spend our lives together,' even though she was terrified about what she was going to do with her life too. So it seemed like a really good idea at the time to get married." If you're not sure who you are yet—and many twentysomethings aren't—marriage provides the means to create that self.

The Search for Connection

Ours is an age of autonomy. If the 1950s was a fixed conformist society of lawn mower men and Tupperware clubs, today's social order is so fragmented that many don't feel part of a common society at all. Our atomized era is marked off by gated neighborhoods, (im)personal computers, privacy movements, cars as big as houses, and houses that look and feel like massive, isolated fortresses. Twenty-six percent of us live alone—twice as many as did in 1960.[6] "I think it's a shame that so many people my age are getting divorced and having to go through this," Robert says, "because there's a failing in modern society that an individual feels so removed from their community that they feel like they have to get married just to be connected to something."

Our childhood families were often characterized by a sense of upheaval and remain confusing into adulthood, as many grown children try to negotiate holidays like Thanksgiving through a thicket of stepfamily obligations. Families are split and splintered or far away (physically or emotionally). James, a multimedia designer from Washington State, explains his wife's desire to marry: "Her parents were both on their third marriages, and there was no security in her home growing up. She told me that was a big attraction for her, the fact that I was so stable and came from a stable home."

A number of young marrieds I interviewed were keen to escape their birth families and establish their own family structure. Some had abusive or substance-dependent parents, or families marred by incessant conflict. Several had parents who divorced shortly before they themselves got married. Clara's parents were embroiled in a messy divorce at the same time she was graduating from college and trying to sort out her own life. She married for the first time when she was twenty-three. "Some of the turmoil that was going on in my life at the time, not feeling like I had a comfort zone, led me into marriage younger and faster than I should have. I was seeking that comfort. His family was really wonderful, and I was drawn to their whole family structure because at the time my own parents were driving me insane."

Our surroundings offer little refuge. We graduate from college, move to a new city—often different from the one in which we grew up or where our families live. The communities formed at college disappear as schoolmates disperse upon graduation, and we're left with little sense of a permanent common ground or a solid, geographical community. Yet 63 percent of Americans agree with the statement "The community I live in is an important part of who I am" (up six percentage points from 1995), and 68 percent agree, "I have responsibilities to my neighbors beyond what is required by law" (up five points).[7]

We long for other people to provide a buffer between ourselves and the world outside. We're afraid of being left behind or losing out. We're frightened by the prospect of AIDS and other sexually transmitted diseases. We're scared of terrorists, we fear outsiders, we no longer even trust our own government. One team of trend trackers identified "desperately seeking security" as one of the "Top 10 Trends for the Future," because "people are seeking a sense of security as an antidote to the accelerating pace of change, turning to the trusted and familiar."[8]

We may live in an age of autonomy, but clearly we don't always like it that way. We're set up to become loners, yet many of us feel adrift. Listen to the bloated, bleeping crowds conversing electronically in Internet chat rooms, signaling people's desire to connect. Glance around any Barnes & Noble or Starbucks on a Saturday afternoon to see people desperate to escape their cocoons. Or witness the popularity of *Friends:* in a world where most people live in scattered single-dwelling vestibules, *Friends* provides the ultimate fantasy. It's what we all long for—a social realm that feels a lot like . . . family. Most of us don't even know our next-door neighbors, let alone cook dinner with them. Most of us have to travel across town to see our friends; we can't just ring a doorbell across the hall and flop down on someone's sofa to watch a video together when we feel lonely. But we wish we could.

People want a place to go to be with other people, to be around like-minded folk—with similar backgrounds, interests, tastes, and sensibilities. There's been a recent community resurgence of sorts, but these new communities—interest-based, and age-based—tend to be more fragmented and isolated than the associations of old. Organizations based on narrowcast interests like quilting, film-noir appreciation, and rock climbing have replaced community centers, neighborhood associations, and block parties. Internet chat rooms are the epitome of this shift, with all sense of physical, real, meaningful closeness absent from the connection.

Americans have always been a very outgoing, gregarious people. During the early twentieth century people's lives were closely intertwined with their workplaces, their neighborhoods, their extended families, and various communal organizations. In the 1950s these institutions were to some extent replaced by the immediate concerns of the nuclear family, but the multiple lines of connection still existed. In the 1960s and 1970s, however, many traditional spheres were broken up or displaced by the more immediate concerns of the individual—this was, after all, the heyday of the Me Generation. And when 1980s yuppiedom took over, self-absorption soared to new heights.

In the 1990s our renewed longing for connection became exemplified—and encouraged—by the Oprahfication of American culture. To have an emotion is to share an emotion. To feel sad is to have someone hear you cry. It's as if we can't experience something without knowing that others are witnessing and partaking in the experience as well. In a talk-show world, where total strangers share their intimate experiences and feelings in order to feel validated, empathy is cherished above all.

Modern social lives do not readily lead to this kind of connection. Outside college and the workplace, people are forced to form their own social institutions under circumstances that do not easily accommodate them. A social life often involves going out to bars where loud music, drunken disarray, and an absence of chairs discourage serious social interaction. Most people have had years of social exploration by the time they're in their early twenties; it's no longer fun to date wildly or bed down a new mate. "I didn't have the stomach for it," says Joel. "Going to see all these packs of women in bars. The same stupid conversations, the same hairdos

and cell phones. It just wasn't my thing." Celina Hex laments in
Bust magazine,

> I don't think humans were ever meant to be kept in a holding
> pattern of adolescent angst for this long—and after a while
> something happens to us, something changes, something just
> gives up. . . . All I know is that my girlfriends and I gather to-
> gether on a regular basis to mourn or laugh over the latest ro-
> mantic fiasco or lack of one, while we get older, our biological
> clocks ticking, worrying about how we're ever going to get the
> boy thing right in time to have a baby. . . . Suddenly we see our
> futures as a mysterious black hole, because we may not end up
> being part of a family portrait like we'd always expected, and
> may instead be hanging out and dating and eating Doritos and
> worrying about our rent until we're ninety.[9]

The path to social, romantic, and eventually marital security is
unmarked in the fuzzy landscape where most people plot their social lives today. With the absence of established courtship patterns,
it's difficult to meet people. Many say the contemporary dating
scene isn't very rewarding or even much fun. It can be demoralizing and exhausting. People feel like they get trapped in a meat
market where they're judging other people according to a set of cri-
teria to which most people don't measure up. What's worse, they
know that they're on display too, being evaluated like any other
product on the market. Courtship advocate Amy Kass notes, "Be-
neath . . . the self-protecting cynicism are deep longings for friendship, for wholeness, for a life that is serious and deep and for
associations that are trustworthy. The young are mainly just
scared, and no one has offered them hope or proper guidance."[10]
Her husband, Leon Kass, writes in an essay entitled "The End of
Courtship":

> Today, there are no socially prescribed forms of conduct that
> help guide young men and women in the direction of matri-
> mony . . . [they] lack a cultural script whose denouement is
> marriage. To be sure, there are still exceptions to be found,
> say, in closed religious communities or among new immigrants
> from parts of the world that still practice arranged marriage.
> But for most of America's middle- and upper-class youth—the

privileged, college-educated and graduated—there are no known explicit, or even tacit, social paths directed at marriage . . . for the great majority, the way to the altar is uncharted territory: It's every couple on its own . . . without a compass.[11]

We find ourselves feeling lonely, confused, and insecure. The tangle of social lives, careers, and personal lives can be overwhelming. "I hated the dating scene in so many ways," says Bethany. "Being a Southern girl, I liked the traditional courting ritual of being picked up and taken to dinner, once a week. But the current variety of dating is weird and undefined. You never know a guy's intentions, and it's hard to get to know each other. It was all too nebulous for me."

"The whole dating scene nowadays is wretched, wretched, wretched," Melissa, a thirty-year-old native Floridian transplanted to New York, complains. "It's a total victim of the agonized relations between men and women. People are ungenerous about introducing other people, and you need that screen. It's hard to meet people; you can't just meet them at a bar. Work-related events are fraught by that quasi-work vibe that makes it weird. You just don't know how much of yourself to put out there. And in public spaces people don't talk to people they don't know. I go to concerts, but the people next to me don't talk to me. I go to the gym; people don't talk to each other. People seem to date in these affinity circles, but they dry up pretty quickly." When she got married as a grad student, she explains, "the sexual dynamics were really complicated and overwrought. It isn't too much of an exaggeration to say that in grad school everyone was sleeping with everyone. I really wanted to get out of that, and marriage was one way to do so."

Many see marriage as an escape hatch. "The thought of only sleeping with my husband was very comforting to me," Elizabeth, a Catholic Midwesterner, recalls. "When I had sex before we got married, I think I justified it by thinking that I would eventually marry him. I didn't have a very healthy or modern view of sex. And unconsciously, I think I was like, 'Gosh, what if I go out in the real dating world and everyone is so fast and sex is taken so lightly and I could get hurt?' " In a 1999 poll, 43 percent of Gen Xers said they "would like to see a return to more traditional standards in their sexual relationships"; 41 percent wanted more traditional standards in social relationships overall.[12] Katie Roiphe calls the current yearning "the dream of a more orderly world": "The progressive whirl of the past few decades, the lifting of one taboo after another, the speed of political change and the resulting freedoms, seem to have left us with a deep, almost perverse nostalgia for the most stifling, moralistic moment in history we can image. Only it doesn't seem stifling and moralistic anymore, it seems *civilized*. We long to reproduce the neatly trimmed rose gardens of Jane Austen's England—the lowered glances, flirtations, innuendos, and felicitous simplicities of the nineteenth century marriage plot."[13]

Roiphe says for her the appeal of Jane Austen's female characters is "the startling neatness and security of their destinies. They fall in love with the man whom history and class and tradition have chosen them for. . . . *This is the way it's supposed to be.*"[14] One of the easiest ways to control your place within society is to create your own society—your own family. As one twenty-three-year-old bride explains, "The world is so unstable. Don't you feel everything around is so unstable? I think dating is emotional abuse. There's something so grounding about being married, saying you will be my mate for life. People need that, people are searching for that."[15]

Social unease has long coaxed people into the warmth of the marital bed. Indeed, some of the factors that set off the marriage boom of the fifties may be encouraging marriage now. An observation from the time, "Why They Can't Wait to Wed," published in a 1958 issue of *Parents* magazine, theorized, "Youngsters want to grasp what little security they can in a world gone frighteningly insecure. The youngsters feel they will cultivate the one security that's possible—their own gardens, their own . . . homes and families."[16] While our grandparents' fear was produced by cold-war tensions, our generation's unease stems from social, technological, and economic uncertainty. But the response is the same. We are heading home, hibernating, shacking up, buckling down, and getting married.

Sociologists have found that children who grow up in single-parent or stepfamily situations have weaker kinship ties overall. They are less likely to rely or depend on their parents, and instead build a network of support among their peers. According to a *Newsweek* study of today's teens, this generation is strongly peer-driven and team-driven.[17] Such children become more easily influenced by a variety of outside parties—boyfriends and girlfriends, the media, and their friends. However, in today's fast-moving society, friends come and go, tribes form and break up, social lives are fluid. The search for unconditional love can result in an unusual eagerness to marry and start a family of one's own, to rebuild what one once had or imagined one had in a predivorce family.

The genuine human intimacy we yearn for can only be attained through constant, close relationships—ones that exist both on a daily basis and with the understanding of long-term devotion. And so we turn toward marriage. "People are rebelling against the idea of being uninvolved in family or community," says Robert Ziller, a University of Florida psychology professor who studies long-term relationships. "Weddings ... are a way to reestablish bonds among individuals, their families, and their communities."[18]

Gen Xers are also fearful of never finding the right person; they fear solitude, fending for themselves, feeling lonely. One young bride explains, "I feel better able to face the world with [my husband] by my side. No one likes to feel alone in the world, and I think my generation more than any other feels alone. And marriage lets you say, 'Hey, I have someone else on my team.' "[19] In her research for *Flux: Women on Sex, Work, Love, Kids, and Life in a Half-Changed World,* Peggy Orenstein found that an overwhelming number of "independent-minded" women were "much more fearful of being 'alone' than of losing themselves in marriage."[20] "I did not like being alone and I still hate it," admits Elizabeth, now twenty-nine and living alone in a New York City high-rise. "I'm a very lonely person in my heart. I essentially went from my parents to my husband because I wanted a steady companion. I liked having someone to always do something with. Someone to go to the movies with or chat with late into the night. I still do, I miss that." Lucy got married because "he really loved me, and I felt like, if I turned him down, he wouldn't stick around. I felt like, this person loves me a lot and I had the feeling that nobody else would ever love me like that. I had low self-esteem and was tremendously flattered. I felt so special."

Quite a few people interviewed were afraid to turn away the possibility of enduring connection once it was on offer. Sam was extremely insecure when he married at twenty-six. "My lifelong fear was that every woman I was with would be the last. I thought to myself, 'This is it, the one woman you're going to meet, and if it ends, you're screwed.'" Melissa married a man she'd only spent time with on a handful of occasions: "I took his asking me to marry him as this great thing that wouldn't come along again," she says. "To say no would have been inconceivable. I liked the idea of having an ally in the world. It seemed like fun, having one other adult around to do things together. And it seemed like a better idea than *not* having someone."

George expressed a similar pull toward marriage, but with some ambivalence. At the time, he says, he was dealing with a lot of "self-hatred" that was alleviated in part by his relationship. "I felt very unstable and uprooted, and she had a total state of grace and effortlessness to her that was very soothing to me. She was very comfortable with her place in the world, and that was attractive to me because I had always had this sense of questing. . . . I guess I got married for this 'neck up' reason that there was so little that was wrong, and even though I didn't feel this big pull . . . I felt like, 'Who am I to turn this down? What makes me think that I should expect better than this? There's a lot here to really hang my hat on.' So I decided to propose."

Marriage provides a firm sense of personal security and comfort. According to *Time* magazine, "Marital feelings of support and stability may account for a stronger sense of well-being" among the married population.[21] "Marriage can make us feel more firmly anchored to something outside ourselves, more strongly tied to the world," muses married author Francine Prose.[22] Jodie explains that when she got married "it was the first time that I remember not worrying about whether somebody loved me. I just knew. There was such security in that I never wondered whether we were on the same page; we were always moving at the same pace."

A spouse is a constantly available resource amidst the unpredictable vicissitudes of modern life. "I liked the idea of finding my better half, the person that completes me," says Ben, thirty-one. "Life is hard enough alone; it would be much easier with someone else." Is it so surprising, then, that once we find that someone—or someone who seems like they're "the" someone—we latch on for dear life? Marriage connects us.

The Search for Meaning

In a culture that sometimes seems to care only for irony, apathy, criticism, superficiality, and sound bites, many twentysomethings long to attach deeper meaning to their lives and their personal relationships.

The Information Age has been glorified for the accessibility of knowledge. Statistics about the info glut abound, simultaneously exhilarating and terrifying: more information is in one day's issue of *The New York Times* than the average person in the seventeenth century accumulated over a lifetime. Over one billion pages of text are on the Internet—more pages of information than were in print in the entirety of history, up until five years ago. We have produced more information in the last five years than was created in the previous five thousand.

Yet it often feels like our minds are merely assaulted with an increasing number of info fragments—bits of data that stream unchecked into our consciousness. A recent study by Pitney Bowes found that 60 percent of workers feel overwhelmed by the amount of information they receive. Even the word that we use to describe this stuff—*info*—is small, slight, and somehow deceiving. People long to know what all these snippets mean, to find something deeper that ties them all together.

With 20/20 hindsight, we regard previous generations as bonded by some kind of underlying goal or movement or ideology. It seems like there used to be something to fight for that gave them a sense of purpose. The Greatest Generation had the Depression, World War II, the Korean War, and the cold war. Baby Boomers had the civil rights movement, the women's movement, and the peace movement. The Boomers also got to knock down a series of belief systems and institutions; our generation doesn't even know these systems and traditions enough to know what it's missing—and that may be part of why we want to build them back up again.

For today's generation there seems to be no united battle to wage or systems within which to wage them. Most don't identify with political parties anymore. We're left wondering how else we can add some kind of meaning to our lives. As one college student complains, "[It's] one of the biggest problems of our generation, the fact that no one attaches meaning to anyone. People say they love whoever they want and have sex with whoever they want, but what it all comes down to is you end up in a void of meaninglessness."[23]

Our longing for ideas and beliefs larger than ourselves has led to a surge in spirituality. In a 1998 poll of college freshmen, 90 percent believe in God, three fourths believe in life after death, most attend religious services, and almost half believe that religion will be more important in the future.[24] Spiritual books regularly top the best-seller lists; Christian entertainment has gone mainstream; and Americans are seeking ways to infuse religious meaning into everyday life. Thousands of religious websites offer everything from online confessionals to service schedules to Christian matchmaking services. Yoga, kabbalah, Wicca, and Buddhism increasingly provide outlets for those dissatisfied with traditional Western religions.

This interest in spirituality is part of a larger effort to find trustworthy belief systems. Filmmaker Lisa Krueger wrote the 1999 film *Committed* as an exploration of what marriage signifies to a generation trying to find meaning in the wake of their chaotic seventies childhoods. She points out the relationship between the quest for meaning in both a higher being and the search for marriage: "The word 'faith' and the idea of being faithful used to refer to a religious ideal, but nowadays people are more familiar with it as a term of monogamy than as a word related to God. But they are totally linked. One is trying to fulfill the space that the other formerly occupied. . . . You cannot ignore or prevent the yearning people have for faith. You can't deny that most people want and think there's more to life than what they're seeing in front of them."

Marriage is the new faith. As Krueger observes, "For a lot of people now, marriage is the most sacred public act or ritual that they will ever undertake. It's the only thing they'll do that will give them that lump in the throat, that knowledge that you are part of a one-thousand-year tradition. Which I think is the high that people get from organized spirituality—that blissfully humbling experience of being infinitesimal in the face of this vast, huge, timeless act. And I think people crave that kind of feeling that there's something bigger than they are." In an essay entitled "Going to the Temple," the self-described "purple-haired, tattooed, nose-ringed feminist" Margorie Ingall explains, "I've heard of weddings where the couple say 'as long as our love shall last.' Um, no. I want to say in front of everyone that this is holy, and legally binding, and I care enough about this person to enter into a very ancient covenant with him. I think I'm far from alone in my desire for both community and continuity. To some degree, I think that's why so many Gen Xers are having big weddings. We feel cast adrift and we want tradition, moorings."[25] Juliet, a Reform Jew living in San Francisco, agrees: "For me, now more than ever, marriage and family values is about having rituals that are underpinned by solid, timeless traditions."

The Search for Permanence

In an era of daily mergers, white-hot trends, and the incessant whirl of technology, in order to keep up you've got to be on a constant race forward. Planning for an unpredictable future is painted as an outdated practice at best and a fool's errand at worst. Things happen so fast we're forced to live in an eternal present. Our lives crash forward from moment to moment, and in many ways we relish the fact that "anything can happen" at any time. Part of us is optimistic about the possibilities change offers. We switch jobs more than any other generation. We believe that something better can surely be found if we just have the courage to move on. Go for it. Get ahead. Embrace change.

The work world reflects this on-the-go, rapid-fire mentality. Every job seems like a temp job because many jobs are. One temp agency found that over a third of American companies now use temps for professional and managerial positions; 45 percent plan to increase their use of temp workers over the next five years.[26] Temp work offers opportunity, but it also leaves people flailing from one office to the next—without benefits, security, or permanence. The temp life, with its unpaid vacations, uncertain paychecks, and irregular hours, can be demoralizing and destabilizing. We may lead flexible lives, but many part-timers, temps, and free agents long for a full-time fix—a full 45 percent of the nation's 1.2 million temp agency workers, according to a 2001 Bureau of Labor Statistics study. Even permanent employees are forced to be constantly on their toes. Once upon a time, switching jobs was a sign of instability; today, moving up means moving on. Ace the interview, secure the offer, and promise yourself to stay for "at least a year" before searching for the next best move. The result is a job-hopping chase throughout our twenties, flipping through entire fields along with functions and titles.

Our sense of home is also constantly shifting. We dart from city to city, often in too short a time to establish real roots. We move with startling frequency—trying out new neighborhoods, changing apartments, rotating roommates, deciding to buy a place—downshifting or upgrading, depending on our work situation du jour. In a recent survey, 61 percent said they believed that "America was a better place when people had a stronger attachment to where they lived and didn't move around so much."[27] For many of us, even our childhood home is inconstant. Our parents divorce, remarry, and relocate; there's no longer even a family nest to which we can return during the holidays.

We yearn for a sense of continuity. To know that something links the seemingly haphazard events of our lives and underpins the passage of time from one day to the next. We want roots from which to begin and ends to which we can strive. Marriage provides that permanent framework—a constant ongoing backdrop to an otherwise shifting, changeable world. "I wanted to know that there was someone I loved who also loved me and that we would be together for the rest of our lives," Michael says. Noelle admits that though she and her first husband had a "rocky, on-and-off relationship," she decided to get married because "that was my way of settling down and just ending things."

On an even deeper level, marriage offers the truest sense of permanence. Getting married enables one to create a legacy through one's children and thereby "live on" forever. Women in particular jump into marriage because they're afraid of "waiting too long" and missing out on motherhood. Panic stories about infertility and the racing biological clock only heighten women's sense of impending disaster. And although most young couples today don't plan to have children right away, the knowledge that they'll be in a situation where they *can* offers assurance enough. "Marriage wasn't my pole star or anything," George explains. "More than anything I buy into the notion of monogamy and having kids in the context of a family. The commitment to a relationship over time and to having children within the context of that ongoing relationship is what really attracted me."

Theoretically at least, marriage is the most enduring aspect of adult life. It's a way of rooting oneself within society, through one's children and one's participation in the community, and in leaving behind a part of oneself when one dies. On some fundamental human level, marriage and childbearing offer the most tangible sense of permanence. Marriage is meant to be forever.

The Search for Fulfillment

One overriding goal overshadows all other desires leading toward marriage: the need for self-fulfillment. While our parents often fled their marriages in search of self-actualization, today's twenty-somethings enter marriage expecting to find it within. "I wasn't looking for a person exactly, I was looking for the answer," one thirty-two-year-old woman explained. "I wanted total enlightenment, to feel connected to everything. But I was seeking something that I wasn't going to find in another person. I think I needed to go on an entire spiritual journey on my own to fill that space. Okay, so now I'm married, I'm a wife. At the time, it seemed like I'd found it."

Americans are famous for their endless attempts at self-improvement, and marriage can seem like just the ticket. Getting married shows that you are loved, wanted, worthwhile. And marriage makes you stronger, more capable, more valued, better. "I think marriage is portrayed as this cure-all solution, the answer to everything," Sam says. "It's like, once you're married, all the anguish in life is extinguished."

What's more, our generation kind of expects this level of happiness. Sometimes it seems we feel entitled to money, success, and career fulfillment. Older Gen Xers have witnessed both the go-go eighties and the dot.com nineties (having conveniently forgotten the recession of the early 1990s), and younger twentysomethings have known nothing but boom times. Even at the dawn of the 2001 recession, Gen Ys continue to hold on to their career optimism. We're enamored with the idea of working hard (but not *too* hard) and reaping fantastic rewards.

Many young people originally think that work will pave the road to self-realization—their career will provide that guiding principle, that overriding purpose, the sense of meaning. And many wind up disappointed. Though financially and personally rewarding jobs do exist, working just isn't very glamorous most of the time. Fabulously interesting jobs are few and far between, and most jobs are downright boring. There's a reason it's called work, and there's a reason we have to be paid to do it. It's not fun to clean counters or to execute menial tasks. Nor is it generally rewarding to shuffle papers, address customer complaints, or make cold sales calls. Columnist Anna Quindlen notes, "Few of us are working to fulfill ourselves anymore. Most women are working to fulfill the banks, the telephone company and the public utilities."[28] Both men and women often find that they just don't feel passionate about their job, nor does it fulfill them. Often they don't have the patience to find out whether one day it will. And in the meantime, *something* needs to take its place as the focal point in their lives.

And so we turn to our personal lives. Seventy-five percent of Americans say their role at home shows more of who they really are than their role at work.[29] One recent study found that despite traditional assumptions about men basing their happiness on their jobs, a man's home life, marriage, and children are just as important to him as they are to women. Men are actually *more* willing than women to trade promotions and raises in exchange for more time with their families.[30]

We look to derive an individualistic form of fulfillment from, of all places, one of the least individualistic social conventions—matrimony. Helena notes, "At least for women my age, all the emphasis is on the idea of marriage and the act of marriage, but never on the relationship itself or the two individuals involved." Marriage is, after all, about giving of oneself and sharing with another, but many look at marriage with the spotlight fixed firmly on themselves. Often what they're really thinking about is what they can get out of the arrangement. "I thought he would bring out the best in me." "I felt that this was the right thing for me." "This was the direction I wanted to go in." "I thought I would be fulfilled."

"I've had a lot of conversations with my friends about why everyone wants to get married," Helena says. "Essentially, marriage is seen as a form of conquest. Especially in our age group. . . . Marriage is seen as the point where everything will come together. Kind of like, This is when my life will start." Jodie and her boyfriend finished grad school together and moved to New York. When they returned, he proposed. "He said that now that he was finally living in New York, he had almost everything he wanted and there was only one thing left—to have me marry him."

Some wedding wannabes say "I do" at a point when they're feeling particularly unfulfilled—unmotivated, insecure, directionless, unhappy. Many have not yet reached a point where they're comfortable with their own lives, so they look for someone else to fill in the gaps. "When I got engaged, I thought marriage meant that I could really make myself vulnerable," James explains. "I could start letting my guard down about the things I was dissatisfied with in myself because this person would accept me no matter what." Marriage feels like something that will make you complete, purposeful, energized, and finally fully satisfied.

Many of the people I interviewed acknowledged that in addition to the cultural and social pressure to marry, much of their desire to marry was influenced by a kind of *self*-pressure. The self-imposed desire to show that they "could do it," they could "get" someone; they could prove they were worthy. After two years, Elizabeth still hadn't told her boyfriend she loved him. "To me saying 'I love you' was so serious," she says. When a friend was shocked by her confession that they hadn't said "it" yet, Elizabeth grew determined to proceed with her relationship in the appropriate way. She thought to herself, "I'll give it a shot. I announced to him that I loved him, and he looked at me and said, 'That's very nice, but the next woman I love is the woman I marry, so I can't say that in return right now.' I got really angry and stomped out. I thought to myself, 'You don't know now, but I'm that woman and you'll marry me.' I think I liked the challenge much more than I ended up liking the success." Marriage fits into the ideal life plan. As Elizabeth puts it, "Women I know talk about meeting men, and the notion is always that you'll meet the man you'll eventually marry. The assumption is always that the end state is marriage and we want to find the right person to get there."

Marriage is for the grounded and emotionally balanced. Once engaged, Elizabeth liked knowing that she would soon be married. "It gave me an air of stability and adultness. It projected a sense of being more mature. You've got that part of your life figured out. I wanted to project that I was more mature than I was. I never wanted anyone to see any type of uncertainty or insecurity." In the high-powered fields of finance and consulting where Elizabeth and her husband worked, marriage was seen as a sign of success. "There's a sense of wanting to be successful in multiple dimensions of your life. Marriage represents better balance. People with good relationships and solid family lives are celebrated. In the office, people say, 'Thank God she's getting married. Now she won't be such a workaholic.' Marriage improves you. It shows you're a success."

Getting married is like crossing the finish line of a relationship. Jared, a financial consultant from New York, says that when he was twenty-four, his twenty-seven-year-old girlfriend pressured him to propose: "She wanted the Cinderella story. She figured that just dating and living together wasn't sufficient; getting married would get her to that next level, so that she was secure and knew that she wasn't wasting her time with me. She wanted kids before thirty and was very hung up on both age and the storybook life. She always wanted more." Because they were already living together, Jared assumed marriage wouldn't change their relationship but says, "The reason she wanted to get married is that she thought things would change. She always looked at the next step ahead as the thing that would ultimately fulfill her. And the reason she wanted to get married, she later revealed, is that she thought the relationship was starting to fizzle and she figured that marriage would make things better. When that didn't work, she wanted to buy a house. The next level was getting a dog. She was reaching out for something, and unfortunately—or fortunately—for me, neither I nor anyone else could fulfill everything she wanted."

Chapter 5

Where Starter Marriages Stumble

CLARA, A TWENTY-NINE-YEAR-OLD COMMUNICATIONS CON-sultant, got married for the first time just after college. She and her husband moved back to his hometown in Pennsylvania, where her husband readily established his own life along his own familiar patterns. "He was in this 'just hang out with the guys' mode. He went out all the time with his friends and spent a lot of time with people from work. And I felt totally ignored. I started to feel like I didn't have my own life, and I just fell into this downward spiral."

"He wanted the barbeque and the picket fence. But I wanted flexibility, openness, new friends," Clara says of their fundamental differences. Clara began to feel isolated and lonely as her relationship with her husband deteriorated. "Eventually I couldn't even acknowledge if anything was good because at bottom, I felt so miserable. The problem was that we never established our own life together. It was always *his life*, and he wouldn't accommodate me at all."

Compromise became a major problem. Clara felt saddled with more responsibility ("I became a mother, not a wife") but believed that though they were "a fundamentally mismatched couple" she was at least willing to grow and try to change and communicate better. She felt alone in her efforts. After several attempts, Clara eventually convinced her husband to go to couples counseling. "I wasn't the easiest person," Clara acknowledges, "but I was more mature. I was willing to try. But after going for a while, the therapist finally told us that it seemed like I was willing to change but that he wasn't willing to make any effort at all. We had come to a standstill." Even their therapist seemed to agree that counseling wouldn't help their marriage.

One day, Clara and her husband were out shopping for bath mats and disagreed over which one to buy. "Another stupid fight over something stupid," Clara recalls with a bitter laugh. Her husband began making a scene. "I walked out of the store, and when he came out with his bath mat I said, 'This just isn't working. I want a divorce.' At that point it was pretty mutual, and I'm the type of person that once I make a decision, I'm there. We took out a piece of paper that night and made a list of all the things we had and what we each wanted."

In retrospect Clara says, "I don't think my husband was a bad guy, he was just immature. Not at all ready for marriage." As for her own part in the marriage's demise, she admits, "On the one hand, I feel like I had an appreciation for what marriage was—had it been the right person. But I wasn't old enough to be a judge of who was the right person. Neither of us was old enough to know what we wanted in life, never mind what we wanted from a partner."

※

Marriage is always a precarious proposition. One measure of just how difficult it can be are the legions of books devoted to its maintenance. The self-help guides set in from the altar onward with titles like *The His and Hers Guide to Surviving Your First Year of Marriage* and *Crib Notes for the First Year of Marriage: A Survival Guide for Newlyweds.* Bookstore shelves teem with volumes to help couples through ongoing commitment: *Getting Ready for a Lifetime of Love; Six Steps to Prepare for a Great Marriage; Till Death Do Us Part (Unless I Kill You First): A Step-by-Step Guide to Resolving Marital Conflict;* and *Each for the Other: Marriage As It's Meant to Be.* Each with competing lists of troublesome signs to watch out for, convictions to hold on to, principles to follow, traps to avoid. Some are motivational or inspirational, others are instructional, and some are critical and dogmatic. All set out to "fix" the marriages that we so eagerly seek out.

To a large extent, the problems that plague starter marriages are those that challenge every marriage. But the youth and inexperience of most twentysomethings, the unrealistic expectations that today's generation holds for marriage, the current gender-role confusion, the competing demands of dual-income couples in a highly mobile society, and the delaying of childbirth all conspire to make starter marriages especially fragile. Above all, starter marriages are often destined to collapse because couples fail to set a stable, durable, mutual foundation before signing up for matrimony. They lack the firm groundwork and commitment essential to weathering marriage's difficulties. Because in all marriages, when problems in the relationship (or in the lives of those living within it) arise, it takes great stores of resolve to confront them without calling into question the marriage itself. Both partners need to hold to the conviction that the marriage bond will not be broken, while other explanations and solutions, often much more difficult to pinpoint and resolve, are found. When you're married, you also can't settle on the solution best for yourself; solutions must work for two people. And many people, especially in their twenties, simply aren't ready, willing, or able to start thinking for two.

The typical marriage follows a certain course. The first year is the hardest, as the saying goes. According to long-term studies of married couples, marital quality suffers a sharp decline over the first four years ("the honeymoon is over" period). In fact, most marriages that end break up within the first five. If they survive, marriages generally stabilize until the eighth year.* In most marriages, passion fades quickly and commitment builds slowly. Once they stumble over and survive the first hurdles—and *because* they stumble over and survive the first few hurdles—married couples are much more likely to survive in the long run.

---

*The "seven-year itch" is more of a myth—and at most a state of mind—than a reality. Divorce rates actually wane and hold steady rather than jump after the seventh year, but because the *median* duration of marriage is around seven years, the misconception remains.[1]

Starter marriages have their own trajectories. They tend to follow one of two paths, the more common of which is the meteor trajectory: taking off quickly, rushing into marriage, and fizzling out fast—the turbo-charged, starry-eyed "Let's get married!"-after-two-months approach. "It felt like the incredibly romantic thing to do," says Joel, who married his wife in a matter of months. "The ultimate expression of love. I said to myself, 'This is it. Let's do it.' You're young and crazy, and you just sort of go for it. It was surprisingly easy."

The second route is the slow, thoughtless plod: long-term dating, often between college sweethearts, likely living together after graduation, and a progression into marriage by default—the "It seemed like the next logical step" approach. A number of people said that they always assumed they would get married and tended to outline the process as a series of directions to follow: college, job, marriage, house, kids. A large percentage of men, particularly those who had dated their partner for over a year, explained their decision this way. As one Texan who married at twenty-five put it: "I thought I was in love, and it seemed like the logical next step. I got a job and I was moving after college, and I thought it was the right thing to do. I guess I was following my mind instead of my heart." Max explains, "I didn't want to be without her, and I didn't want to be alone. We'd been together for four years, and I couldn't imagine not being with her. It was safer to get married than to break up."

In either scenario, people don't give the idea of marriage itself much consideration before leaping in. "I went into marriage with blinders on," says Zoë, who married at twenty-three after dating her husband for a year. "I didn't think about anything. Do our ethics and values match or complement each other? If not, where do we differ, and how will we handle those differences? How do we feel about money? Am I a spender and he's a saver? Why don't we think about these things? We assume that everyone is just like us. And so when it becomes a problem, we have no idea what to do about it." She concludes, "Though I think my marriage could have worked out if we both had worked harder, we were probably ultimately destined for failure because we were both too young and too unaware of who we were as individuals, let alone as a couple."

Starter marriages almost always start out wrong, and the marriage fails altogether very quickly.

"I Wasn't Ready for Marriage"

Whether they married at nineteen or at twenty-five, almost all the starter marriage veterans I talked to realized they were too young, too immature, or simply too unprepared to be married. "Emotionally and personally I was too young," says Elizabeth, married at twenty-three. "On the surface I appeared extremely mature and put together, and it's a shame because the outside didn't match the inside. Thinking now, how different I am at twenty-eight, it's extraordinary. I think if I met [my ex-husband] today, it may have been very different. But at the time, I didn't have the knowledge about what I wanted in a relationship. And I had no idea how to make a relationship successful."

Even when couples were older than the average wedding age, they often felt they lacked the maturity marriage requires. According to Sam, married at twenty-six, "I was old enough, but not emotionally stable enough. I don't think I was mature enough." George was twenty-seven when he walked down the aisle. "I wasn't so in touch with myself at the time," he recalls. "I didn't have an accurate gauge of the requisite level for one to want to get married. I sort of lunged at it and then justified it afterward. I think I was busy trying to talk myself into the whole thing." Olivia had only a smattering of romantic experiences before her wedding. "Maybe my divorce was avoidable, but I didn't have the skills or the willingness at the time to make it work," she admits. "If I were in the same situation now, I could probably make it work. Now I know that nothing is easy in marriage, but at that time, I wasn't emotionally prepared."

They didn't know what they were getting into, they didn't know how to deal with it once they did, and they weren't able to handle the problems marriage posed. Zoë thought she had it all mapped out. After her wedding, she and her husband would move from California to Florida to finish college and become financially secure. "And then we would eventually have kids and live happily ever after," she says. "But both of us were very young, and we hadn't thought about how hard that would be. We didn't think about how well I would handle the transition, or get along in an alien culture, or how much time he would be investing in school while I had to work to pay his tuition, or how hard it would be for me to even find a job. I wasn't at all prepared for how many struggles were coming." Lucy, who married her live-in boyfriend of six months at age twenty-five, also felt overwhelmed by the reality of marriage: "I wasn't ready or prepared. I wasn't comfortable with what I was doing with my life. And I thought I was taking marriage seriously at the time, but I wasn't. All the things I said didn't matter to me at the time—like jobs or money—matter to me now. I want someone I can depend on."

Others felt like they were mature enough for marriage but not mature enough to choose the right person. Or they believed they were ready but their partner was not. Ben complains that his wife "was too much of a child. She always had been and maybe always will be a child. And looking at marriage through a child's eyes . . . well, it was too much to deal with." Many of the women who married young felt their husbands were even less ready than they were. Some had husbands who were actually younger, but most found their mates were simply unfocused, immature, or insecure. Women discovered their husbands just weren't up to the task of marriage. "He's too immature," "too self-absorbed," "couldn't handle his anger." He "never faced issues" or "didn't know how to talk about things."

Sometimes one partner can't cope and will simply opt out of the marriage or excessively maintain independence within it, leaving the committed spouse grappling for a sense of marital interdependence. Studies have shown that people with a low evaluation of their spouse's dependability report a decrease in marital happiness and stability.[2] Lucy says of her ex, "He was really irresponsible and unwilling to settle down and work for things. He had always gotten things easily, been bailed out by his parents. He didn't want to face problems. I think our divorce was the first time he didn't get what he wanted."

Studies also identify low expressiveness (or lack of "femininity") on the husband's part as a factor for low marital happiness.[3] Bethany says her husband "had a total inability to communicate. I had to do all the emotional work. He didn't want to take responsibility. He just wanted to hold on to this ideal he had in his head and live in denial. I would sit him down and talk to him as if he were a child." Jodie's husband retreated into his own world. "He actually became a different person," she recalls. "His personality changed. He went through a clinical depression. He just stopped being the man I fell in love with and became a stranger. He lost his love for life, his joy at doing anything, even simple things. He seemed numb." Jodie says she assumed responsibility for their entire marriage because otherwise, nothing would get done. "I had to become the grown-up. I felt like I had to take care of everything, whether it was paying the bills on time, handling any problem with the car or the apartment, any major decision. I had to do it or it simply wouldn't get done."

Many attributed their marriage's problem to one partner "not getting his act together," "not accepting responsibility," or "not taking the marriage seriously enough." Often that meant drug or alcohol abuse, excessive partying, or financial irresponsibility. Lucy was heartbroken to find out that her husband had taken speed right before their wedding ceremony. Melissa's husband began drinking heavily after a few months of marriage. "Our relationship died in a fast, ignoble way," she explains. "There was no discussion, no anger, no arguments. He just started to stay out all night drinking. I kept asking him why, but it became clear that he wanted to self-destruct without even having an audience. He clearly didn't want me there, so I left." Both Melissa's and Amy's husbands turned out to be alcoholics. Ben complains of his wife, "She was living in a fantasy land. She would smoke dope and think that everything was just hunky-dory. But meanwhile, she wasn't working, she wouldn't cook, she'd just sit in bed stoned. And when she talked about kids, I was like, 'No way! Not until you stop smoking dope and get your life together. What kind of mother do you expect to be?' She was *not* the kind of mother that I envisioned."

"I Thought Marriage Would Change Things"

Many ascribe to the act of marriage transformative powers—marriage can make a bad relationship good, transform an iffy obligation into solid commitment, turn a drug-abusing boyfriend into a corporate superstar, make a straying mate settle down. Consciously or unconsciously, they thought, hoped, and desperately wanted to believe that marriage would change things. Young divorcés mused in retrospect: "I thought marriage would give me focus." "I hoped that now that she got what she wanted she would stop complaining so much." "I figured our problems were just part of the stress of planning a wedding." "I suppose that subconsciously I thought marriage would bring us closer together." As George explains, "In a way, rather than having been transformed by the relationship and then looking toward the wedding as a public confirmation of that fact, I was instead—and so was my fiancée—looking toward the wedding as being the transformative thing."

People see marriage as a guarantee that though there may be problems in the relationship, the relationship itself will endure. The fact that two partners want to commit through marriage means they are also committing to working things out. Ben and his wife had major fights before the wedding, even breaking off the engagement at one point, but as Ben says, "I figured marriage would change everything—that was one of the deciding factors in proposing. She wanted to get married, and I figured that it would be the solution to all our problems." Zoë confesses, "I thought that when we got married, he might become more responsible and more committed to the relationship. I thought that if we had problems, he would really try to work them out, and he said he would. What I found out later was that saying and doing are two very different things."

One of the major mistakes is believing that marriage will heal existing wounds or solve ongoing problems. Starter marriages in particular tend to suffer from this expectation. "Sex was always lousy," Sam complains, "but I assumed it would get better once we married." James had a difficult relationship with his girlfriend, but when she gave him an ultimatum, he decided to take the plunge. "The things that were wrong, I thought would get better," he recalls. "I treated them like projects that we could work on together. But I overlooked a lot of things, and I didn't realize that at that point in my life, I still had my own issues to work out, let alone helping her with hers." George realized from the start that his year-and-a-half-long relationship lacked a certain spark. But he assumed that the passion he had with previous girlfriends wasn't necessary or even beneficial to marriage and that perhaps he needed something "calmer and quieter." At the same time he hoped marriage might shake things up. "I think on a conscious level, you don't go into a marriage hoping that someone will change. But unconsciously, I think I thought that it would quicken the relationship into life, wake her up, and get rid of this fundamental passivity. Which, of course, was not the case."

Couples may have an idea of existing differences, if not their severity, before they marry but assume matters will work themselves out. "I guess the problems in my marriage were issues before we got married," says Michael, who married his girlfriend of three years when he was twenty-eight. "But at the time they didn't seem like issues because we didn't have enough history together. And since we'd managed to work through differences up to that point, I assumed that we would always be able to do so." "I wish I had known that marriage was not the solution that was going to improve our relationship," says Elizabeth. "It was really just a continuation and intensification of the relationship that already existed."

Of course marriage does change certain things, but few people have a clear idea of just what that change will be or how it will affect them, both individually and as a couple. "We figured a lot of our fights were coming from the insecurity of being in a new relationship," Lucy recalls. "Even though we were engaged, we figured that there was this thing—marriage—that would answer all these questions between us. Marriage would make things a lot more solid."

Juliet even took a marriage class with her fiancé to uncover any problems they might need to work on. "We had to take a test at the end of our marriage course and then go over it with a therapist. Our results were terrible, but the therapist made it seem like most couples had similar results. It wasn't that we had personality differences, but we had such different ideas about each other. We were so off in terms of how we perceived each other. It was scary." But at the time she decided it didn't matter.

"I Thought He Would Change"

People not only thought marriage would transform their relationship; they expected marriage to change their partner. "I thought he would become more responsible." "I thought she would become more adventurous." "I hoped marriage would keep him from looking around so much." As Melissa explains of her alcoholic ex, "My husband had a very hard childhood. He was like this sad little person, reserved, depressive. I thought that once he had a stable, loving marriage and a good family to support him, he would come out of himself a little."

Young marrieds, caught in the throes of galloping courtship and youthful optimism, often have idealized images of their spouses—and that feels rather charming and romantic. "He honestly thought I was perfect," muses Bethany, whose husband asked for a divorce after less than two years of marriage. The charm quickly wore off. "He had an idea of me that wasn't based anywhere in reality. Once he realized I wasn't perfect, everything came to a halt." Idealizing a spouse is particularly understandable when you don't know him well or haven't known him very long. "I was a nightclub promoter and he was the new deejay," recalls one woman who married at twenty-two. "The moment I saw him, I knew I was going to marry him. I actually said to my friend, 'See that guy? I'm going to marry him.' And so she did, three months later. Joel proposed to his wife after a few weeks. "For her to look at me and decide to marry me just like that, it doesn't seem like she gave it much thought. She may have been wrong to marry me because she may have had the wrong idea about me—not that I had any better idea of myself either." A great number of people marry before they have a chance to really know their mate and what kind of relationship they will have together over the long term. "I have a sheet of Instructions for Life pinned on my refrigerator now," Amy says. "And number four is 'Know the person for at least six months before you get married.' I should have known him better. I should have taken the time to talk to my mom and heard about and learned from her experiences in marriage. All I can say is, don't rush into marriage."

Because they frequently didn't know each other well, some

people discovered their spouse "changed" in ways they didn't like. "I always think of this person who I married who I didn't know at all and don't know to this day, and then this person who I knew for the four months before, who was really funny and outgoing and adventurous," says Sam, who married at twenty-six. "We'd gotten engaged after only a few months. If we hadn't rushed in, we would have discovered over time who we really were and that we just weren't good together." According to Olivia, who moved in with her boyfriend after three months of dating and was engaged seven months later, "Once we got married, my husband changed a lot. He became really possessive and thought we had to do everything together. Whereas I still wanted to spend some time with friends on my own." He started dictating to her in ways she hadn't expected. "We worked at the same place, and he didn't like that at all. I quit even though I didn't want to, and I guess I was pretty resentful." Sam found that after they got married, his adventurous girlfriend transformed into an old-fashioned kind of wife. "She became everything that she had thought she left behind. All the edge was gone. It seemed like she was now in competition with all her friends from home and was trying to fulfill what her parents had always wanted her to be." Another man discovered that once his wife left her hometown, "She turned into a different person. She became more manipulative, more materialistic, completely different once she was out from under her parents' control. I think she actually finally developed into who she really was." He adds, "And I don't think she should have gotten married until she had done that."

Some felt that not only did their spouse change in unwelcome ways, but that as that person's partner, they were expected to change along with him. "I knew my husband for all these years, and it seemed like first he was one person and then another," says Noelle. "But I was always who I was, and when he changed, I was like, 'I'm not going to change to become more like you!' He went through all these phases, and I just felt like I couldn't keep changing and trying to keep up with this person."

Others *wanted* to see change in a spouse who couldn't, wouldn't try, or downright refused to entertain making any accommodations at all. "I thought he'd become more responsible about work," Lucy says of her salesclerk husband. "And he told me he would. But even though we're married, we're still the same people. As it turned out, it was a lot harder for me to have a husband with no job than a boyfriend with no job."

Once people figure out who their spouses really are, many feel they don't belong together at all. Husbands find themselves living with women who are very different from themselves. Wives are married to men who aren't at all who they want. One woman explains, "I really didn't know until we got married that everything in life was about work for him. . . . I realized that he saw everything in black and white, and I saw the world as gray. He saw life as being about work and money; I saw it as family and friends. The root of our incompatibility was something I couldn't change in our relationship. The way we looked at life, at what was important, our spiritual values, was completely different." Yasmin, a Berkeley-based psychotherapist, witnessed her husband transform almost immediately following the wedding. He stopped writing poetry and started up his own business. Soon he was buying sports cars and smoking cigars. "I was like, 'Oh my God, who is this man? He's become everything I hate. How am I going to live with him for the rest of my life?' I hated him and I was in despair."

"We Had Different Ideas About Marriage"

Some people see marriage as a great leap forward, and some fall back into their parents' patterns. Others imagine that marriage won't change a thing. The flip side of one partner hoping that marriage would change her spouse is that many young marrieds didn't expect anything to change at all—often because they didn't have a very good sense of what they anticipated from marriage to begin with.

Though Yasmin and her husband knew each other well before they got married, they found that their ideas of living within a marriage were quite different. Yasmin says her businessman husband became very interested in "stuff." "He wanted a Lexus, he wanted me to wear a big diamond ring, he wanted a winery in Napa. I couldn't care less about wealth. I wanted to have some real conversation. He just wanted to come home and have me take care of him. I ended up having to do all the emotional work." Though they struggled through therapy, Yasmin says the marriage was doomed. "He just wanted me to accommodate his vision of the marriage, which was very different from my own." Neither could compromise on their ideal. George says he simply "wanted more out of marriage than my wife did." He felt like he "had higher expectations of the marriage. On a fundamental level, she had never fully pulled herself away from her family, so she actually didn't really need me emotionally. And I had a very hard time trying to create our own family rituals, to carve out a little niche for just the two of us."

Many of the couples I interviewed hadn't given any thought to how marriage would fit into their own long-term goals as individuals, let alone whether or how their spouse would accommodate them. They often didn't even bother bringing up children, finances, home ownership or location—these things just seemed too removed from their reality at the time. "Most of the major problems came from the usual stuff you have to deal with as an adult," Joel says. "I realized marriage just isn't these two fun and crazy kids hanging out downtown. There are a lot of things you have to do in dealing with the present and preparing for the future, none of which I had given much thought to at the time. We never really talked about long-term goals."

These marriages often underwent a kind of early-marriage crisis. Four years into their marriage, Noelle's husband decided that he wanted to move to Africa to be a missionary. "His dream was for me to follow him and live the life he led, and I wasn't going to do that. That's not what I wanted." In retrospect Noelle realized they never talked about their long-term plans or formed mutual goals. "I wasn't even looking into that when I got married. It turned out that there were lots of things I wanted that he didn't want. He didn't want a house or children, but we had never discussed that. His idea of married life was completely different from what I wanted."

Several people felt that their spouses had married in their parents' shadow or under the influence of their upbringing and divorced once they realized they could—and perhaps ought to—

rebel. One man's wife was twenty-three when they tied the knot. "She was from a very strict Catholic upbringing and had never lived outside her home before we got married," he explains. "But once we had moved and she was in grad school, she started to see other cultures, and began to think in the way she wanted to think, rather than the way her parents forced her to think. . . . Pretty much everything went to hell. She started going out all the time, making new friends, and she didn't want me to come along. She told me she needed to see 'what else was out there' and 'what the world had to offer.' And eventually I realized that 'what else there is to offer' meant 'not me.' " His wife asked for a separation so she could date other people, and the marriage plummeted rapidly toward divorce.

"We began to have very different ideas about how we wanted to run our lives," one Beverly Hills–born law student complained. "He began to have a more ethereal, less materialistic concept of life. He wanted to live more simply and he wanted to have less responsibility because he felt like he was under too much pressure, whereas I was a much more urban, ambitious type. I have the attitude of work hard, consume, invest. I'm very oriented in following more of the superficial, financial, real estate world—and he had no interest in that. It's like he suddenly found himself. He wanted to go off on silent retreats, meditate, and do yoga. It was like *Dharma & Greg.*" She laughs. "Except *I* was Greg. *I* was the man."

"Money Was a Major Issue"

Surveys show that most married couples cite money as the number-one source of marital conflict. So while matrimony provides real economic benefits, it also creates a fertile breeding ground for problems. "We always fought about money—that was a constant," Ben says. "She always complained that I spent money but that she couldn't spend money on anything. But she did spend a lot of money, I thought. We were incessantly bickering over it."

For many young couples, there simply isn't enough cash to go around. Joel remembers, "At first I thought it was romantic, having to struggle over money. It seemed like one of those things young married couples go through. But as much as I thought I would be this carefree person, the debts really concerned me. She was still recklessly spending money. She'd come home with new shoes, and we were thousands of dollars in debt." Joel managed to get his career going, but his wife hopped from job to job and eventually stopped working altogether. "She was home all day and the place was just a mess. Meanwhile, I was at work all day and then I would come home and I had to clean up. I did the cooking, which I like to do, but I was also like, 'Hey, you're not even working, maybe you could help out and clean up a little.' " By the time they divorced, their credit card bills had accumulated to nearly fifteen thousand dollars.

Money rears its ugly head within marriage in more ways than one. Married couples often discover they have different attitudes toward money, different spending habits, different priorities. They find themselves arguing over money—even when money itself isn't a problem. For some, financial troubles arise when one partner doesn't seem to pull his equal weight. Amy's husband was neither as ambitious nor as responsible as she was. "He was never really motivated to do much beyond sitting around drinking," she says. "I kind of pushed him along because I didn't want to be married to someone who was a failure. So I had him do what I wanted him to do, in terms of furthering himself. I wrote all his essays to grad school and the Peace Corps. I essentially turned into an enabler. I took care of everything."

Inequality works both ways. According to the Bureau of Labor Statistics, in 1998 almost a third of married women earned more than their husbands. In some cases, men resent that their wives are the primary providers; women sometimes begrudge the fact that they have to take on this role. Clara says that her family's money negatively impacted her relationship. "He resented the fact that I came from money. I mean, he enjoyed it sometimes, but he also liked to throw it back in my face. And he knew that I was particularly sensitive because if people know that you have a successful father, they assume all sorts of things about you. And he knew that those preconceptions bothered me, so he would use it against me when we fought."

Even when it's not a question of enough or equality, finances can lead to fights. Some couples decided not to share resources and responsibilities, a decision that many felt stemmed from underlying problems, usually involving trust and power. "We kept our finances completely separate," Helena recalls. "It was a huge issue for me to be able to trust someone enough to give up my financial independence, and I guess I didn't really trust him. At the same time, I resented that he kept his money separately. We were clearly not of the mind that what's mine is his and vice versa. Neither of us was willing to give up that independence or security. . . . That we couldn't even pool our financial resources was a big red flag. And I think it was a mistake. We should have at least had one joint account."

The decision not to share funds can exacerbate an existing imbalance of power. Isabel and her husband constantly fought over finances. "He made ten times what I made, and I ended up having to pay for so much and had nothing for myself," she recalls. "But I didn't want to have a joint bank account because I didn't trust him. Every month I just pushed it off." Isabel felt that her husband used money to wield power. "He actually wanted to give me an allowance," she says, laughing. "One time we went away to Las Vegas for a weekend and we got into a huge fight while we were there. I had won this money at a casino, and he made me use it to pay for the entire trip."

Couples can focus so much on money during their marriage that they lose sight of the marriage itself. "I was the one who was always, 'Push, push, push,' " says Juliet. " 'We've got to work, we've got to save'; we were on the fast track. I wanted our marriage to be perfect. I didn't stop to smell the flowers, I kept thinking, 'We've got to be here, we should be at this point, we should be doing this, we should be doing that.' I was trying so hard to get to this place, and I'm not even sure where it was I wanted to get to." High achievers working in demanding fields are particularly prone to tackling marriage like a project, focusing on its success as if plotting a career path. Juliet fell into this trap. "The idea of working so much and focusing so much on money and professional success is not such a good thing when you're considering marriage," she says of the lesson she learned. "You need to focus more on the marriage itself. We all work so hard on our professional lives, but not on our personal lives."

The bottom line is that money isn't the real problem in marriage. Arguing over finances is usually just a symptom of larger issues; tensions about money generally translate into an underlying inequality of love, commitment, or power. "Everybody always says that money doesn't make you happy," says Isabel, "and a little part of me didn't think that was true. But it is. . . . I was miserable."

"We Couldn't Communicate"

Power struggles are almost always partnered with communication problems. John Gottman, psychology professor at the University of Washington, has conducted extensive research into what types of behaviors predict marriage failure. Gottman heads the high-tech Love Lab, which claims to predict which couples will divorce with a 90 percent rate of accuracy. From his observations of married pairs in action, Gottman has identified what he calls the "Four Horsemen of the Apocalypse," the major factors leading to divorce: contempt, criticism, defensiveness, and stonewalling—all examples of poor communication.

Communication is the backbone of marriage, and not surprisingly, many divorcés conclude that one or both spouses lacked the proper skills. "Neither of us would ever give in," Isabel says. "I definitely had a problem with compromise. We both did. We couldn't communicate at all." Poor communication is potent because it inevitably escalates any form of disagreement or difference: criticism leads to fights and fights subside into bitterness. That bitterness leads to a lack of trust, which in turn devolves into depression or anger or resentment—and leads to fights. The cycle begins anew, repeats itself, and always gets worse.

One man complained that marital disagreements followed an inevitably unproductive path. "It was always me. She turned things around to where it seemed like *I* was always in the wrong. I was always wrong for thinking the way I did. So she would give me the silent treatment as a punishment, while I would just be trying to talk to her, trying to apologize. I think I apologized on average five times every time there was an incident, just so that we could get past it." The result was an escalating competition fueled by anger. "It seemed like everything I did was wrong, so that it got to the point where I just wanted to nail her on something."

Michael says of his own marriage, "My wife always felt threat-ened by certain ways in which I communicated, which would cause her to overreact.... I don't know what changed, but it seemed like she felt increasingly threatened and she would be-come very aggressive. We started to fight more and more. She said that the way I spoke to her made her feel 'less than' and that I al-ways had to win. I thought I had always tried to offer some kind of opinion or solution to resolve the problem but that she just wanted to dwell on the problem itself. She would end up getting so angry that she would start venting about present stuff *and* past stuff, which I didn't think was fair. It's like she kept a little checklist of all my faults. And then I would get angry because she would rage at me. So I would either shut down or get really angry back." In spite of his efforts to hold on to a "mental ethical guideline" about what was and was not permissible in a fight, their arguments even-tually dissolved into name calling and door slamming. The mar-riage ended in anger.

"She Didn't Know How to Compromise"

Many marriages devolve into an ongoing series of unresolvable conflicts. One partner feels like the one who has to shoulder all the responsibility or always do the apologizing. Or one partner has to control everything and have the upper hand while the other plays a more passive, accepting role. Some marriages witness a switch or a rotating flip-flop in dominance. A husband may get the power position because he earns more; one spouse may have more sexual power; a wife might be constantly jealous and vulnerable; a hus-band may threaten to leave every time his wife complains.

Arguments become something to win; fights turn into con-tests; tallies of battle triumphs are kept in order to score off the other spouse. "She would always get defensive, and our arguments would escalate," Jared says. "I'm not saying I was high and mighty, but I cared about her, so I wouldn't throw things blatantly hurtful in her face. But she didn't have any such reservations. She would do whatever it took. She had to win—and let me know it."

"Neither one of us knew how to compromise," Zoë recalls. "My idea of compromise was giving in. But neither of us could ever

really figure out what we wanted or articulate that desire, and neither of us could figure out how to get what we wanted. We just
were too young and immature to know how to find a middle
ground." A pattern developed. They would fight, she would grovel,
and he would send her flowers in the aftermath. "But I started
being like, 'Stop sending me flowers. Flowers die—they don't
make up for the shortcomings in our marriage. I wish you would
just talk to me.' "

Charlotte's husband seemed incapable of compromise. "He
was very much like my dad," she explains, describing his rigidity.
"Very stubborn and cold, really set in his ways. Even with little
things. Like he wouldn't ever want to go out for breakfast. He just
didn't like doing that. If someone said, 'Hey, let's all go out for
breakfast together,' he'd say, 'I don't go out for breakfast.' I was like,
'Loosen up! It's just breakfast, just this one time.' But he wouldn't
budge on the smallest things. It took a lot of the life out of me. I
was much more of an adventurer." When her husband dropped out
of college to pursue his music career full-time, Charlotte found
herself alone in the house from the day after her honeymoon, providing the sole steady income. Problems with compromise became
a major theme of their marriage. "He had the freedom to say whatever he wanted and make all the decisions," Charlotte says. "I knew
I wanted to have kids at some point and he didn't. I thought he
would change over time, but the topic would intensify. If we saw
someone with a baby, he would turn to me and say, 'Don't get any
ideas,' and that really bothered me. That started once we got married. He started really mocking me about it. But there wasn't a way
to discuss anything with him. He would say, 'I was just joking.
Drop the subject.' "

Charlotte felt like she constantly sacrificed. "I wanted to have a
church relationship with him, and he didn't want anything to do
with that. He refused to go with me, so I went alone." In the end,
her husband's inability to make any sacrifices left her feeling like
the marriage couldn't survive over the long term. "The kid issue
was a big thing. The nonspiritual aspect of the marriage was *not*
okay with me. There wasn't any hope for him in either of those
ways, and that was extremely discouraging for me. Neither of us
was willing to compromise, but I felt like I compromised most of

the time. He was just so stubborn." When Charlotte ran into her ex-husband two years after their divorce, he told her, "You know, I've realized that there were a lot of things about myself that I could have changed to save our marriage." "That really blew me away," Charlotte says. "Because he would never admit to anything like that at the time."

"Our Relationship Was Completely Unequal"

Some power struggles seem to stem from the current confusion over gender roles. Spouses aren't sure what they're "supposed" to do in marriage, and often one partner ends up feeling like he's doing everything. Husbands fear being perceived as domineering or old-fashioned and often retreat into a defensive stance of passivity or indifference. Wives find that they slip into what they had thought were outdated roles from the pre–women's movement era. Call it Fear of the Shrew. A wife resolves from the beginning, "I will not nag him. I will not bother him all the time. I won't disparage him." But then she finds herself muttering under her breath, "But damn it, I *don't* want to do it all by myself." Nag, nag, nag. Confront, fight, retreat, provoke, and confront. The dismal dance of a bad marriage breaking down.

Many failed marriages are characterized by unequal partnerships between strong women and weak men. Several women I talked to admitted that they may have inadvertently "bullied" their husbands into marriage or led fundamentally passive men into something they weren't ready for. "People talk about the traditional male and female roles," says Jodie. "Well, I had both of them." Lucy thinks that may have been the case with her husband as well. "My biggest problem with the marriage and what really ended it was that he had no work ethic," she says. "I had grown up with a strong work ethic, but he would just quit his job if he had a bad day at work. . . . He was always looking for a quick fix. Maybe that's one of the reasons he married me."

Amy's husband was neither as ambitious nor as responsible as she was. He was "incapable of doing anything by himself," so she ended up cleaning the house, taking care of the car, handling the finances, and cooking dinner. "Looking back, I have no idea what he did," she says. "I always hoped he would change after we were married for a while, but he never got a job. When I forced him, he would get jobs at Wendy's or McDonald's. I hoped he would have higher expectations for himself. When I told my parents we were getting divorced, they said they had always anticipated this day coming. In fact, they said that I'd essentially raised my husband as my son."

Studies have indicated that wives with high levels of "instrumentality" (or "masculinity" in the traditional sense) report significant decreases in marital satisfaction.[4] Perhaps not surprisingly, these women were frequently the ones to initiate divorce. "I had more responsibility in the household, which was okay with me," explains Laurel. "I was ready to make a sixty/forty or even a sixty-five/thirty-five deal. I was fine if someone else would take care of certain things. I didn't need or want to do it all, but my husband just wasn't working hard enough to provide for me. I had certain obligations around the house and socially, but I had a job and I was really busy. So we had to be able to afford a housekeeper, and certain things should have been shared. I liked to cook and he didn't, so I was happy to be in charge of that. But then he was supposed to take care of bills, which he didn't do. The deal was, if I gardened, he would do x, y, or z in exchange." The problems in Laurel's marriage grew progressively worse. "Toward the end of the marriage, I was doing everything. He thought a wife was just like his mother, but he wasn't willing to be the kind of guy that would be needed to provide for that kind of person. I started to get frustrated with who he wanted me to be and the role he wanted me to play. He'd be watching TV all night, and I would find myself out in the garden watering plants after cleaning the kitchen and thinking, 'Oh my God, this is my life.' "

Laurel's frustration finally led to confrontation. "I'm a big talker, but his reaction to feeling pressed and pushed was to go into hiding. He was pedaling backward on purpose. My expectations were forced lower and lower. 'Just be the bill guy, please,' I said to him. But then two months would go by and he wouldn't have paid the bills. So it was still effectively my job to do the bills because I had to remember to remind him to do it. I got meaner and meaner, and he grew less and less involved. I think he was depressed." Laurel and her ex-husband saw a marriage therapist after filing for a separation. "The therapist asked him why he got married, and he said, 'I don't know. Because she wanted to.' My ex just floats through life like it's being done to him. As if life is this force that just impinges upon him."

"I Got Depressed"

Starter marriages can sink very quickly. People who have less-than-wonderful long-term relationships lurch down the aisle hoping marriage will perk things up; when it doesn't, they droop swiftly into defeat. For others, vows are taken during the early, blissfully happy stages of the relationship, when all they know is unadulterated pleasure. Once the inevitable normalization occurs and the first few letdowns loom in, marriage itself can become the culprit. And this can push a bout of sadness into a full-blown depression: You're sad. It's because of your husband/your marriage. And you're trapped.

When people realize that marriage doesn't make everything bright and shiny, they find themselves feeling increasingly dejected. Olivia's marriage fell apart almost immediately. "He would badmouth me to the point where my self-esteem plummeted. It must have been really low because I didn't even stay pissed-off. I just kind of retreated. I was so miserable I gained forty pounds. Early into the marriage he warned me that if I ever got fat, he would seriously consider cheating on me. I guess I hoped it would come true."

A number of people I interviewed became clinically depressed; several were put on Prozac or other antidepressants. Bethany got married after a few months of dating. About a year into her marriage, Bethany says she got depressed. "I would come home and crawl into bed, and he didn't know how to deal with it. He was rather sheltered, I think, growing up. He couldn't deal with his own emotions, so how could he deal with mine? At the time, I felt utterly abandoned; it broke my spirit. This is the man I'm supposed to spend the rest of my life with, and he can't be here when I really need him, to pick me up and help me."

At first Noelle thought her husband was the depressed one in her marriage, but eventually she began to suffer as well. "I'm usually really happy and energetic," she says. "But I started to get depressed and he was definitely depressed already. I would find ways to snap out of it, like going for a run because I was always the strong person. I knew the situation between us wasn't going to change, so all I could do was try to make myself happy. But it was hard."

Depression and its treatment often highlight existing problems in the marriage. One's spouse may act as an enabler, inadvertently encouraging depression by taking on a caretaker role or creating the marriage structure around that depression, rather than trying to treat it. On the other hand, sometimes a spouse acts indifferent, insensitive, self-absorbed, or unwilling to make sacrifices for the depressed party. A wife becomes afraid that the person she fell in love with will never return, or a husband can't handle that his bouncy bride isn't always a perky wife. In other cases, the healthy spouse turns the situation onto himself and imagines he's making his partner unhappy or is in some way to blame. "I didn't understand why I couldn't make her feel better." "If she weren't in this miserable marriage, she'd be okay." "I felt totally powerless." "If he *really* loved me, he wouldn't be depressed."

Some people felt like their spouse simply opted out of the situation, preferring to see it as *the depressed person's problem* as opposed to *our problem*. Such marriages, like many starter marriages, devolve into alternating rounds of accusation and apologies; frustrated tension and silence; helplessness and indifference. One person is sick and the other is off the hook. It wasn't *my* fault the marriage ended. One person is sad and I can't make her happy. For many, if depression didn't occur during their marriage, it followed at some point after the marriage dissolved.

Chapter 6

When Starter Marriages
Fall Apart

TODD, A TWENTY-NINE-YEAR-OLD BOSTON-BASED LAWYER, married his childhood sweetheart when he was twenty-five. "The time had come," he explains. "We couldn't go on being boyfriend and girlfriend forever." When they married after ten years of dating on and off, he assumed "we would overcome our problems and be married forever."

Trouble arose the day after their engagement and only got worse over the course of their two-year marriage. "Being married can be tough," Todd admits. "You're working really hard and you're tired and you still have all life's problems to contend with. But my wife had this gingerbread-house view of our relationship. Life would not intrude in any way on our marriage. We'd live in this dollhouse, play in the dollhouse, live happily ever after. When that didn't happen, I think it was shocking to her."

Their marital troubles grew increasingly serious. "She would bring up all these problems with me but then wouldn't want to deal with the consequences. At one point she said to me, 'What happens if it doesn't work out?' I said, 'We get divorced.' And she started to cry." When their problems became overwhelming, Todd decided to join his wife in therapy. "I think I was in denial of her mental state at the time," he says. "I ignored the fact that she was totally insecure and emotionally vulnerable. When you're with someone for that long, you think you really know them, so you may not pay as much attention."

In many ways, attending his wife's therapy sessions forced Todd to take notice. "In therapy, she told me that she felt like we had nothing in common. She said she was attracted to someone else. The therapist felt that it was because the object of her affection was the complete opposite of how she saw me. He was this happy-go-lucky guy. And she saw me as this serious, unhappy person."

They decided to see a marriage counselor. "It was very tough," Todd recalls. "Things came out that were very hard for me to hear. The night we separated, the therapist asked her, 'What is it about Todd that you're not attracted to?' and she said, 'Everything.' I went out of my skin. I said, 'You heard that! She just said that! How could you say that?' When we left, I said to my wife, 'When was the last time you wanted to reach over and kiss me?' And she said, 'It's been a very long time.' We got home and I said to her, 'Just tell me on a scale from one to ten, how much do you want me to kick you out?' She didn't even answer. That's when I knew it was over. An hour later I told her to leave. 'I want you gone,' I said. And when she had left, I just sat down and cried."

Matrimony can be the loneliest state in the world. A troubled marriage leaves its participants in a precarious frame of mind; it's often impossible to turn within the marriage to solve it, and it's terrifying to face the world outside. Disclosing marriage problems can feel like spilling out one's worst fears and exposing one's failings—with irrevocable repercussions. And once a failing marriage is split open for public consumption, it's almost impossible to imagine sewing it back together.

Joel eloped without telling his parents, so when his marriage began to crumble, "I didn't have anyone in my family to talk to because they didn't even know we were married. I was so miserable. I felt so lost. I was completely devoid of feeling for my wife even though I knew I had felt so much for her before. It was painful to look at her and think, 'Ugh. We're occupying this dirty, little, cramped space, and we have so little money and so little feeling for one another.' . . . I felt very much alone."

Even under the best circumstances, marriage relies on the support of a network of friends and family. Without the ongoing involvement of outsiders, couples become isolated along with their problems, their arguments, and their misunderstandings—a situation that usually makes matters much, much worse. There's a strange contradiction between the social pressure to marry and the subsequent lack of social involvement in marriage itself. As George observes, "There are tremendous pressures to get married . . . and yet we are more atomized now. We don't have the buttressing, the support, the networks, or even the reinforcement of the shame of divorce—though that was mostly a bad thing—that helps hold people together."

Starter marriages in particular lack the support system so essential to a marriage's survival. Marrying before one's peers, eloping without family involvement, or retreating to the confines of a table for two can leave couples feeling dangerously isolated. Young, insecure, perfectionist spouses are the least likely of people to admit to shortcomings or, heaven forbid, defeat. One woman recalls, "I felt like I was living in this personal hell that I couldn't get out of. I had no one to bounce ideas off for a long time because I thought that if I told people about the problems we were having, they would say, 'I told you so.' And I couldn't bear to hear that on top of all the other problems. I just couldn't handle it at the time. But the less I reached out, the more cocooned I felt. It was only when the relationship got abusive and I grew desperate that I felt like I could reach out for help. And at that point, people had started to witness scenes between us, so it had become too hard to hide anyway."

Suffering in Silence

Whether out of pride, fear, shame, or anger, couples feel inhibited
by the unspoken taboo against speaking out about a troubled marriage. It *feels* wrong. Talking with others about what your marriage is really like feels like poking around a cadaver; there's a
distinct sense that such inner workings ought to remain unseen. "I
was very infrequently able to talk to people about the problems we
were having, and that was a mistake," a thirty-one-year-old man
from Texas admits. "My father gave me the advice that before getting married, he and my mom decided never to say anything bad
about each other to other people. Not bad advice, but I think I took
it way too far. I felt like that meant I couldn't talk to anybody about
our problems. It might have helped me to acknowledge some of
the problems and address them instead of hoping they would go
away."

Just as getting married signals personal success, exposing a
failing marriage makes you look like a failure. Serious marital
woes conjure an almost unbearable sense of shame. "I didn't talk
to anybody at first," Lucy recounts. "I didn't want anyone to know
that it was going downhill so quickly. I was really embarrassed. I
was ashamed. I actually felt lucky that I was able to hide it from
my friends and family back home." Bethany pretended to everyone
else that things were fine. "It would drive my husband crazy because we'd be in the middle of this horrible fight and then the
phone would ring and I'd pick up and act like nothing was wrong.
I guess I felt a lot of shame about what was happening to us."

And talking about problems within your marriage decidedly
means that your marriage is bad. Isabel recalls, "I didn't say one
word about the problems we were having until the day I walked
out. I figured, A, if you don't say anything, then they're not true,
and B, this was just not supposed to happen to me. I thought the
way people viewed me was that I had this perfect life with no problems. I didn't want to let anyone down. And C, I didn't want to turn
people against him. I didn't want to feel stupid badmouthing my
husband and then end up staying with him for twenty years. So I
just avoided my friends when I was with him."

Badmouthing marriage feels decidedly dangerous. Assuming
that problems will ultimately be resolved, one doesn't want to risk

undermining the marriage by exposing it. "I felt like I couldn't talk to anyone," Olivia says. "I had alienated all my friends by not spending any time with them. And I still felt nervous bad-mouthing him because if things did work out between us, I didn't want people not to like him. Especially my family." People feel protective of their spouses or fear that their loyalty is somehow at stake. "I didn't want people to think badly of him," Jodie says of her husband. "But then again, I didn't want to have to defend him to other people because I was so angry with him, it would be too hard. I mean, it was okay for me to be angry at him, but it wasn't okay if other people were."

Jared was afraid to talk to anyone because "I felt like if I told people how things really were, they would tell me to get out." When your friends seem happily married, it's hard to admit to your own difficulties. Many young marrieds beat themselves up wondering why their marriage was so screwed-up while other couples seem to float permanently in the honeymoon phase. Not only is it scary to talk to them, often other couples don't want to face the prospect of marital collapse.

Charlotte tried to talk to friends, but "our mutual friends didn't want to hear about it. They would just change the subject." She adds, "We got married first and then these two other couples got married and our next-door neighbors had recently married as well. All three of those couples are divorced now. But at the time they didn't want to hear about my problems because they felt like, 'If one of us leaves, how could the rest of us be sure we'll stay together?' " Charlotte's divorce ultimately ended one of those friendships. "One of my married friends felt like I was abandoning her. She let me have it. She told me that she didn't agree with what we were doing, that I should give it more time. When we split up, she wouldn't have anything to do with me." Later on, Charlotte learned from that friend that "she was having her own marriage problems but she didn't want to face them at the time. Once she got divorced, she was ready to be friends again."

For children of divorce, admitting one's own problems to a divorced parent can incite feelings of shame, embarrassment, and overwhelming guilt. Nobody wants to burden one's parents with the idea that the divorce is somehow *their* fault, that they failed to lead by example. Parents—divorced or not—are hard to turn to when marriage is supposed to mean you've grown up and are on your own—especially if they didn't support the marriage in the first place. "My family didn't like my wife," Ben explains. "And that had a very negative effect on the marriage. It's a difficult position to be in when you don't have the support of your friends and family." Amy's parents were furious when she eloped during college. "My mother was my only friend, and I wanted her approval so much that I didn't want her to see the bad things happening in my marriage," she remembers. "I kept to myself or talked to my husband—even when the problem was him. It was so hard. You need a support system outside of the marriage in order for it to survive, and I didn't have that."

Even supportive parents can be difficult to confide in. Jodie's parents were close to her husband and pleased by their daughter's marriage. "I was terrified to tell my parents," Jodie says of her decision to divorce. "I thought they'd be disappointed in me, or think I hadn't done everything I could. . . . I was afraid they'd feel sorry for me, and I didn't want that."

As hard as it can be, discussing marital problems and getting others involved provides much needed perspective. Lucy says that it wasn't until she began to talk to her friends that she was able to confront her marital problems. "When we moved back home, all of a sudden my friends started witnessing us together and I realized just how bad the relationship was and how badly I was being treated," Lucy says. "My best friend finally said to me, 'What is going on? Why are you staying in this?' And I told her how I was feeling. I told her I felt trapped and that I was afraid to disappoint my family and that I didn't think I was trying hard enough. So then I started dealing with it, and I started going to counseling." In a way, Lucy was motivated to end things because she feared how a bad marriage reflected on her. "For some reason, it wasn't enough for me to just be unhappy. I would feel foolish for my best friend to know how unhappy I was and not do anything about it," she explains. "My friends had an image of me as this strong woman and to be just letting myself feel so crappy was embarrassing. It looked like I didn't respect myself."

Exposing the innards of a marriage can also quicken its demise—for better or for worse. Whether it's a single friend who just doesn't "get" marriage, a family member all too ready to blame your spouse, or someone unintentionally offering biased advice, sometimes talking to other people might be good for you individually but not necessarily right for the marriage. "Once when we had a horrible, blowout fight, my husband stormed out and went to talk to his older brother, who was single," Kate, thirty-one, recalls bitterly. "I was glad that he was talking to an outside party because I thought he would have had some sense talked into him, that he would have been encouraged to work things out, you know? Told to do whatever it takes. So I was shocked when he came home as furious and self-righteous as ever. I said to him, 'Didn't he advise you that we ought to work things out?' And he said, 'No, he told me that I have to watch out for myself and do whatever makes *me* happy.'"

People are frequently told to do "what makes you happy" or "whatever you need to do" rather than to do what needs to be done in order to make the marriage work. Outsiders can be so fearful of interfering in what they consider a private matter that they hold back, scared of being perceived as judgmental or taking sides. In a marriage, taking sides is usually destructive—the "side" is the common ground of the marriage, not the self-interest of either individual. Objectivity seems impossible. Often couples enter therapy because friends and family seem either unwilling or unable to help.

Marriage Therapy

Couples' therapy can be the best remedy for marriage misery. Many long-lasting unions credit their endurance to some form of counseling, be it a regular retreat, weekly sessions individually or as a couple, or some form of group couples' counseling. As of 1995, 4.6 million couples a year visited 50,000 licensed family therapists, up from 1.2 million in 1980.[1] At the same time, up to 25 percent of divorcing couples never go through marital therapy at all.[2]

The road to therapy isn't always easy. Common wisdom holds that it can only work if both partners are dedicated to it, but sometimes one spouse refuses to go or to take it seriously. "For me, it was inspiring to try to change and work out the problems so that we could communicate better," Michael says. "I learned so much about myself and my own communication habits during therapy. But even though [my wife] always said she liked therapy, I got the sense that it was threatening to her. She would only allow herself to go so far." Charlotte asked her husband to come to therapy with her, but he always refused, until she finally asked for a divorce. At that point he insisted on going. "By then, it was really apparent to me that it was over," Charlotte remembers. "Someone told me that you would know right away in couples' therapy whether you needed to continue with the therapy or whether the relationship was over. And that's what happened with me. We only went once."

As helpful as marriage therapy can be, it can speed the divorce instead of saving the marriage. Unlike traditional therapeutic practice, which treats the individual, in marital therapy the marriage is the "patient." Unfortunately, sometimes the highly self-centered methods of individual therapy are mistakenly applied to the two selves in a marriage—either by one half of the couple in individual therapy, or by a bad couples' therapist. "I brought my husband to my therapist," one woman recounted, "and when I went alone to the next session my therapist told me, 'Get out of there! You're only twenty-eight. Don't try to fix this if you're not happy. If you're happier by yourself, what are you doing? Go find out what you want to do.'"

Lucy had to convince her husband to go to therapy. "We saw this man who was really great, but he ended up facilitating our divorce because he would make me say how I really felt. And I would say that the marriage wasn't working and I wanted to break up. It was much easier for me to say in front of the therapist.... The therapist eventually asked to see me alone. And he explained to me, this is what I'm seeing and this is what I think you need to do." Whether the person giving this advice was simply a bad therapist, guided by his own personal motivations, or honestly believed that Lucy was better off ending an early, childless marriage is unknown. In any case, Lucy decided on divorce. Noelle and her husband saw a counselor through their church. "It helped, but only temporarily," she recalls. "We weren't willing to work on any of the issues once we left his office though. We ended up going to counseling for so long that the counselor finally told us to just get divorced."

Yet therapy often facilitates divorce not through any direct action by the therapist but because problems previously ignored or belittled become exposed and legitimized (and, the hope is, worked on). A twenty-seven-year-old man from Boston explained, "When my wife and I went into counseling, she said in the session that I had been the best of what was offered in the area and though she had wanted more, she settled for me. . . . Which told me that I was not the person she wanted and that even if we got through our problems, I would always feel like she was looking for someone else. So that's when I requested that our marriage sessions be turned into divorce sessions." One woman says she used couples' therapy as a way to confront her husband about things that had been bothering her. At one point, she recalls, she tried to "induce some kind of reaction in him. I yelled the magic words, 'I want a divorce!' This had never come up before. But the therapist, instead of asking me what made me say that or what I was feeling, just started talking about the logistical requirements of divorce. And that was a turning point. If somebody had asked me, 'What are you really feeling?' 'Where is this coming from?' the focus would not have been on divorce but on what my needs were and how we could meet them. All I really needed was some attention." She adds later, "If I had to say I had any regrets about my marriage, it was standing up and saying that in therapy, instead of approaching the real issues. It hurt my husband terribly."

In the cases cited in this book, marital therapy failed to "save" the marriage, but many say it helped them tremendously as individuals. A few said that the most positive consequence of their starter marriage was that it finally got them to confront their own problems. As a result of marital counseling, people explained, "I figured out how to have a healthy relationship." "I learned a lot about myself." "I became the person I am today."

Whether therapy provided them such individual benefits or not, many couples feel that by the time they agreed to counseling, the fate of their marriage was a foregone conclusion. After Zoë and her husband were separated, she proposed that they see a therapist together. "But he forgot to write down the name, address, and the directions. I was following him in his car, and we just kept driving and driving in circles. When I got out of the car to ask him what was going on, he got mad at me for trying to discuss it 'in the middle of the street.' I felt like, here's somebody who does not want the marriage to work out. So we never ended up going to therapy. We got lost along the way."

Marriage's End

Marriage is not a consistent enterprise, and while most couples profess awareness of this, or at least pay lip service to the old stock phrase "Marriage is work," their behavior often proves otherwise. Even happy marriages suffer blowout fights, lingering silences, deep resentments, and recurrent bickering. The lows can last for months—in some marriages for years. With marriage so hard to pinpoint or judge at any given moment, how does one know when the low signifies a permanent defect rather than a temporary phase? What looks like a bad marriage one month might turn out to be a good marriage the next.

It seems like nowadays fewer marriages endure the inevitable rough patches. On a positive note, we're less willing to tolerate unhappy lives and are more optimistic about our rights and abilities to attain personal happiness. A more negative interpretation is that we no longer have what it takes to make marriage work over the long haul; we're spoiled, impatient, selfish, and lazy. The truth probably lies uncomfortably between the two, as many divorcés will reluctantly admit. Whatever the case may be, starter marriages are either unwilling or unable to either succeed with their marriages or to make themselves miserable by sticking to an unhappy one.

At some point people in starter marriages realize that the problem with their marriage is the marriage itself. "*If* our marriage breaks up" becomes "*when* the marriage breaks up." It's decided not to struggle through problems but to abandon them entirely. To help oneself instead of helping the marriage. "My wife says she left because she wasn't happy and she didn't think she could make me happy," one thirty-three-year-old man recalls bitterly. "On the one hand, I would *never* get divorced for that reason, which doesn't seem like reason enough to dissolve a marriage contract. On the other hand, what could I say to that?"

Knowing when it's over and making the decision to end a marriage can be brutally difficult. "My parents had a ritual where every year they ask one another on their anniversary if they wanted to re-up for another year," Zoë explains. "Then they would assess their marriage and talk about any problems or changes that needed to be made. So I tried to do the same thing with my husband. On our first anniversary I asked him if he wanted to re-up another year, and he just said, 'Do we have to talk about this right now?' I thought, 'Oh God.' That was the first time I saw we were in trouble, or at least the first time I was willing to admit it. I remember thinking, 'Oh, no. This is the beginning of the end.'"

For some couples, the marriage gets so bad that the decision to divorce seems relatively quick and painless. "I never would have wanted a divorce if my husband hadn't told me that he didn't want to be married anymore," explains one woman, divorced at thirty-one. "But I knew I had to do it. I had put my heart and soul into preserving my marriage, and it was clear through what my husband said and the way he behaved toward me that he just did *not* want to be married. And I wasn't willing to be treated like that anymore. I just couldn't bear the pain. It was making me insane. . . . To finally go to a lawyer and file for divorce was actually easy compared with what I'd been through."

But most marriages suffer through a more convoluted, difficult collapse, stretching out, splintering, resolving to leave, and then reconciling. Back and forth, arguments and apologies, and anniversaries and promises. Someone says the unforgivable. Throws an ashtray, kicks the door, walks out the door.

A dying marriage often goes out fighting. Michael became aware that his marriage was in trouble in the middle of a typical argument. "It suddenly occurred to me that maybe we couldn't work this out, and that was devastating to me because it went against my whole belief system. I don't even remember what the fight was about. I just remember that I was really upset and crying because my thoughts had changed from the fight itself to the realization that maybe the marriage couldn't be worked out." George realized that the "volcanic fights" he was having with his wife were not only destructive to the relationship, they were bringing out the worst in him, a side of himself he had never seen. "I started going to a therapist because I was feeling very blocked. And I was unnerving myself, because I felt like with all this horrible yelling in these fights, I wasn't centered anymore. I felt like I was not as in control of my emotions as I wanted to be." He also began to realize the impact of their debilitating blowouts. "My biggest regret is that in my own unhappiness, I blamed [my wife] for a lot of things. And I succeeded in making her feel responsible for things that she shouldn't have. One of the reasons I wanted to get out was that I felt myself grinding her down and making her feel terrible, when she shouldn't have felt that way at all."

Vacations, time apart, work changes, family conflicts, financial woes, and moves often provide the dramatic tension that leads to marital trauma. One woman's husband was away for several months on business when she discovered that she wanted a divorce. "I realized that I was actually glad when he left. I had kind of shut off my feelings until then, but suddenly my emotions came up and it was a nightmare. And when I thought about him coming home, I became massively depressed. I was a total basket case. I knew that I needed to get a divorce. It was actually our anniversary, and he was supposed to fly in for the weekend, but I told him over the phone that I wanted to end things. He was completely blindsided. He had no idea I had these feelings."

In a shaky marriage with poor communication, two spouses can judge the state of the union very differently. A marriage seems to be going well for one while the other is suffering. "I felt like I was the town crier for our marriage," Yasmin says. "I issued the weather reports. And we were in such different places that he didn't have a clue what I was talking about until I was literally at the breaking point.... We thought that we would get closer after our conflicts, but that closeness was never sustained. Sometimes I tried to engage in conflict even if only to show how empty our marriage had become. He didn't think anything was wrong, but he just wasn't paying attention. To me, it felt like death."

Often the people I interviewed found themselves desperate to leave, and did so at the next, inevitable provocation. "We would have these fights where we would sit on the couch all day Saturday barely able to talk," Yasmin says. "It got more and more hostile as the marriage wore on. At that point we positively hated each other, and I think that's what we needed in order to be able to leave one another." Zoë and her husband decided to separate after sixteen months because, she says, "I knew that one of us had to move out before we killed each other." "We got married in October, and by January things were shaky. And that continued and built," Charlotte recalls. "Finally, about a year and a half later, I said to myself, 'This is over.' I was in summer school at the time, and I remember on the way home wishing that when I got there, his car would be gone. I just wanted him to go. I wanted him to leave. I was so sure it was over, but I was too busy to deal with it. I didn't want to have to disrupt my plans by having to move, so I made this little schedule for myself. Certain things had to happen by certain points in time. And if they didn't and if he wasn't gone by the end of summer, I would leave." By summer's close, Charlotte had packed her things and gone.

Actually having to deal with a marriage's demise is so traumatizing that people flee into excuses, procrastination, and sheer avoidance. They fantasize that "something would just happen" to end things. "Every day I'd wake up and try to figure out a reason not to get divorced," Amy recalls. "I knew I had rushed into my marriage, but divorce just seemed like something I could not do. I wished something terrible would happen to him, even though he was my best friend. I wished he would die or something, so that I could be free. I wanted him to just go overseas and die. It sounds so horrible, but I felt so trapped. But divorce, no, never. It wasn't an acceptable thing in my family. People just did not quit. And he was so in love with me, I knew he wouldn't be able to accept it." Finally Amy made a decision. "After almost five years of marriage, I couldn't even pretend to be happy anymore. I told him, 'You deserve to be with someone who's in love with you. It's not fair to you. You deserve so much more.' And at that point, I asked for a divorce."

Some find themselves searching for an excuse to end their marriages. "After we decided to separate, he had an affair," Lucy says. "And that sped everything up. I felt completely upset and betrayed, even though, ironically, I think I wanted it to happen. It gave me a solid reason to leave, whereas everything before felt nebulous. I would say to myself, 'He's not necessarily mean to me. He doesn't beat me. But if he cheated on me . . . *then* it would be understandable.' Of course, when it really happened, I was crushed."

For most people, the hardest thing about their marriage is facing the finality of divorce, with all its details, legalities, and decision making. "I thought about divorce all the time," Charlotte recalls. "But I resolved that I wouldn't get divorced as quickly as I got married. I made promises to myself that I would make sure it was the right decision. I wanted to give it all the chances I could. After three months of marriage, I outlined all these rules that I needed to follow to ensure that I tried as hard as I could with the marriage." Two years later, Charlotte asked her husband for a divorce. "Going through the divorce was a huge pain. I took care of the whole thing. I got a packet and I typed it all up. I didn't have a computer at home, so I had to do it out in public at Kinko's. And I saw myself sitting there out in the open, and I thought, 'Man, I really *do* want to get this divorce if I'm going through this hell.' But it actually felt good to be so sure about something, to do something that I knew was right."

Deciding to divorce can also be immensely satisfying. Many people feel incredible resolve in making their decision, like they've finally figured out how to solve the problem or make a clean break. Often it's a huge relief. Olivia was only eight months into her marriage when she first filed for divorce. Her husband begged her not to leave. "But when I stayed, I grew even more miserable. I didn't care about myself anymore. I was only twenty-two and I thought that I was stuck in a bad marriage for the rest of my life. I just resigned myself. 'Okay, this is my destiny.' " After graduating from school and starting a new job, she began to see the possibility of changing her situation. "I had been in this trap. But then I had this epiphany where I realized I wasn't stuck. I could end things and everything will be still be okay."

Ending a bad marriage early can be its own reward. "For me, my greatest failure was also my greatest gift to myself," says Laurel. "Because my unwillingness to live with his way of life meant that I got divorced and got a second chance, rather than ending up in a five-, ten-, or twenty-year marriage that would have been a lot worse."

D Day

The day that divorce comes home stands out sharply in every divorcé's memory—especially for those caught off guard. When one partner decides of his own accord to end a marriage, there's a terrible sense of betrayal. Sam learned that his wife was planning a divorce after noticing money missing from their joint bank account. He discovered that she'd gone through his wallet, taken his credit cards, and changed all their mutual accounts. Then he found "to do" lists in her dresser drawer breaking down their common expenses and assets, along with legal actions she planned to take. "I was really mad," he says. "So I confronted her and asked, 'How long have you been planning this?' And she said, 'I've been thinking about it for a while, but I wasn't sure.' I was in shock."

Jodie was stunned by the way her husband chose to ask for a divorce. Following their first session of couples' therapy, "I was at work and we were having this argument via instant messaging. Basically, I kept asking him the same question over and over. All I wanted to know was, was he willing to try to make the marriage work? I wasn't asking if he was going to guarantee that it would, just if he was willing to try, but he kept refusing to answer. Instead, he sent me a message that he wanted to get divorced. I was stunned. Not only that he wanted a divorce, but that he wrote it on an instant message. I felt so small. Like our marriage was so meaningless it didn't even merit being discussed in person."

Often when one partner wants to divorce, the other feels like the dissolution is inevitable. After all, marriage is, by its very nature a contract between two willing participants; how can it succeed if one partner wants out? "We might expect that both partners would be ready to end the relationship by the time one leaves," remark sociologists Frank F. Furstenberg, Jr., and Andrew J. Cherlin, "but the data suggest otherwise. Four out of five marriages end *unilaterally*."[3] And in these starter marriages, when one person decided it was over, the spouse felt compelled to agree. Jodie's husband initiated the divorce process, and she felt she should go along, even taking over the paperwork in the end. "He had made up his mind and that was it," she says. "It never would have been my choice, but I think he always saw it as a way out—even when he proposed. . . . Marriage was like an experiment for him. He just wanted to know if he could do it."

Facing divorce and admitting defeat when the decision isn't one's own to begin with is excruciating. During their separation, Zoë's husband unexpectedly served her divorce papers at her office. "I was in shock when I got them," she recounts. "I was like, 'Wait a minute.' I thought we were just talking about divorce but that we weren't really going to *do* it. He had decided completely without me that no, our marriage could not be saved. I had the biggest panic attack of my life. I had no idea how I was going to survive on my own. . . . It was absolutely surreal; I couldn't believe it was happening. I brought home the divorce papers, and I just sat there looking at them, like they were some kind of mythical creature that couldn't possibly be in front of me. It was like, 'Look, a unicorn! How the hell did *that* get in here?' "

Being on the other end can be just as tough. "My husband was very kind to me, and to this day I have a very hard time hurting him," Elizabeth says. When she told him she wanted a divorce after two years of marriage, "he got so distraught. I was devastated because he had never been unkind to me. When you have someone who is so good and so loving, how do you turn around to them and say, 'We don't have that spark. We shouldn't be married'?"

Sometimes the decision is mutual. Bethany recalls the moment divorce became a reality. "My husband came home one night, and I could tell by the look on his face that it was over. I was watching *Friends.* And he sat down and said, 'I just don't know. We fight all the time. We haven't had sex in months.' I said, 'First of all, we don't fight all the time, not anymore, and secondly, we're working on the sex thing.' But he just silently got up and went into the bedroom and lay down. I knew right then that he was going to leave me, and I knew just as surely there was nothing I could do about it. So I just sat there watching the end of the show. Then I went into the bedroom and said, 'Do you want a divorce?' And he started crying and said, 'I'm so unhappy.' I crawled on top of him and held him and we both cried together. Then I asked him to be gone by morning because I had nowhere else to go."

Why Starter Marriages Fail

JAMES'S WIFE LEFT HIM AFTER A YEAR OF MARRIAGE FOR A man she'd met only eight days before. She and James had dated for almost four years before getting engaged, at which point she had given him an ultimatum. "She said to me, 'I think we need to get married, or I don't know if I can stay in this relationship.' " He duly proposed, and they were married eight months later.

"I don't know what she expected from marriage," James says. "I guess I don't know what her ideals were for marriage. Looking back now, I think that all she knew or wanted was immediate gratification. Growing up, she was always the center of attention and basically it was always about her and her immediate needs. She was very egocentric."

When James found out about his wife's affair, she asked him for a divorce. "Most couples today seem to forget that once you're married, you have a foundation, and while you inevitably sway away from it from time to time, you'll still come back to it eventually," James says sadly. "Today people lose sight of that foundation and the moment they start to sway, they forget all about it. They get caught up in looking for something outside the marriage and give up on it. And the reality is, whatever they're looking for can probably be found within the marriage at some point; it's just not right in front of them at that moment. But people just go off in their own direction and call it quits." James was shocked by his own divorce. "I had pretty strong values. . . . I thought that even in the difficult times, you do whatever it takes to make the marriage work. No matter what it involves—talking to friends or family or counseling—you've got to do it. You shouldn't give up easily."

But he's not surprised many marriages today fail. "A lot of my friends are going through divorces. There are too many things that seem to threaten marriages these days—whether it's outside stimuli or other working opportunities—people run after whatever they want without trying to work within their marriages. People don't try their hardest. They think everything should be easy, that there shouldn't be a struggle. And yet you have to go through those struggles because that's where you'll find long-lasting love and a durable foundation."

Today's marrying generation has very high expectations of matrimony. We assume the major marriage battles have already been waged, the big mistakes made, by previous generations. Now our generation will figure out how to reconfigure marriage in a post-fifties, post-hippie, postfeminist, postyuppie era. We'll be able to juggle and balance our hectic lives, our careers, our interests. Our marriages won't be boring or static or numbed; they'll be adventurous and dynamic and passionate. *We* will be the ones to make marriage work.

The current marrying generation has a lot to prove. We want to succeed even though the odds are stacked firmly against us, even though children of divorce seem susceptible to divorces of their own. Even though divorce is happening to everyone. Even though critics charge Gen Xers with being amoral slackers and Gen Yers as spoiled brats. Even though few of us have seen a modern marriage last a lifetime.

Is Marriage Harder Nowadays?

Are our marriages unhappier nowadays, or are we less willing to tolerate that unhappiness?

The question itself is misleading. We know that marriage is not a stable institution, that matrimony isn't an eternal truth existing across time. Modern marriage is in fact quite different from our idealized notions of what marriage is supposed to be. We have constructed a vaunted ideal with no idea how to re-create it in real life. "I don't think that marriages worked any better in the past," Jared says. "People just were more accepting of what their roles were. Today women want more from themselves and from their husbands, which is not a bad thing. People aren't settling anymore. If things don't work out, it's a lot easier to say, 'Okay, let's move on.' "

In today's complicated, ever-changing society, marriage too is a lot more complicated. According to sociologist Pepper Schwartz, "Today's woman is not as naïve as a woman in the fifties, but that woman had fewer variables to contend with. She and her husband probably had the same view of marriage. Today, couples might move. They might work. There are a zillion more things to complicate it. So it's a more challenging world in which they're trying to manage a marriage."[1] Our own ways of thinking about marriage have added a great deal of pressure to the institution. David Popenoe of the Marriage Project points out:

> The nature of marriage has changed so much. It has become a kind of close friendship with a sexual relationship between a man and a woman. That's a change. Before, it was a multifaceted institution. A partnership that was legally bound, typically a religious partnership, and a partnership between two families. Just because the husband and wife didn't get along wasn't a reason to break up. Also, in times past, men, by and large, had mostly male friends and women had mostly female friends. Today, we're together in an entirely different way. It's stripped down, mainly to the two of them. They're best friends, often isolated, alone, and this is something pretty new.[2]

It's not that we don't take marriage seriously—or think we do—when we're heading in. But we often unintentionally don't do so enough once we're inside. To a large extent, that's not our fault. Many of us don't know how to deal with marriage. "I firmly believe that marriage should be for life," says Bethany, who divorced at age twenty-five. "I don't think people take it very seriously anymore, and that's a terrible thing. I *did* take it seriously. I tried very hard. We went into therapy together and tried to make it work, but we just didn't know how."

Chapter 4 touched upon some of the explanations for why young people marry: the search for identity, connection, meaning, permanence, and the all-encompassing quest for self-fulfillment. At the same time that we long for these things, we are shaped by and taught to strive for their opposites. We aspire to certain ideals but are hemmed in by both societal and personal norms, by ways of thinking and behaving that have become so prevalent in our culture we've absorbed them wholesale. Some of the reasons we jump into marriage turn out to be the very reasons we jump right back out.

We have higher expectations for marriage than ever before, but fewer means to attain them. And that *does* make marriage harder nowadays.

The Search for Identity Versus the Cult of Self-Renewal

Self-renewal has become a modern mantra. We live in an era of makeovers, mood-altering pharmaceuticals, cosmetic surgery, and mid-twenties, mid-thirties, and midlife-crises-driven changes of direction. We may long for a defined role, but we balk when we find ourselves within it. We eschew anything that labels us, categorizes us, or makes us feel limited in any way. So even as we search for our identity, we reserve the right to change at will. And we glorify it.

We can alter our circumstances at any moment. We can acquire a new skill, take a cooking class, climb Mount Kilimanjaro. We decide that we *really* are a "creative person"—we quit our jobs as business consultants and take up filmmaking. At age twenty-nine, we decide we're on the wrong track. We have a mini-mid-

midlife crisis (*The New York Times* has dubbed this trend the new "young-life crises")[3] and realize we're heading in the wrong direction. We take six months off, travel around Southeast Asia, reconsider everything, mull over our past choices, and make new decisions. We return and join an Internet startup, then leave to start our own startup.

Today the average worker changes career—not just jobs—several times over the course of a lifetime. A résumé listing six different positions used to reflect instability; today that same résumé describes someone who knows when to move on to the bigger, better, next thing. We transfer from city to city. We change apartments. We buy new, bigger homes the way previous generations bought new cars. Most college graduates are excited by the possibility of moving wherever they want to begin their new, postcollege lives. We may complain about feeling rootless and insecure, but we also relish our mobility. According to Clara, "As it turned out, my husband and I had very different ideas about marriage. He liked having firmly planted roots, and I liked *not* having roots. I liked to constantly try new things."

"I moved her from place to place with my job and I thought things would get better when she was away from her family and friends, but nothing changed," says Ben, a New Yorker married to a Floridian. "I wanted to move up North, but she wasn't too pleased with that. That's when I knew we weren't going to have much of a future. I decided I would move to Ohio on my own." Just as we can quit a job or change apartments, we can leave a marriage if it doesn't take us where we want to go. If it doesn't turn us into the person we want to be.

Once upon a time, identity in marriage was chosen for you, with simpler, less flexible roles. One twenty-eight-year-old man explains, "In the fifties there was only one choice. If you were a woman, you were a housewife. If you were a man, you married and supported your family. Today . . . Americans have a long cultural menu to choose from. If you're a woman, you can be a single woman, a career woman, a lesbian, a single mom by choice, a live-in lover, a married-for-now wife, a married-forever wife. And the same for work: I'm on my third career."[4]

Today people jump into marriage without knowing which role

they want to play. A woman decides to be "the perfect wife" only to find out she doesn't know what that means or is unable to deliver on the meaning. A man aspires to be a devoted husband only to discover that what he really wants to be is a globe-trotting banker or a workaholic entrepreneur or a backpacker in India. Many people see changes within themselves following their weddings that don't jibe with how they liked to view themselves: "I became really passive." "I didn't want to be who he thought I was." "I lost my sense of who I was." Or they find that once they marry, the role they thought they wanted to occupy makes them desperately unhappy. Bethany admits, "I turned into this screaming-banshee wife that I didn't even recognize. I was angry all the time, angry at him. I don't think I'd ever felt such rage in my entire life. . . . I didn't know how to be 'wifey.'"

Relying on a spouse to forge one's identity ultimately proves destructive at worst—futile at best. "Over the course of being married, I really lost touch with my identity," says Sam. "I basically became someone who was just there to take care of my wife's needs. I sort of stopped being myself—whoever that was—and just became what she wanted. And when things weren't working out, I thought that if I did what she wanted, I would get her attention. I basically sublimated myself to her to the point where I was just a well-mannered doormat. . . . I think I was responsible for the failure of the marriage in that I failed to maintain my own identity. I thought that was what she wanted, but in the end it was problematic. She was bored with me."

It's particularly hard to know whether marriage will accommodate who you are when you're not even sure who that is. "I didn't know exactly what I wanted from life," Joel explains. "Maybe I should have known at that age, but I was coming out of an intense relationship with my folks and was still trying to find myself. I just wanted to please other people. But if you're not doing anything for yourself, you start to feel extremely unfulfilled and you don't know why, and it's very, very confusing."

Many young marrieds thought they weren't able to grow emotionally, psychologically, or spiritually within the boundaries of marriage. They felt hampered by their spouse, by the institution itself, or by their own expectations. "To this day, I maintain that it was the state of marriage that freaked him," Melissa says of her ex-husband. "He just completely freaked out. He didn't take well to the constraints, to the responsibilities." In order to help support them, her husband had to take an unrewarding job. "Instead of having a sense of humor, or seeing it as a midpoint, he got depressed. He saw his capitulation over the job as just one, in what he thought would prove to be a series, of sacrifices or losses that he would have to make in order to be married."

While one partner may still be trying to figure out who he is, his wife probably assumes that he *is* the person she married—and may be none too pleased if he suddenly changes after the wedding. Noelle's husband started out as a computer programmer and decided to become a missionary in Africa. Charlotte's husband was taking college courses and working as a store manager; the day after their honeymoon he decided to drop everything and hit the road with his rock band. Yasmin says her ex "went from being this bleached-blond, dreadlocked, skateboarding, Take Back the Night protesting, depressed poet to this right-wing businessman in a suit that was hooked to a pager and a laptop and a cell phone and who couldn't give a shit about anybody else."

Marriage may change a person in many respects, but it doesn't *create* an identity. If you're too young or insecure or unsure of who you are, what you want, and what your needs are, being married to someone else won't help you figure it out. "Nobody should go into marriage before figuring out who they are and how to take care of themselves," Zoë reflects. "You need that sense of stability and self-empowerment before you start to give yourself away." People who try to find themselves in marriage only succeed in getting lost.

Our therapeutic, New Agey culture often makes the mistake of looking at every stage in life as a means toward self-development, as if life were no more than a personalized, custom-built obstacle course created solely for the individual's benefit. Yet looking to marriage exclusively as a path to personal growth is a selfish mistake. Using marriage to find oneself is all about the individual, reducing the relationship and one's spouse into the means to an end and letting the marriage dissolve when it no longer serves one well. If marriage means giving up your identity or becoming someone you dislike, then disposing of marriage lets you be true to yourself—to the person you really are deep down, to get rid of something that isn't "working" for you. America celebrates those who know what they want and are willing to do what it takes to get there, damn the consequences. Divorce becomes a way to turn over a new leaf, reinvent oneself, rethink one's priorities. It can even sound good.

The Search for Connection Versus the Independent Ideal

Our generation is fiercely independent. We pride ourselves on our self-reliance. In a 1996 poll, Gen Xers expressed a degree of self-sufficiency exceeding that of previous generations, with 69 percent agreeing with the statement "I have to take whatever I can get in this world because no one is going to give me anything." (Only 43 percent of respondents in their fifties and sixties felt the same.)[5] But in our narcissistic culture, in which the individual is exalted above all, autonomy is often a guise for selfishness and irresponsibility.

The traditional American icons are the rebel, the revolutionary, the inventor, the frontiersman. Today's buccaneering entrepreneur is all about flexibility and rule breaking. Internet pioneers built smaller, looser companies while scoffing at the monoliths of the old economy. They ignored dress codes, traditional workday hours, and standard hierarchies. They dubbed themselves civil libertarians: no government messing with their affairs, no old-style big business interfering with their business, no one getting in the way of them doing exactly what they want to do.

But there's a fine line between exercising one's options and excusing irresponsibility. When Max and his wife separated, she asked him to go to counseling with her but Max refused. "I thought it was just another ploy to get me back," he says. In retrospect he admits, "I could have gone to couples' counseling or seen her through her own counseling, but I was fed up. When we were married, I used to drive alone down the road in our town and I would just think about how great it would be to keep driving and never come back." He adds, "It sounds so dumb and typical, but I just wasn't ready to settle down. I had a wandering spirit. I wanted to be able to do so many things, and I wasn't ready to make sacrifices."

The prevailing American culture fosters a mind-set that encourages people to value selfishness above generosity, independence above community, self-satisfaction before compassion. Capitalism is all about freedom and individualism, not duty and community. My dues. My wallet. My time.

This primacy of the individual can also undermine our efforts toward connection and community, preventing us from building a form of social capital and establishing associations. It's not that we don't like to care for others or that we're not sympathetic. Nor is it that we're incapable of love and nurturing. But having grown up in the give-it-to-me-now eighties, we believe we can forge these bonds without ever making the kind of personal sacrifices or compromises that meaningful relationships require. Forming serious attachments is difficult when the bottom line is, how are *my* needs being served? "Is this worth it?" means "Is this worth it *for me*?" One woman conceded that she "was in no way ready to share a life or compromise or do anything fifty/fifty. I was still a kid doing everything my way, and everything that we had to do together I saw as taking away from my own personal decision. Like I would have been able to do it my way, if only I weren't married."

Sociologist Larry Bumpass attributes the high divorce rate in part to this "increasing cultural emphasis on individualism."[6] "Everything was about him," one woman who married at twenty-three complained. "His career, his job, his feelings. . . . I wanted to get out, find out who I was, go on my own journey. And that was not going to happen with him around. I just grew apart and so I moved on." A twenty-eight-year-old divorced man concluded with dismay, "I always thought that you make whatever sacrifices are necessary and you do what you've got to do to preserve the marriage, but my wife suddenly decided that she wanted to do something else. And so for her it had to end."

That we are unwilling to make certain compromises is by no means a bad thing, but modern couples often excessively maintain their respective independence within marriage. Amy, divorced after four years of marriage, explains, "We were just so different. I tried so hard to reconcile it, to be proud to say, 'This is my husband.' But I had all these desires and wanted to do all these things with my life. All he wanted was to have this house, come home, drink beer, and watch TV. That was just *so* not what I wanted from my life. . . . He wanted to build a log cabin in rural North Carolina and settle down about an hour from his parents and start having kids. That was not what I wanted to do. I wanted to travel and then get my medical degree, and after putting in my time in the States, I wanted to move overseas to India."

The marriage contract at its most fundamental level means that two people agree to share their lives based on the same set of values and expectations. When people's lives were fairly limited this was a relatively simple promise to uphold. In the old days, a man chose a career and stuck with a single company or profession over the course of a lifetime. A woman, if she worked, tended to stick to a single profession. The couple would buy a home, furnish it, and raise their children there. Moving house was a fairly big deal; changing cities was usually the result of a husband's company relocating him (his employer would at least remain constant). In an era when people's lives did not change all that much, expecting couples to hold on to a similar set of values and expectations over the course of a lifetime wasn't so far-fetched.

Fast-forward fifty years. We've got many, many more choices— and that makes lifelong commitment, no matter how secure, extremely difficult to uphold. A twenty-eight-year-old graphic designer in San Francisco explains, "Today's hype is that 'You can get it if you really want it'—a mate, career, and love still sell a lot of tickets. We're the Generation of Individual Choice. Which? Which? Which? But the bottom can fall out from some of those choices. And in the end, we're orphans. We're supposed to take care of ourselves. That's our only choice."[7] But just as marriage is not "all about the other person" or total self-sacrifice, neither is it just about ourselves. Starter marriages are often justified or explained by arguments about the individuals rather than the relationship: "I've changed"; "I wasn't ready for marriage"; "I'm not happy"; or "You'll be happier without me."

If a marriage is to succeed, some degree of autonomy is necessarily lost. The marriage sometimes takes precedence over individual preferences; the We sometimes has to triumph over the Me. Indeed, the Love Lab at the University of Washington focuses on "We-ness" as a defining factor for marital success. The marriage needs to exist in and of itself, as a common entity, and as an idea that may temporarily supersede or submerge the individual.

But we're scared of letting go or—heaven forbid—giving in. We've been taught by divorce and by other destabilizing aspects of our society that we can't depend on anyone but ourselves. And having become sexually active earlier than previous generations, today's twentysomethings typically go through several monogamous relationships and countless casual affairs before heading to the altar. We have been used, bruised, hurt, and bewildered by the opposite sex a lot more often than the maidenly women and bachelor men of yore. We mistrust others. In America's cult of the individual, we-ness doesn't necessarily feel natural or necessary. Autonomy is not always want we want; it's what we've gotten used to. "People used to get married right after college, but now they live on their own for a long time," says Bethany. "I think it's harder for us to accept that 'living together' thing. If you walk in the door at the end of the day, you don't always want to have to talk to somebody. You don't always want to do what you're supposed to do for the other person's sake."

For some people, fear of dependency is what discourages them from marriage; for starter marriages, it's what thwarts them within it. "I felt so dependent in my marriage," Amy says. "I didn't have to go out and date. I didn't have to try to make new friends. I could just be with him. I didn't have to confront anything or think about who I was. I didn't have to confront my own sexuality. I was totally sheltered. . . . I finally realized that I could do things on my own and that I didn't need someone else. I told him that I couldn't be married anymore. Marriage was a symptom of my own weakness, my own lack of self-esteem. I viewed marriage as a dependency."

Marriage *does* make people dependent—or rather, it eliminates total independence—and we don't want to be tied down. We're afraid that interdependence leads to "codependence" and then to plain old dependence. We're not only unaccustomed to that, we're told it's a bad thing. In modern society, bonds tend to be transient and superficial. We get together, hook up, hang out, and consult instead of sticking together, establishing relationships, and committing ourselves. When we attempt to go beyond the superficial links that we grew up with and that our society reinforces, we often fail from lack of practice. Or society tells us that we're looking in vain, that such bonds will only limit us. You may feel secure, but really you're just closed off to opportunity. You may feel safe, but really you're suffocating.

Starter marriage veterans claim they were too young, too selfish, too self-involved to be married. Time and again, exes remark that marriage made them feel "trapped" or "limited," they were "no longer free." "I had no sense that I would have to give up anything by getting married," one woman admitted. "The idea of him influencing me or being allowed to share in my decisions had never occurred to me. I had no sense of having to share a life. I thought I could have my cake and eat it too." Several people expressed discomfort with either their own increasing dependence or that of their spouse. Noelle notes with distaste, "After we got married my husband became attached to me, and so as a consequence, I became detached."

Once that detachment occurs—when the Me trumps the We—marriages inevitably slide downhill. "Things were going to hell, and she started talking about counseling," Sam says. "I was really excited. I said to her I'd been thinking about it for a long time and was glad that she had come around to the idea of marriage counseling. But then she said, 'No, *you* need counseling on your own. Not me.' That's what she had meant by going to counseling. She wasn't willing to work at it together."

To stay in a bad marriage is to limit one's own freedom, and to refuse someone else the desire to leave is to commit an equivalent sin: limiting the freedom of another individual. One woman says she divorced because "I just wanted to get out and not have to report to anyone. I just wanted to be free to do whatever I wanted, to travel, to meet people. That's the real reason I got divorced. To be free. . . . I didn't have enough respect for the whole marriage thing. I was completely indifferent to it." When asked why she sought a divorce, another woman replied, "I was tired. It took a lot of energy to keep trying to work things out and keep the game going that we were playing. And I wanted the freedom to just leave and pursue the things that I had wanted to pursue before I got married."

If marriage means limiting our choices, we can simply eliminate the marriage. "I wanted flexibility to do things," explains Laurel, who filed for divorce after three years. "I couldn't because I had this house payment to worry about and this jerk of a husband who wasn't even paying his fifty percent. I wanted to explore, but he was like a ball and chain." Some people simply decide that something else will make them happier and they should be allowed to go for it. "Now I'm free to play golf every Saturday and Sunday, and I couldn't do that with her around because she gave me grief," says the newly divorced Ben. "I could not do everything that I wanted to do when I was married. I like not having to answer to anybody." He adds, "I guess that's a little selfish on my part."

The Search for Meaning Versus the Limits of Conviction

In the Information Age, attention spans are short. Often we don't take the time to figure out exactly what we know or think or believe. And we reserve the right to change our mind, alter our perceptions, and reconsider our convictions on an ongoing basis.

Our maverick generation eschews the idea of a prescribed set of beliefs inherent to most traditional "belief systems." Unwavering faith is suspect, and with our distrust of institutions, we don't readily identify with established religions, political parties, or intellectual movements. Instead of submitting to dogma, we lean toward a kind of cut-and-paste spirituality, picking and choosing elements from various religions in order to establish our own "indie spirituality." This isn't necessarily a bad thing, but it's also rather convenient when you want to overlook certain doctrinal standards, such as those imposed by the legal, social, and, for many, spiritual institution of marriage.

Yet our iconoclastic cynicism is often a mask for an underlying fear of being let down, a fear that causes many couples to avoid marriage in the first place. Instead, they gravitate toward trial marriages, which are supposed to protect you from making a commitment that you can't or won't want to keep. The idea is that cohabitation will lessen the chances of divorce because instead of divorcing, you can simply part ways if the relationship falls apart.

And this is probably true. But at the same time, by creating a short-term, casual mind-set and individualistic approach to relationships, trial marriages may end up encouraging divorce. Trial marriage breeds a mentality of letting go, moving out, moving on, and starting anew—making it psychologically easier to end long-term relationships. It becomes less difficult and more justifiable with each turn. If you've been able to break up the serious commitment of cohabitation, isn't it just one small step to breaking up a brief, unrewarding marriage? Getting used to having an out can become a self-fulfilling prophecy for a real marriage down the road.

Many couples base their expectations of marriage on their co-habitation experiences. Often couples who lived together before marrying remark that they thought there would be "really no difference between the two." And though one may know that a very real difference exists, it's hard to make the mental adjustment fit in line with the new reality. As William Doherty, director of the Marriage and Family Therapy Program at the University of Minnesota in Minneapolis, notes, "I wonder what [cohabitation] teaches people about commitment and about working through problems. Fifteen years ago, I might have said, 'It's a good idea.' Five years ago, I would have said, 'Who cares?' But now, I'm hoping my own adult children do not cohabitate."[8]

Serial monogamy and cohabitation lead to a persistent sense of failure among their participants, who watch again and again as *yet another* relationship doesn't work out. We learn not to sacrifice, not to risk, not to get hurt. We erect barriers and defense mechanisms because we know that whatever we give will eventually be taken away. We hedge our bets, we hold back, and we refuse to commit. When we do commit, we do so on our own narrow, inconstant terms. Trial marriages usually end because the relationship fails to make one party happy. There's no cause, ideal, or commitment—no "for the sake of our marriage" complication—outside the well-being of the two individuals involved, whereas in a marriage, the marriage itself acts as a third, overriding entity.

But sometimes it feels like marriage as an ideal has lost any meaning. Or its naïve, immature participants have little sense of what that meaning is—or could be. Starter marriage veteran Kari Jenson Gold writes,

[I]t may well be that marriage "till death us do part" is simply a doomed enterprise. In a world so ruled by the jargon of therapy there is little room for a permanent relationship. In this ever-optimistic world there are no external absolutes, no original sin, only the relentless pursuit of "health" and "fulfillment." If what we all aspire to is health rather than virtue, gratification rather than strength of character, how can we hope to find a foundation for a lasting commitment? If I have "grown" and my mate hasn't kept up, is even impeding my own "growth," what possible reason could I have for remaining faithful? The "healthy" choice is clear: find someone better suited to my current needs. The notion that a man and woman should be devoted to the other "through sickness and health," should place their good as a couple over the good of each individual, is then just silly.[9]

"What has happened to commitment as an ideal?" Juliet wonders, after divorcing at twenty-eight. "Getting married should be harder, just as becoming a parent should be harder. People need to really think about what kind of sacrifices and work these commitments entail."

Many couples expressed disappointment in the lack of meaning their marriage bond seemed to inspire, both in themselves and their spouse. They didn't attach enough weight to the marital bond or didn't understand the importance of marriage. Elizabeth says she "was too young to really understand the importance of marriage as both a civic and religious institution." She eventually sought an annulment because, she explains, "in the Catholic sacrament I don't believe I was ever married. I had not made a commitment to this person in my mind even as I stood in front of God and the Church and said so. Legally, yes, I was married, but I think that emotionally and spiritually I never was." "I wanted to look at things from a deeper perspective than my husband did," Zoë complains. "I have to look at the darkness to be able to see the light. For him, the darkness was much too scary. He wanted to live on a more superficial level, and he thought of marriage in those kinds of terms."

The Search for Permanence Versus
the Insistence on Instant Gratification

We live in a one-click culture. Everything happens faster, and if it doesn't, we're impatient. A recent report by Zona Research, "The Need for Speed," describes "the eight second rule," which claims people will only wait eight seconds to get onto a web page. If the site doesn't load, they'll leave. And if we don't get instant gratification in our marriages, we're gone. "She asked me if I was willing to try to work things out," one man admitted after two years of marriage, "and I said no. I felt like I had been miserable with her for so long already—unappreciated and unwanted. The next day, she told me she was going to file for divorce."

Ritalin, anyone? Our collective attention span has shrunk to puny proportions. We like headlines, not in-depth analysis. We read plot summaries and book reviews instead of lengthy novels and historical tomes. TV sound bites are down to an average of nine seconds because producers fear we'll switch channels if forced to listen for longer. We can handle only one major news story at any given moment (which we stretch and strain and expand into Elián González–sized proportions), but once the initial wave of hysteria passes, we move on with reckless indifference to ongoing circumstance and long-term impact.

We are an extremely impatient generation living in an increasingly impatient society, a circumstance that frequently prompts us into marriage in the first place. Sarah Bernard explains in *New York* magazine, "A kind of ubiquitous been-there-done-that impatience has made marriage the new frontier of the moment."[10] Unfortunately, it often makes divorce into the next. "We went to a marriage counselor," Olivia says, "but it was kind of too late. I was already finished with the marriage in my mind and thought there was no helping it. Looking back now, I can see that we could have worked through a lot of the problems. But I was just too young and too unwilling to do what had to be done to make it work." In our throwaway culture, people change the channel, click the mouse, or toss items indiscriminately into the wastebasket when they fail to gratify or meet expectations. Socks that were once darned repeatedly before disposal are now chucked at the first sign of fraying, just as casually as we throw away videos that no longer entertain and appliances that lack the latest upgraded feature.

And so we dismiss freshly minted marriages with relative ease. As Neil LaBute, director of such marriage-phobic movies as *Your Friends and Neighbors,* observed in a recent interview, "During my mother's era, you got one shot at marriage. . . . You made your bed and that was it. Now we see a whole different mindset. You see Charlie Sheen in *Us* magazine, after a disastrous, or semi-disastrous run of relationships and marriages, saying about his recent failed marriage: 'You buy a car, it breaks down, what are you going to do? Get rid of it.' That's a vast change in sensibility in a relatively short time span of forty years ago."[11] In the anthology *Generations: A Century of Women Speak About Their Lives,* a ninety-two-year-old woman says, "Today a lot of marriages break up because people are not willing to recognize certain differences in their characters and make compromises. I don't think there's enough willingness to put up with the pain and differences in a marriage. You can't have a relationship with a person for a lifetime and be a complete human being yourself without painful things happening. They have to be faced and handled. Today's human beings, I think they are too frivolous about this. Marriages fall apart too easily. It is very sad. It's preposterous."[12]

Long-married couples frequently testify that at one or several points during their marriage, divorce was seriously considered and ultimately rejected. And these are often *not* bad marriages. After all, though it may sound simplistic, marriage is just a part of life, with all its attendant ups and downs, its giddy highs and long, and slow, dull mediums. Starter marriages, on the other hand, tend to take off in a hurry and fizzle out fast—a terrible premise for long-lasting marriage. The PAIR (Processes of Adaptation in Intimate Relationships) Project, a thirteen-year study of marriage based at the University of Texas, found that marriages that start out particularly romantic and blissful are most doomed to divorce in the long run. The less of a love-fest the relationship is to begin with, the more likely the love that is there will endure, decreasing the negative impact of the process psychologists refer to as "disillusionment."

Almost all of us become in some way disillusioned with our

spouse over time. It's a typical process in most marriages, as the petty annoyances, failings, and differences that may have been effectively submerged during the courtship process emerge over time. Idealism gives way to realism. And reality can lead to disappointment. In a starter marriage, that disappointment hits faster and harder. As *Cosmopolitan* magazine explains, "Young couples might have a more idealized notion of relationships. So when they find themselves in a reality that falls short of perfection, they want out."[13] One man admitted that rather than start couples' therapy, after less than two years of marriage he gave up. "At that point, it would have been an awful lot of work to patch things back together," he explained. "Why put in all the effort for something that's not so great anyway?" Zoë wanted to salvage her marriage but says "[my husband] thought it would be easier in the long run if we just got divorced. He just wanted to end the suffering. I felt like it was a cop-out. Like it was easier for him to throw in the towel rather than work on the marriage. We had gotten married for a reason, and I was really angry that he didn't even want to try.... His biggest crime was his lack of commitment. That really sums it up."

While earlier generations aspired toward a range of benefits, opportunities, and rewards, today's generation *demands* them. Many of today's teens and twentysomethings feel entitled to a rather lofty height of happiness. In some ways this is a positive development. Better to have high expectations of oneself and one's rights than to suffer from defeatism. But this entitlement mentality also does a great deal of harm. While it's good to have high aspirations, it's wrong to expect to have them served up without dedication and hard work, never mind sacrifice. The research firm Youth Intelligence notes that Gen Xers "don't feel they lose their identity by getting married, and they're not looking at marriage as an end to their fun."[14]

But marriage isn't fun all of the time. Our generation seems to have a hard time accepting the old "You can't always get what you want." You can almost hear us collectively mutter under our breath, "Well, *I* can." Zoë explains that when she thought about marriage, "I had this vision of all the good stuff without any of the bad stuff." Olivia, whose parents have been married for thirty-six years, says, "I think the divorce rate is so high because people don't really try hard enough anymore. I don't think people realize that the bad times in a marriage can last months. You could have four really horrible months; it's almost inevitable. People either need to put up with those problems or deal with them. But I don't think they do either anymore."

Marriage by its very nature requires long-term thinking and coping skills that many of us have either lost or not yet developed. You need to know intuitively how to wait things out, realize when to attack an issue head-on and when to hang back or let things go, to develop the patient understanding that you'll have plenty of time to deal with it at some more appropriate point in the future. But many young people no longer seem to believe in process. "I was done with it," Max explained bluntly. "I just saw that my marriage was going to be mostly miserable. I didn't want constant issues that we were trying to work out or to always have some kind of confrontation. I didn't want to deal with that. I figured, you only live once and I was still young."

In many ways, the life span of a starter marriage mirrors the trajectory companies during the dot.com boom, when every business's goal was to develop a model, then to have another company buy it up and deal with actually making the business work. Everything focused on inception, rather than process or execution. And like starter marriages, many such startups flopped in the absence of a solid foundation. One woman explains, "My parents at least knew what marriage was, and they had a clear sense of what they were committing to. They knew that that commitment necessitated hard work. I had no concept of commitment—that this was for life. In an offhand way, I didn't really see it as a lifetime choice. Nor did I see it as something that required effort over the long haul. I wasn't really seeing beyond the date of the wedding."

Today's twentysomethings seem unable to visualize a lifelong scenario for themselves. Life changes so quickly; it's hard to imagine anything enduring—and even harder to attain it. None of the starter marriage veterans believed that they would ever divorce, but a few admitted that they knew deep down that marriage didn't *have* to be forever. "Growing up, divorce was all around me," says Max, who asked his wife for a divorce after a year and a half. "I definitely saw it, even though my parents were happily married. I didn't think my marriage wouldn't work out, but I knew that when things got rocky, I could get out. I guess I went into marriage knowing that divorce was an option." For those who claimed to stick to their convictions, it was often their spouse who gave in. "I think the permanence of marriage scared me," Jodie says, and concludes that her husband felt the same way. "The idea of fighting for and trying to fix a marriage was too scary for him. He was very immature. . . . He always had these wild dreams but no idea of how to attain them. He thought he would become this CEO, but he didn't actually work hard enough. He just thought that if he thought these things, they would happen. He just expected that people would recognize his brilliance and his desire for it."

Gone are the days when reward is seen as the product of hard work. We believe that you can become instantly rich by making the right pick on the stock ticker. We can buy, access, or acquire things with the zip of a credit card or the click of a shopping-cart symbol. Perseverance and persistence are looked down upon alternately as intractability, stubbornness, or plain old-school thought. And those who persevere are seen as plodding, nagging, unadventurous, stuck. "People used to struggle more to stick with their marriage," says Joel. "My parents' first years as married immigrants must have been incredibly hard, very stressful. I wonder if I could have done the same thing. I don't think kids growing up now understand all the work that it takes."

Can Marriage "Fulfill"?

Our failure to succeed in marriage is often fated by our expectations. As the 1999 report "The State of Our Unions" puts it: "Not so long ago, the marital relationship consisted of three elements: an economic bond of mutual dependency; a social bond supported by the extended family and larger community; and a spiritual bond upheld by religious doctrine, observance, and faith. Today many marriages have none of these elements."[15] Instead, we have new elements—and they're much more demanding. The 2000 report explains: "If anything, they've raised this standard [of marriage] to a higher level. Young men and women today want to marry a best friend and 'soul mate' who will hear and understand their most intimate feelings, needs and desires."[16] The 2001 report includes a survey of twentysomethings that found 94 percent of twenty-somethings agreeing "when you marry you want your spouse to be your soul mate, first and foremost."[17]

The expectation of this kind of emotional intimacy—virtually emotional assimilation—in marriage is almost entirely new. Naturally, earlier generations of women wanted to be close to their husbands, but the degree of closeness expected or even desired was much smaller. A woman wanted to be in love with her husband, to spend time with him, for her husband to understand and respect her, and in return she hoped to provide her husband with love, sympathy, and comfort. At most, couples longed for what they might call a kindred spirit or a similarity in spiritual outlook. What they didn't talk about was emotional intimacy, deep connections, personal growth, or mutual self-actualization. Yet today we expect precisely those things from a marriage—and think we can get them. George felt that his marriage would never provide what he needed. "We didn't have much of a shared emotional life. We were much more lonely together than we were apart. It just wasn't authentic. We didn't feel like each other's soul mates. . . . It just felt like this thin gruel of our shared emotional life was not a substantive meal. I was sort of starving to death."

We ask modern marriage to deliver on a whole range of psychological and spiritual needs. According to Whittier College psychology professor Chuck Hill, "The high divorce rates, rather than implying that marriage is doomed, instead partly reflect the higher standards we have for marriage. . . . Now people want their psychological needs to be met in marriage."[18] Instead of looking toward a stable job, a home, a supportive community, intergenerational family, religious creed, or other traditional institutions to serve our needs, we turn to marriage.

And we add yet more to the formula: we want marriage to bring us unalloyed happiness, total fulfillment, a sense of purpose—in short, complete self-actualization. We want marriage to make us feel intellectually stimulated, emotionally fulfilled, socially enhanced, financially free, and psychologically complete.

"People today seem to think that marriage is all about being happy," Robert notes with dismay. "But it has nothing to do with that. A good relationship is something that scares the hell out of you and is hard and has real downs. It's not going to make you a happy person suddenly. And it bothers me that marriage is portrayed in pop culture as this state that, once attained, makes you forever blissful."

According to the National Marriage Project, "Increasingly, happiness in marriage is measured by each partner's sense of psychological well-being rather than the more traditional measures of getting ahead economically, boosting children up to a higher rung on the educational ladder than the parents, or following religious teachings on marriage. People tend to be puzzled or put off by the idea that marriage has purposes or benefits that extend beyond fulfilling individual adult needs for intimacy and satisfaction."[19]

When marriage becomes a vehicle for personal happiness, we measure it accordingly. And with the bar raised so high, it's inevitable that marriage will fall short. As Pamela Smock, a sociologist at the University of Michigan's Population Studies Center, puts it, "If something doesn't contribute to our individual growth, then we leave it. Our threshold has somehow changed."[20] Elizabeth recalls the way she felt while married: "I was very moody and sad and I didn't understand why. I'm very analytical, so I kept thinking to myself, what is the logical solution? Here's a man who is kind to me, a very good provider, devoted, financially very secure, attractive, and all those things that should have been a perfect mate. And yet I wasn't excited. I assumed something was wrong with me. . . . The day of the wedding I felt very sad. I got home from my honeymoon and saw my bouquet hanging and I just threw it out. One night I was hungry, so I ate the anniversary cake. I kept doing these mean things, and I'm not a mean person. Marriage should make you a better person, not what I was becoming. And I think these things were all signs that I was confused, conflicted, and very, very sad."

Many young marrieds discover that marriage just doesn't live up to or deliver on their ideals. Noelle explains why her marriage fell short: "When you're young and you're dating somebody, you have that warm happy feeling all the time, and I thought that's what marriage would be like—*all* the time. But eventually that warm and fuzzy feeling went away. I wasn't happy. I didn't feel fulfilled."

Yet marriage is about incorporating, and sometimes subsuming, one's own mercurial wants and needs with those of another person. It's not about freedom, personal pleasure, or independence. It's about compromise, empathy, and interdependence. At root, it's about commitment to another person, not to oneself, or at least commitment to oneself *through* one's commitment to another. As divorced and remarried filmmaker Lisa Krueger explains, "There used to be givens—values, like family—that created a sense of grounding. Nowadays, we're raised on the idea of limitless possibility—you know, 'Do what you need to do, and if you're not being fulfilled, then move on.' "[21]

Elizabeth summarizes her decision to divorce as follows: "I just think we decided that getting divorced was the best thing for both of us. We were not happy. It was not the right match. And if you're not interested in being married to each other, it doesn't behoove either of you to hold on and struggle for it."

No Reason to Stay and the Reason to Go

Whether having children is avoided or delayed, starter marriages break up before children are involved. And marriages are much easier to end when they are not bound together by that common responsibility.

For previous generations, family building was the immediate, primary function of marriage. Even when wives weren't pregnant at the altar, marriage usually led to children within the first few years. And children helped solidify the marriage. As Charlotte Mayerson notes of traditional marriages in *Goin' to the Chapel,* "Children provide both a distraction from marital problems and also the cement of the family they value. Cooking dinner for them, attending their athletic events, making decisions about their health or their schooling—these constitute family life and may cover up or at least push aside acknowledgment that there's not much going on between husband and wife. In these marriages, whether they eventually break up or survive, it is as parents of their children that the couple functions best together."[22]

In 1970 the average age of a first-time mother was twenty-two. By 1993, she was twenty-four,[23] and according to the U.S. Census Bureau, the average age of women giving birth continues to rise. One of the reasons behind the delay is that women are confused about how to juggle marriage, career, and motherhood. There's still no clear pattern (nor does it appear one will likely emerge any time soon). In the meantime, many couples simply hold off: "I knew I wasn't ready to be a mother." "We'll have them five years down the road." "We weren't ready for children yet." "We didn't even *think* about starting a family."

Another reason we postpone childbirth is because we can. With medical advances springing up every day, fertility has been expanded and extended—we can avoid pregnancy when we're young, then we can have more babies, later—and they have better chances of survival than ever before. This has brought miracles to infertile and older couples desperate to have children. But for healthy younger couples it's also one more reason to procrastinate. Women don't have to worry about sacrificing their careers, their bodies, their independence, and their "young married just-you-and-me" lives until much later. Men don't have to feel as guilty about postponing childbearing (almost) as late as they want.

While childbearing is delayed, it's still seen as an eventuality. Most women want and expect to have children (in fact, many women who marry on the later side seem to think of marriage as a kind of preemptive strike against single motherhood). Gen Xers hold that expectation at the top of their life priorities. In a 1978 Roper survey, 21 percent of respondents ages eighteen to twenty-nine declared that they never wanted to have children; by 1995, the figure had dropped to 8 percent. "I had very definite ideas about when we had to have children," says Juliet, who married at twenty-six. "We were going to wait at least three years. I wanted him to be a dad by his thirtieth birthday, and I wanted to be twenty-nine. I even said that to him."

At some point couples start to wonder whether they share similar thoughts about raising children. They begin to question how they'll manage the division of labor necessitated by a two-career household or contemplate the possibility of living on one income. (Surviving on a single income also used to be a lot more financially feasible for young families, but that's another story.) When childbearing was a more immediate priority in marriage, these issues were usually confronted before the wedding day. Today many people don't think of them until much later—sometimes not until the moment they're ready to have children. A shocking number of people interviewed had never even discussed children before getting married. They often didn't bother to ask their potential husbands the crucial questions about fatherhood—or even ask *themselves* those questions. Too late in the game, a wife will begin to contemplate childbearing and the contours of her prospective family and realize that her spouse (even if he is her ideal husband) may not be the ideal father. "I knew I wanted children," Zoë says. "But I remember mentioning it to my husband, and his response was, 'If *you* want to have a kid, that's okay.' That scared me because I wanted someone who was as into it as I was. But I figured it was still years off yet."

Many people realized their marriages weren't stable enough to support a family. One woman, now remarried with a one-year-old baby, says of her first marriage, "The more I saw of our marriage, the more I wanted to put childbearing off. I wanted having children to be fun, and I knew that [my first husband] just couldn't be fun about it." Charlotte says that as she became increasingly estranged from her husband, "we stopped having sex and I went off the Pill. He was always bugging me to sleep with him, and finally we did once, even though I wasn't on the Pill, and I thought immediately after, 'If we get pregnant, I'll be stuck with him.' It felt like I was selling myself, like I had become cheap. By the end, he made my skin crawl. I remember thinking, 'I do *not* want to have kids with this person!' "

When talk turns to baby-to-be, many spouses start to panic. One woman began having an affair a month before she and her husband were supposed to begin trying. Others found themselves sneaking birth control, avoiding the subject, putting it off. Not having children is not only a reason why couples fail to stay together, it becomes the very reason many starter marriages fall apart. Max says of his wife, "Her moods would just snap. And there was this whole history of alcoholism and emotional abuse in her family. When she started showing those traits, I started thinking, 'I don't know if I want to have kids with this person.' And then I started to think, 'Where am I going with this?' " Ben explains his decision to divorce in the following terms: "After three years of things not changing in our relationship, I was scared of moving to Ohio together and risking children together. Then we'd really be in trouble. That's when I finally decided that I wanted a divorce."

It's easier to let a marriage fall apart early without the glue that held together marriages in an earlier era. By jumping into marriage at the same age as previous generations but delaying childbirth until much later, young couples find it much easier to justify divorce. It certainly doesn't mean "breaking up a family"—which to children of divorce is total anathema. As the daughter of divorced parents, George's wife was haunted by that possibility. Says George, "Divorce was very painful for her because she was determined that the same thing wasn't going to happen to her. That she was going to make it right. So ending things was very tough for her in that respect."

"One of the reasons I eventually decided to get divorced is because I thought it would be better to do it now, before we had children," Elizabeth recalls. "I really thought long and hard about that. I felt like if marriage wasn't the right thing now, then I had no right to continue with it because in the future, I might be affecting others."

Chapter 8

Divorced Under Thirty

JULIET WAS TWENTY-EIGHT WHEN HER HUSBAND MADE THE decision to end their marriage. "He woke up New Year's Day. We hadn't gone out for New Year's Eve because I had the flu. That morning he walked into the bedroom with a weird look on his face. He said, 'I don't think I love you anymore. I hate my job. And everything else sucks too.' I was shocked. I said, 'You're kidding.' "

The next month passed by in a haze. "I don't remember when the word 'divorce' first came up," she says. "My birthday was in a couple of weeks, so between New Year's and then, he stayed in the apartment but moved into the second bedroom. We got back together briefly and went on a trip for my birthday, but I was living in a fantasy world. I thought everything would be fine, that we didn't need therapy. We came back and tried to work it out, but we really didn't. We were both out of it. By the end of the month, he was gone. He went to his grandparents', and that was it.

"I guess I went through a lot of hysterics, though I didn't throw things or call him screaming. I dragged him to therapy once we started talking about divorce. I thought, 'Okay, we're going to see what the hell's going on here.' But it was as if my husband had literally died inside. He looked dead. I remember as we went into the therapist's office, he said to me something about paying a Visa bill. And I thought to myself, 'What the hell are you talking about? He's bringing up the Visa bill, and our marriage is ending!' "

The absence of an explanation was particularly devastating. Juliet is still baffled by what went wrong, because her husband chose not to discuss it with her. "There was no affair, he wasn't gay, there were no drugs; those were all ruled out," she says. "To this day, I still don't really know what happened. We went to the therapist, but when we got there, I was sobbing away desperately and my husband just said nothing. It was like he was completely comatose. He eventually left the office and I stayed and talked. My therapist thought I was suicidal and sent me to a doctor to put me on Prozac."

Juliet had a hard time recognizing that her marriage was over. "I completely, totally resisted the idea of divorce. I couldn't believe it was happening to me. I kept thinking to myself, '*Nobody* is going to know.' I felt like I had to be so perfect. So I lied about it. I didn't tell anybody. I kept up a façade at work for six months—until I moved from Los Angeles to San Francisco. I put on my wedding ring every morning before I went to work. It took a good month before I even told my two best friends.

"Afterward, I felt like I had a scarlet letter on my chest. I kept thinking, 'Oh my God, I'm divorced.' I had always thought that I would never date someone who was divorced; now I thought to myself, 'Why would anyone ever date me?' It's a terrible feeling. I felt scarred.

"I think divorce is both too easy and too accepted," Juliet says. "I don't think that the government should be playing a role in our personal lives, but I do think that divorce should somehow be harder to come by. On the one hand, I want divorce to be more acceptable because I don't want people to look down on me, but on the other hand, I don't want people to think, 'Oh, no big deal' about my divorce. People *do* need to make more judgments. . . . I remember a friend's boyfriend found out I was divorced and it turned out that he was divorced too. So he said to me, 'Well, you got your first one out of the way.' And I couldn't believe my ears. It was like nothing to him. To me, it was everything. I would have done everything I could to make it work. I had the belief that marriage was that important."

❧

Americans are afraid of divorce. We fear it because we've assigned a host of social ills to its fallout. We fear it because it runs against our deeply ingrained idealism. If marriage means everlasting love between two fabulous, accomplished individuals; a two-car, four-bedroom home; obedient children and happy, multigenerational family gatherings, then divorce means all that is lost forever.

Most of all, we fear divorce because we fear that it will happen to us. Every time someone gets divorced, each of us is forced to acknowledge its proximity and frequency; each of us is forced to realize, if only fleetingly, "Oh God, it could happen to me."

Divorce is one of the most painful experiences a human being can undergo. "I had no idea how awful a divorce was until I went through it myself," says Yasmin, a psychotherapist who divorced after two years of marriage. "It was the worst thing I ever experienced, the worst two years of my life. I was in shock." According to psychologists, divorce results in a process of mourning similar to what we experience with the death of a loved one. In its own way, divorce *is* a kind of death—the death of a marriage, the death of love, the death of one's place in the world. "Divorce felt very odd to me," Helena, a travel editor living in Washington, remembers. "I felt like I didn't have an identity anymore. I'm not somebody's wife. I felt lost."

Young divorcés I interviewed tell stories of insomnia, migraines, weight loss, and panic attacks. The words they used to describe themselves during the aftermath were "lost," "lonely," "alone," "devastated," "shocked," "bereaved," and "hopeless." Most of them began therapy afterward and said it took a year or two for them to get over the pain; some said it took up to three years, and most felt they still hadn't fully recovered. "You don't ever really get over something like this," several people explained. A few became clinically depressed and even felt suicidal. One man admitted, "Before the divorce, I had never felt that sense of being overwhelmed by guilt and anxiety and depression. Anxiety to the point where your mind shuts down and you can't do anything. That happened frequently during the first few months."

Perhaps the best reason to discourage a "divorce culture" is that, quite simply, divorce hurts. And it's a form of pain many see as entirely avoidable. "It was searing for both of us," George recalls. "I was absolutely devastated. It was agonizing—by far the most painful thing I have ever gone through."

The pain of divorce exists on three, interwoven levels. There's the pain to the self—the fact that one is now alone, unloved, vulnerable, depressed. The pain of the other—losing someone who, even if unwanted now was once the pivotal center of one's life. "When you marry someone and take seriously their well-being, their hopes, their past, their ideas about the present, and your mutual future, you permanently draw an emotional line between yourself and another human being," Melissa says. "And when you lose that, it's absolutely devastating—more devastating than I can describe." And there's a third pain, the social pain—one has sinned, failed, screwed up. "I felt dirty and tainted after the divorce," James remarks. "Even today I don't like to hear myself say that I'm divorced."

If marriage is for winners, divorce is surely for losers. For people who are meant to be in the prime of their lives—when everything's supposed to come together—divorce shows a life that is falling apart. As Michael describes it, "Divorce seemed like a black hole to me. I did not want to be a divorcé. I had no idea what to do with my life or what would happen to me if I got divorced. It just wasn't an option. It seemed like I had been on a railroad track all my life, proceeding, proceeding, and then all of the sudden I derailed."

Postdivorce Disaster Tales

Recent divorcés are assaulted by two disaster scenarios, both commonly cited in women's magazines, psychological journals, and political diatribes. Yet when viewing them side by side, one can't help but question their wisdom. After all, in one case you never marry again; in the other you can't stop marrying. Surely they can't both be true.

The first one runs like this. You screwed up. You abandoned a lifelong commitment, so clearly you have no understanding of commitment. With your disrespect for the sanctity of marriage, you'll end up one of those aimless, rootless individuals, setting a bad example to the next generation by cohabitating or engaging in a series of short-term romances, bent on destroying a peaceable, family-value-filled society. Your type is afraid of commitment. You've been burned once and you won't let it happen again. You'll never have the optimism and faith in the institution of marriage that led you down the aisle in the first place. You'll never be able to "believe in marriage" again. Expect to be alone or feel alone for the rest of your life. "I want to remarry," says Juliet, thirty-two, admitting she now has problems with trust and abandonment. "The question is, will I ever meet someone? I used up my one chance, that's how I feel. It makes me cry. I was given one opportunity and I screwed it up. I'm constantly asking myself, Will it ever happen again? It's scary. I try to remind myself that I can't live my life like that. But I do think, 'I did it once and that's it. I'll never have that chance again.'"

In other words, you had your chance and you lost it. You'll never get another shot at marriage.

In the second scenario, you're told that recent divorcés are in a state of heightened vulnerability. You've grown dependent on the security and comfort that the state of marriage provides. *Psychology Today* describes postdivorce behavior in the following way: "The divorced individuals wanted sustained, meaningful relationships and were not satisfied with a series of superficial encounters. The formation of lasting intimate relations, involving deep concern and a willingness to make sacrifices for the partner, as well as a strong attachment and desire to be near the person, was a strong factor in happiness, self-esteem, and feelings of competence in sexual relations for both divorced men and women."[1] According to this theory, you will crave the close companionship of marriage and do everything you can to secure it again. William F. Doherty, director of the Marriage and Family Therapy Program at the University of Minnesota, explains, "Partners bring to remarriage the stupidity of the first engagement and the baggage of the first marriage."[2] You'll rush foolishly into a second marriage, bearing a suitcase of emotional needs, if only to assuage the emptiness left in the wake of the first. You risk becoming a serial marrier, ever ready to waltz down the aisle, blindly repeating your mistakes, possibly over and over again.

In other words, you are the ultimate disaster date. A walking wound ready to latch on to the nearest Band-Aid. Potential loves ought be warned not to touch a recent divorcé with a ten-foot pole lest they end up tied down in a miserable rebound marriage with a dependent loser for the rest of their lives.

In both scenarios, divorcés are doomed. Fortunately, neither case need be true. Veterans of starter marriages are neither condemned to a life of solitude and superficial sexcapades nor fated to an ongoing series of minimarriages. In fact, many happily remarry. However, both disaster scenarios contain elements of truth. The challenge is to recognize those truths in oneself and one's situation and deal with them constructively so as not to make the same mistakes again.

"I Never Dreamed I Would Be Divorced"

"I remember thinking that if someone told me five years ago where my life would be at age twenty-four, I would never have believed it," Clara says. "I never expected anything like that to happen to me because I had always been so in control of my life."

Divorce is a strange situation to find oneself in at age twenty-four. Or twenty-eight. It feels utterly inappropriate, like having arthritis or glaucoma or being widowed while still trying to decide whether to go to grad school. As Lucy says, "I felt like some kind of joke to be divorced before any of my friends had even gotten married." This isn't supposed to happen now. I'm not ready. I'm too young. I still have single friends who party all night downtown; how can we be the same age? "I thought of divorced guys as these desperate, forty-year-old men, kind of loser types," Max admits. "It made me feel really old. I was like, 'Oh my God, I'm twenty-eight and divorced.' I was divorced before most of my friends were married. When I thought about it, I felt like a loser. It made me feel tainted."

The first impulse after divorce is often to retreat, usually to go back to one's childhood home. A University of Michigan study found that 50 percent of people under twenty-five move back home after their marriages break up; the shorter the marriage, the more likely they are to return.[3] Though many find it difficult to tell their parents, particularly if the marriage itself had generated a rift, for most, family proves an enormous refuge. Sam sank into a deep depression when he found out his wife wanted a divorce. "I called my parents and they were very supportive, but I fell apart completely the moment I got off the phone," he says. "So I called them back and begged, 'Can you just tell me that I'm a good person? That I'm actually worth something?' And they just said, 'Come home.' I was a screaming, blubbering idiot by that time. I felt so alone. I went home immediately."

Spreading the news about one's marriage is one thing; spreading the news about one's divorce is quite another. Friends can have a hard time dealing with divorce among their peers, and married friends often react most sharply. The happily married, devoted in their mutual commitment, can have a difficult time understanding how other people could make such a decision and then abandon it so quickly. One of Juliet's married friends had difficulty accepting her divorce. "She was pretty shocked and perplexed. She kept asking me, 'But how could this just happen?'" Kate, divorced at age twenty-eight, was afraid to tell married friends. "First of all, I was embarrassed. Like I had let them down. Or just that I had failed where they so obviously were succeeding. What's worse is that I felt like the entire act of my divorce was an affront to them. I worried that they would take it personally somehow, as if I were saying to them, 'Bad idea! Wrong choice! Get out while you still can.' And yet I myself didn't feel that way at all. I even thought they might not want to be friends with me anymore, like I was some kind of bad-luck talisman that you wouldn't want to keep around. It sounds ridiculous, but I felt like this threatening agent that could spread divorce against my will."

For the unhappily married, news of a divorce pushes uncomfortable buttons. "Some of my friends had a hard time with it," Laurel recalls. "One unhappily married friend in particular seemed really upset because she felt like she couldn't do it herself. She was actually quite offended and upset, and totally objected to my decision." Another woman explains, "I was the first divorce, and I ended up losing all the friends I had gained through the marriage. There was one couple that was so threatened by our divorce that they completely avoided me. I heard through others that it was scary for them because there were a lot of similar doubts on the wife's part."

Young marrieds, who exchange their vows with such optimism and conviction, smug and self-assured while in marriage's secure hold, often find themselves angry and bitter once it's gone. It's exceedingly difficult and painful to suddenly transform from a paragon of personal and social success into a symbol of personal and societal failure. "I never told anyone about what was going on," Elizabeth says. "I just put up a front. I liked to appear buttoned-up. So I was kind of anxious about telling people about the divorce. The whole process made me learn how to open up more. It took my being able to make the statement 'I should not have gotten married; I need to figure out what happened,' which was very embarrassing for me to say, but it also took a lot of courage because I had never done anything wrong before. And here was a public admission that I'd done something very, very wrong."

The stigma of divorce was something many had only thought of from the safe confines of the other side. Elizabeth admits, "I thought of divorced people as selfish. Not successful. Hard to deal with. Not grounded. A fifty-year-old man who now wants a younger woman. I had very negative thoughts. . . . If you had said to me when I was a little girl, 'Oh, you're going to be twenty-eight and divorced,' I would have said, 'Ridiculous!' " Elizabeth confesses that she still attaches a bit of stigma to divorce "except in my case," and questions whether she would date someone who was divorced. "We all think of divorce in terms of our own learning experience," she says finally. "It's taught me to be more forgiving and not to assume anything about divorced people. I guess I would want to make sure that he had had a similar learning experience. I would want to understand the circumstances." Robert, now thirty-two, says, "I didn't think I was the kind of person who would get divorced. I thought that that was someone who came from a broken family and wasn't serious about their life. I attached such a heavy stigma to divorce that I didn't want to think of attaching that stigma to myself. But the reality is, when we're judging others, it really comes from ourselves and our own fears. When I first got married, I became very critical of people who got divorced." He laughs. "But that was based entirely on the fact that I didn't want to be married. I was really just judging my own insecurity about the wrongness of my own choice to marry."

Many psychologists say that men tend to be more distressed by the disapproval of friends and family following divorce. "You're 'the divorced guy,' " says Joel, who had always thought of himself as a true romantic. "It was very unsettling to me that that would be my identity. I'll have that always." Another man admitted, "I was mostly concerned with what people would think. I was really concerned with my family judging me. I didn't know what they would think specifically, but I had images in my mind of one relative whispering to another, 'Did you hear what happened?' I thought they would think I wasn't a good person, that I gave up too quickly or that I had made a foolish decision in the first place. And I had a very hard time with the fact that I had invited all these people to my wedding and got up in front of them to proclaim an everlasting love that only a year and a half later was suddenly gone."

While people fear familial and social approbation, the sense of personal failure is the harshest. "Before, I had never really looked down on divorce," says Bethany. "I thought it was other people's problem anyway. I just thought it was a fact of life. I didn't understand why people got so upset about it. And in any case, it wasn't going to happen to me. But once I went through it, I felt like such a failure. It wasn't just a breakup—it was A DIVORCE. I felt like damaged goods. It was the most painful thing I had ever experienced in my life. I was shocked by the tremendous weight it had on my life."

The prognosis for divorcés can look pretty bleak. Divorced people experience more health problems and undergo psychiatric treatment more often than their married or single counterparts. The young divorcés interviewed explained that divorce left them confused and disoriented, their self-esteem plummeted, and they felt depressed or withdrawn for a long period of time. Many said they were in shock. When asked how they felt after their divorce, almost everyone gave the same answer: "I felt like a failure." One man explained, "I'm not familiar or comfortable with failure. That was the hardest thing for me to come to terms with. I was a failure. I was unsuccessful at marriage. I was an undesirable person. She didn't want me. I thought I was hideous." Zoë recalls, "I thought that getting married only happened once. And I felt like I was a failure. Lesser people than me managed to make a marriage work and I blew it. I took a lot of responsibility."

After a period of recovery, many young divorcés felt relieved, particularly once the legal aspects were resolved and the divorce papers signed. "It took almost two years," Max says, despite the fact that he and his wife owned no property or common assets. "By the time it was all done, emotionally it was all over for me. I think I was just excited that the legal stuff was finally out of the way." Everyone agreed that the experience led to a necessary period of growth. "Getting divorced made me learn ways to find myself," says Olivia. "It kind of forced me into it. I feel like I'm kind of ahead now, having gone through all that." When Zoë got divorced at twenty-five, she despaired. "How am I going to do it? I was scared, depressed, angry, petrified, elated, relieved, but mostly very, very sad. It was probably my first inkling that I had to take care of myself, for the first time in my life. It was scary as hell at the time, but in retrospect it was probably the best thing that ever happened to me."

Even though *every single person* interviewed believed that divorce was ultimately the best thing for them, no matter what they learned from their starter marriages, they did not want to see their loved ones—or one day their children—go through the same experience. Getting divorced is not the recommended process for personal or societal growth; divorce is not the lesson we want to teach. Divorce can become a legacy, but it doesn't have to be.

Generations of Divorce

Divorce has become a common component of our culture, indeed an almost expected pattern in the typical American family. It is such a ubiquitous reality that one popular book for married couples is actually called *Divorce Busters.* Two former editors of *Wed-*

ding Bells left and formed *Divorce* magazine. Roseanne and the Fox network both have new "divorce shows" in the works, in which couples battle their divorces on-air. In the meantime, tune in to *Divorce Court.*

One statistic angrily flung about is that 50 percent of marriages will end in divorce. Actually, today it's probably closer to 45 percent, and while that's still a dismal prospect for the newly nuptialed, it's important to understand what the numbers really mean. The divorce-rate calculation takes into account *all* divorces that occur within forty years of marriage; until recently most marriages didn't even last forty years because people died before they could toast their fortieth. Today our marriages have to last much longer to match our expanding life spans; divorce rates are higher in part because divorce is largely displacing death as the cause of marriage's end.

Though it sometimes feels like we're on the brink of disaster, the divorce rate actually hit its high point over twenty years ago, in 1980, when the number of divorces per 1,000 married women reached 22.6. But the divorce rate has since decreased. By 1998 the number of divorces per 1,000 married women dropped to 19.5.*[4] Nonetheless, even with this recent reversal, the divorce rate is painfully high. Every month, .4 percent of the U.S. population gets divorced.[5]

Looking at these numbers, some people have decided that divorce is too easy, but the truth is a bit more complex. True, divorce is increasingly easy to come by on a technical or legal basis, but more fundamentally, people do not *need* marriage as much as they used to. Men used to need wives because they weren't trained to do the intensive labor of housework. They didn't know how to bake bread from scratch or iron shirts into acceptability. Nor did they have the time; housework used to require more than flipping "on" switches and wiping up spray cleansers. To work all day in an office or factory and then come home to an empty stomach and eight

---

* Unfortunately, the recent decline is commonly attributed to the overall decline of marriage rates and to the rise in trial marriages, which end without the process of divorce. In other words, fewer marriages equal fewer divorces.

more hours of work around the house—who wouldn't need a wife?

Women needed marriage to get by financially; their husbands were their primary source of income. They needed their husbands psychologically, to provide them with an identity as wife and mother. They needed their husbands socially; married couples formed the basic building blocks with which a social life was constructed.

Some people say that without these strict gender roles and their attendant requirements, people have no use for marriage. Marriages are defined by a male-breadwinner/stay-at-home-mom model and don't function well outside it. This argument accuses women's entry into the workforce of increasing the divorce rate. According to this theory, women work after marriage, and particularly after childbirth, not because they want or need to but because they're afraid. They fear that if they stop working, they'll no longer be developing the skills and contacts they'll need if their husbands leave and they have to rejoin the workforce. These arguments claim that men are the primary beneficiaries of divorce. Freed from their marital responsibilities, men retain the economic power and emotional resilience to simply move on and start anew. Looser divorce laws have actually decreased men's financial obligations to their ex-wives, lowering alimony settlements and limiting the bias toward mothers in custody cases. And statistics show that divorced women are not particularly well-off financially—certainly the decrease in average household income provides them no economic incentive to divorce. In other words, work falsely leads women to think they'll be better off in case of divorce when actually it just makes women poorer and men richer.

Yet it's not always men doing the dumping. Work or no work, women predominantly initiate the divorce process. According to a study by economists Margaret F. Brinig and Douglas Allen, "These Boots Are Made for Walking: Why Most Divorce Filers Are Women," two thirds of divorces are filed by wives. Nor is there convincing evidence that women's work *caused* the divorce rate to rise. Just because women can survive a divorce more easily doesn't mean they divorce *in order* to assert this power. Few happily married women would divorce to prove their financial prowess.

Rather, an independent income offers women the ability to leave a bad marriage, rather than stick with it out of desperation. Even if women's work *did* cause divorce, is the solution that wives drop out of the workforce postwedding in order to prevent their husbands from leaving? Aside from the obvious flaws inherent in this argument, this would force men to stay married out of pity, fear of social stigmatization, or resigned obligation, surely no recipe for marital bliss.

Another favorite culprit targeted by explanations for the high divorce rate is society's lenient view of divorce. Blame it on those crazy Boomers, hippies, and feminists, who sabotaged the institution of marriage by making divorce cheap, easy, and fun. Such critics contend that we promote and encourage divorce, considering it "just another lifestyle choice." In *The Divorce Culture: Rethinking Our Commitments to Marriage and Family,* Barbara Dafoe Whitehead argues that "a high divorce society is a society marked by growing division and separation in its social arrangements," complete with single mothers, deadbeat dads, complex custody arrangements, throwaway kids, and divided and confused households. According to Whitehead, this mentality is perpetuated by the "divorce industry," a booming economic sector comprising lawyers, psychiatrists, financial advisors, and social services.

A related theory focuses on the changing social and cultural attitudes that arose as the country expanded civil rights and liberalized social attitudes. The resultant tolerance of different backgrounds and experiences has led to a toleration of different lifestyles. Others point out that changing gender roles mean that in a modern society people don't know how to function in marriages that continue to rely on a traditional gender divide. According to this theory, now that working women are the norm, marriage will adjust accordingly and social stabilization based on these new patterns will lead to a decline in divorce.

These theories have their attractive elements, but nailing a culprit for the divorce rate is not as easy or simplistic as many social critics would like to believe. According to sociologist Larry L. Bumpass, an expert on marriage and divorce patterns, "The duration of [the divorce] trend suggests that the roots of current patterns of marital instability are deep, and not just a response to recent changes in other domains such as fertility, sex-role attitudes, female employment, or divorce laws."[6]

In some ways, the divorce rate is most convincingly explained by our changing definition of marriage. When marriage was primarily an economic arrangement, divorce could mean impoverishment. When marriage was socially and legally required, divorce meant ostracization. But now that marriage is so heavily defined by individual happiness and love, divorce simply means that love has died; a loveless marriage isn't a marriage at all. As E. J. Graff asks in *What Is Marriage For?*, "Once emotional expectations rise, once marriage's inner life *is* the marriage, mustn't the death of love undo the marriage? And if marriage is immoral without love, then mustn't a moral society change the rules of—and expect a dramatic rise in—divorce?"[7]

Death to Divorce?

It better not, because according to the "pro-marriage," antidivorce crowd, divorce screws you up, ruins your kids, breaks down society, encourages bad governmental policy, wipes out the private sphere, and destroys the economy. For them, the solution is to make divorce more difficult, less accessible, and more socially condemned.

Divorce has been put on a deathwatch. A series of books came out in the 1980s and 1990s decrying the liberalization of divorce law, among them *The Divorce Revolution: The Unexpected Social and Economic Consequences for Women and Children in America* by Lenore Weitzman, and *The Equality Trap* by Mary Ann Mason. In 2000 *The Unexpected Legacy of Divorce* by Judith Wallerstein joined the shelves. These books argue that divorce laws have not only hurt women and children but, by making divorce "easier," have damaged the state of the American marriage.

They argue that destroying divorce begins with an attack on the legal system. The main target is no-fault divorce, which has been used to mobilize public opinion and create public policy aimed at minimizing divorce. Such efforts are paying off. A 1998 poll revealed that 59 percent of Americans believed that divorce should be harder to obtain,[8] up from 42 percent in 1974.[9] The result is a growing grassroots movement to remove no-fault divorce from the books. In 1996 nineteen states introduced bills to repeal their no-fault divorce laws, and in other states measures have been passed to extend the waiting period before divorce is granted.[10]

Actually, no conclusive evidence proves that no-fault laws had any causal impact on the divorce rate. In fact, during the 1970s divorce rates in most states with the new no-fault laws were no higher than in other states.[11] Furthermore, the majority of no-fault divorce laws were enacted fifteen years *after* the divorce rate began to rise again (in 1965). Sociologists tend to agree that the changing divorce laws were the *result,* rather than the cause, of changing attitudes toward divorce.

No-fault divorce was in fact created to correct some of the abuses of the past wherein, for example, a woman wasn't allowed to request divorce or the man automatically retained custody of his children. The new laws granted women more control over their marital status, giving them greater independence and flexibility. Wives would no longer be required to stay in unhappy, demeaning, or abusive situations, and battered women would be able to seek legal action while avoiding protracted court battles. They gave women access to divorce lawyers and produced more sympathetic courtrooms. Husbands could no longer just abandon their wives and children, leaving them little legal recourse or financial cushion.

Opponents argue that the opposite has occurred—divorce has become so easy to obtain and widespread that its tragedy has been diminished and the sanctity of marriage destroyed. Maggie Gallagher, author of *The Case for Marriage,* argues for an end to "unilateral divorce," asserting that no-fault divorce laws have done no less than "outlaw marriage."[12] Gallagher claims that the easy divorce undermines the idea of marriage as a covenant. In her view, higher barriers to divorce will increase marital commitment.

The message behind these arguments is clear: a woman's independence destabilizes the traditional roles in a marriage, stripping men of their identity as producer and provider. Women need to stick to their designated function as a civilizing force on the more aggressive, unstable male.

Many of these arguments tread along the same evolutionary-biology lines that explain why traditional gender roles are crucial to marriage's survival. With divorce easy to obtain, the naturally wayward man will inevitably drop his wife to search for younger, fresher prey. Evolutionary psychologist Robert Wright claims that the only effective way that societies can restrain the male's propensity toward polygamy is through strong social sanctions—the "shaming" of divorce such as in Victorian England or present-day Japan. Yet even if this Tarzan-and-Jane model fit reality, surely a mere restriction of divorce practices wouldn't be a sufficient restraint on such stampeding biology. And to argue against egalitarian marriage—overwhelmingly preferred by both men and women these days—because it has the side effect of enabling women to survive divorce is a pretty roundabout way to bolster matrimony.

Even if one ignores the "scientific" claims behind these arguments and subscribes to their prescriptions, making divorce laws stricter could have the unintended consequence of transforming a bad marriage from a three-year mistake into a ten-year disaster. A prolonged marriage may well lead to children, and a later divorce into a tragic legacy—the very error starter marriages avoid. "I actually viewed divorce at my age as something positive," Jared, divorced at age twenty-seven, says. "I'm still young. I still have time ahead of me. And better to get divorced now than to wait five years and have two kids. Better sooner than later if it's going to happen."

Viewed from the flip side, the high divorce rate can be seen as a positive indicator of the elimination of bad marriages. "It feels sad being divorced so young," Isabel, now twenty-nine, says. "When you tell people, you can see that they pity you. But I feel pity for people who are in unhappy marriages and never get out. In the end, I feel lucky to have been strong enough to get out of a bad situation."

People in bad marriages who still believe that good marriages exist tend to be the ones *most* eager to divorce. They trust that marriage can still bring them happiness even if the particular marriage they are in cannot. Instead of being "committed to marriage," people who remain in bad marriages have often just lost faith in themselves and the very institution of marriage. And social critics who would force such unhappy couples to adhere to a miserable state of matrimony must think marriage is pretty bad if you've got to punish people in order to make them stay.

So who's pro-marriage now?

The Right to the Right Divorce

To be pro-marriage does not mean being pro- *all* marriages. Even Barbara Dafoe Whitehead, no fan of divorce, favors no-fault divorce laws. "It would be a cruel irony indeed if a pro-marriage policy unintentionally became a pro-bad-marriage policy," she warns, "giving aid and comfort to the critics of the institution."[13]

The concept of no-fault divorce is actually rather enlightened. Before no-fault divorce laws, someone always had to be blamed for the marriage's failure, yet most failed unions are not one person's fault or responsibility. The truth is usually much more complicated than the black-and-white picture that fault-based divorce laws force parting couples to paint. It's more realistic and humane to assume that the apportioning of "fault" is a private matter between the couple and the best scenario is to allow people to divorce amicably rather than in argument.

No-fault divorce laws are also effective in avoiding the overly litigious atmosphere so poisonous to the state of marriage. Without these laws, couples often lie anyway in order to justify divorce. Many divorcés interviewed confessed to creating fake accusations and scenarios in order to expedite their divorces in states without no-fault. In New York a favorite is the trumped-up "constructive abandonment" charge, in which one partner has refused to have sex with the other for a year or longer. And those who advocate waiting periods for divorces, in the hope that couples will reconsider and reconcile, might listen to the voices of divorcés who overwhelming insist they considered their marriages over from the date of separation; the rest was basically "paperwork."

If divorce cannot be stemmed through formal laws, some argue it can and should be changed by a conscious shift in societal attitudes and behavior. They contend that divorce is looked upon too lightly by our culture and people are not as discouraged as they once were from choosing it. These accusations are very often right on the mark. And many divorcés agree wholeheartedly.

However, some people want to go a step further by *stigmatizing* divorce the way we do adultery, incest, and social crimes. Their motivation may sound reasonable enough, but the implementation of such impulses is misguided and its implications frightening. Melinda Ledden Sidak of the Independent Women's Forum suggests that landlords discriminate in favor of married couples and argues that "to the extent that there is any hope at all of arresting America's moral decay, conservative elites must take the lead not only in lamenting the consequences of the sexual revolution, but in actually enforcing a sense of shame." She proposes specific legal and social means of doing so, including "sanctions ranging from chilly social greetings to total social ostracism and even the loss of a job."[14]

The idea that divorcés deserve some kind of punishment is objectionable in and of itself. Some of the proponents of stigmatizing divorce must have in mind the typical divorce "bad guys." The philandering husband. The power-hungry career woman who left her husband for a job. The careless youth who made a foolish decision. The deadbeat dad. Yet marriages are much more complex than these cardboard stereotypes suggest. Suppose the philandering husband's wife was a sour, nasty woman who constantly undermined him. Suppose she turned over in her bed every night before they went to sleep and told him he repulsed her. There are reasons behind people's divorces that the marriage police can't know of, unless they sit down with a couple at breakfast every morning and join them in bed at night. Who really knows what goes on in a couple's lives and inside their heads?

If we stigmatize divorce as a lifestyle choice, we would be stigmatizing not only the downright roguish, but their victims as well. "My husband just up and left me one day, and sometimes I *do* wish he were stigmatized," admits Kate. "But at the same time, if he gets a stigma, then so do I, and I don't think I deserve it. After all, I never would have chosen divorce if it hadn't been chosen for me. I tell myself that at least everyone we knew when we were married knows what kind of man he is. Our families know what really happened. And he has to live with himself—that's the most important thing."

The husband whose wife abandoned him for a wealthier man should not be viewed as a lesser person because he's—for shame!—divorced. A battered wife needn't feel morally degenerate because she finally had the courage to leave her spouse. More often than not, "good" divorces are hard to weed from "bad" ones and blame isn't easily assigned. By proclaiming certain reasons to divorce like adultery, alcoholism, abuse, addiction, and abandonment appropriate, one ignores the more nebulous but often valid reasons like depression, rage, animosity, and lovelessness.

Do the marriage police propose that an independent commission judge who justifiably got divorced and who ought to be excused from societal disapproval? Would these proponents of Victorian values really want to watch their own daughter cry tears of shame because her husband left her for another woman or because she wasn't able to live up to her parents' ideals? To see her dishonored because of someone else's mistake? Those who aren't "at fault" can't just pass for single or widowed. They don't get to wear a placard explaining, "I wasn't the bad guy." Even the most "innocent," committed, pro-marriage person has little recourse when her spouse decides marriage isn't for him.

No matter how much we decry a culture of divorce and no matter how open, liberal, tolerant, or carefree we pretend to be, most people who actually go through a divorce find it is neither encouraged nor sanctioned in our society. As a 1997 *Newsday* report entitled "Marriage Is Back" put it, "Want to be hip? Stay together."[15] The "prodivorce" mentality epitomized by the 1970s bible *The Courage to Divorce* disappeared just as surely as the book went out of print.

Divorcés are still looked down upon, pitied, and pilloried. Divorce may even be *more* stigmatized among Gen Xers because not only do we share the general societal condemnation of divorce, our children-of-divorce generation is particularly bitter and disapproving given our own childhood experiences. "I always thought divorce was for trashy people—trailer-park types. I had this image of the forty-two-year-old bleached blonde with long fingernails, smoking a cigarette and driving a Camaro," says Olivia, who divorced after three years. "I think that's why I stayed married for as long as I did even though I was miserable. I just didn't want to be twenty-four and divorced."

It may seem like an easy fix, but making people feel even worse about their divorced status will *not* discourage divorce. Nor will making divorce more difficult. An unhappy couple doesn't say to themselves, "Well, we'd like to get a divorce, but it's just too complicated. Let's stick together until the laws change and there's less paperwork involved." Most couples seeking a divorce are unhappy enough to put up with the required procedures, and certainly no happy couple would be coaxed into divorcing by looser laws and pared-down paperwork. It's a typical afterthought, Band-Aid solution to a much deeper problem. Rather than being strengthened, the institution of marriage is weakened by the assumption that in order to sustain it, its participants need to "suffer through" and "stick it out" in spite of their misery. "When you're in a bad marriage, it's just unbelievably depressing to get up every morning," Charlotte, who is engaged to be married again, recalls. "You know that you have to be with this person, and you desperately don't want to be. It makes happiness impossible. . . . I wanted to have a normal, healthy life and to have kids, and I couldn't in that marriage."

Starter Marriage Divorces

Divorce is often stigmatized for reasons that have nothing to do with starter marriages anyway. Much of the debate isn't really about divorce per se, but about its effect on children. According to the antidivorce crusaders, the real victim isn't the individual woman or man but the "fatherless" children.*

---

* It should be noted that the impact of fatherless families on children is a highly contentious, much disputed area of study. Some studies claim that children who grow up in single-mother households are less healthy, less emotionally stable, and less likely to succeed in their education, their careers, and their own relationships. Other studies show that much of these negative results are really due to the impact of one less salary contributing to the family's welfare. If you control for income, you will find that children who grow up without fathers present in the primary household do not suffer any more than their two-parent-family counterparts. Nonetheless, this is still a major problem. Most fathers contribute more than just another income, and even if their contributions are limited to the financial, those benefits can be tremendous.

But the fact that starter marriage couples don't have children doesn't let us entirely off the hook. While most of the negative effects of divorce stem from its effects on children, divorces in marriages without children are not completely absolved of wrong. While divorce needn't be stigmatized, it might well be taken more seriously—by those who go through it, by society, and by our culture.

When we give up on marriage, we lose our dedication to the principles of trust that those relationships require, and our faith is shaken. Sophia, a thirty-five-year-old mortgage loan originator from Ohio, felt this on two fronts. "This is such a huge issue. After I found out my husband had been lying to me, I went to therapy with him and said, 'We went cliff jumping while we were engaged. I was afraid, but you put your hand out and said, "You can trust me with your life!" I trusted you with my life—and look at how our marriage is filled with lies.'" She recalls, "Before I walked down the aisle, my father asked me if I was absolutely sure this was what I wanted to do. And I turned to him and said, 'Dad, I've never been so sure of anything in my life.' It's like a double whammy to have been so sure and so wrong. I made vows before God that I couldn't keep. It makes matters worse to know that you can no longer even trust yourself." Sophia didn't date for three years following her divorce. "How could I date or marry again after I said those vows before God?" she asked.

We lose our sense of compromise and commitment to others to the mentality of me, here, now, mine. We elevate a self-centered mind-set that esteems self-reliance, self-fulfillment, and self-serving above empathy, kindness, and sacrifice. And we rob marriage of meaning. Sophia explains, "I was brought up with the idea that marriage is sacred. That it's built on ground rules of respect and commitment. When I realized those values were missing from my own marriage, it was devastating for me." As the devoted wife in the film *Committed* says of marriage, "I'm still a committed person. If you didn't take things to certain extremes, how would you know what we're made of? Where we stand? Where anyone else stands? It would be a mystery."

Young divorcés have strong, if often contradictory, opinions about divorce. Many still struggle to reconcile their own experi-

ence with their larger beliefs. After our initial interview, Laurel
sent an e-mail saying that starter marriages shouldn't be treated
like a "pop theme" or something "cool" because "the idea of starter
marriages is dangerous in my eyes." She explained, "I think the
starter-marriage trend is indicative of our social disregard for the
consequence of action. In other people's lives this plays out dangerously, in different ways, like with criminals who have no regard
for human life/no sense of implications, and little depth or exploration of the meaning of action and thought and consequence."

Laurel initiated her own divorce. At the time, she says, "I was
initially so relieved that there was the option of divorce that could
get rid of this problem. . . . I didn't have any sense of shame or
guilt."

Ironically, several divorcés interviewed still considered themselves opposed to divorce, and some of the most ardent opponents
had initiated their own divorces. For some ex–young marrieds, and
particularly those who are remarried, there can be a failure to fit
the uncomfortable fact of their own divorces into their ideas about
divorce in general. "I still think marriage should be for life," says
Noelle, remarried at thirty-three. "When you think about it, people
take divorce really lightly. . . . I believe in commitment, but if
you're not happy, then get out." When her own divorce went
through, she says she felt relieved. She remembers calling up her
friends and screaming, "Yay! I'm divorced!" Yet in general she believes that divorce is "too easy," that "there needs to be commitment," and that "people don't try." Noelle, who got a thirty-day
no-fault divorce, complains that "the problem isn't with the law, it's
with people. The first little argument, they go to a lawyer. People
don't take marriage seriously enough." But she's aware of her own
inconsistencies. Seconds later, she laughs uneasily, "I know—I say
one thing and then contradict it."

Not only do some people have difficulty accepting their own
divorces, they are shocked by what they see as an acceptance of divorce in certain corners of our society. "It was so strange," Juliet
says. "Nobody asks you questions when you get divorced. Nobody
sends you to a therapist. It was so easy. To get a Jewish divorce and
not even get a call from the rabbi. Nobody even called me to check
in or find out what happened. It's now so accepted to be divorced

that it's treated like no big thing. I couldn't and still cannot under-stand it."

More accepting attitudes toward starter-marriage divorces may be attributed to the fact that because we are young and childless we'll more easily be able to move on and create new lives—and new marriages. Part of the reaction by divorced parents is relief that at least no children are involved, that their sons and daughters aren't repeating their mistakes. Nonetheless, the current accept-ability of divorce leaves many people feeling like, "What did my marriage mean, anyway, if its dissolution is no big deal?" A few people said their divorce experiences somehow cheapened their ideas about marriage. "New York doesn't have a no-fault option, but you can kind of cheat. There are ads in the paper for people who'll do it for two hundred dollars," explains Joel. "We were talk-ing about that option, but then she got upset that it would be over so quickly. We ended up doing it in a more proper way, which made me feel better about it. Part of me just wanted it to be over quickly and painlessly. But having to go through the real process gave it more dignity."

Elizabeth got a no-fault divorce in Massachusetts. "Divorce was one of the simplest procedures I ever went through—simple to the point of being comical. Simple to the point of being sad that it's so easy. You fill out a form and you get a court date. . . . We stood in front of the judge for two minutes. We didn't even have lawyers. The judge said, 'I read your case. Is there no chance for reconcilia-tion?' and we said no, and he said, 'I grant you a divorce.' It was really humorous—no, that's not the right word. It was bizarre. You feel like, 'I just got a divorce and it's no big deal.' " In the end, Eliza-beth sought an annulment from the Catholic church, a process that was a great deal more meaningful to her.

One Conservative Jewish man was deeply moved by the get ceremony, in which the husband drops the *ketubah* (the Jewish marriage contract) and when it passes through the wife's hands the marriage is over. Yet Isabel found the ceremony humiliating and unnecessary. "The language was very derogatory toward women," she says. "It made me look like the biggest slut. . . . It was very degrading." She left the ceremony feeling angry, bitter, and shocked. "I will never get married by a rabbi again after that experience," Isabel says. "It's the opposite of everything a modern woman believes and everything marriage is supposed to be about."

Most dismissed the state's treatment of their divorce as mere paperwork and considered their marriages long over, usually dating the end to the date of separation. Despite the supposedly lenient divorce laws and the fact that most of these divorces went uncontested, the majority felt their divorces were unnecessarily difficult from a procedural point of view. Jodie thinks no-fault laws should be passed in New York. In order to get divorced, she had to sue her husband for refusing to have sex. "If you're grown up enough to get married, then you're grown up enough to know if you don't want to be married anymore," Jodie argues. "I don't like the fact that the state seems to be making a moral judgment on whether or not you should stay married. Marriage is a legal contract between two people, and if they want to end it, that's not the state's business." She adds, "If it's a religious marriage, I can understand that the religious leader would want to get involved in the divorce, but the state is another matter."

Many were shocked and dismayed that divorce was a lot harder to come by than marriage. "There were so many bureaucratic holes to jump through and so much paperwork that by the time it was finally done, I just felt a big sense of relief," Amy says. "I can put that whole part of my life behind me. And it's made it easier on my current relationship because it was hard to reconcile our commitment with my divorce still hanging over us." Charlotte agrees that the divorce paperwork was extremely difficult but says, "For me, it was such a pain to do that it really put a lot of things about marriage into perspective. I thought, 'I have really had to work to get this divorce, and if I ever get married again, I'm going to really work at that marriage.' For me, it was a turning point in my life. I realized that you really have to work hard on things. And I knew that the first thing I had to work on was myself. It gave me a new sense of direction in life."

Whether their divorce was easy or difficult, sought after or unexpected, not a single person interviewed regretted it. And almost without exception they felt their divorces had been unavoidable. As one woman puts it, "I look back at all the decisions I made, and knowing myself and how I came to each of those decisions, I know I had to do it. I had to get married—and I had to get divorced."

While they were keen on not romanticizing the concept of divorce or excusing it in any way, they felt much more strongly that their marriages—*not* their divorces—were the real problem. Rather than focus debate on divorce, which puts the emphasis on preserving bad marriages, we could concentrate on preventing bad marriages and strengthening good ones.

Chapter 9

Lessons from a Starter Marriage

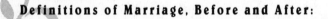

Definitions of Marriage, Before and After:

MAX BEFORE: "I guess I thought marriage would be the same as living to-gether."

MAX AFTER: "Marriage is a union of two people who love each other and want to share their lives together."

AMY BEFORE: "I don't think I really thought about what marriage meant when I did it."

AMY AFTER: "Marriage is loving one person and only one person whole-heartedly and being willing to do anything for that person without losing track of who you are."

ZOË BEFORE: "I knew that he was the husband and I was the wife, and I didn't know what any of that meant."

ZOË AFTER: "Marriage is a legal and spiritual union between two people of like minds."

MICHAEL BEFORE: "I had this idealistic view that marriage meant that we were going to just be together and travel and have a great time for a few years and then start a family, have kids, and live this great life."

MICHAEL AFTER: "Marriage is a relationship between two people where each of them communicates their wishes, desires, thoughts, feelings, pain, and joy; where each of them listens and empathizes; and where each person loves the other unconditionally."

ROBERT BEFORE: "I thought about it for all of three days. In my mind, we were creating this whole new notion of being this married couple who was Latin and American and artistic and educated all at the same time. That we could do anything, be anything, free of consequence."

ROBERT AFTER: "Marriage is the union of two families expressed by two individuals and their idea of how they hope to share their lives and their aspirations with and within their community."

Starter marriages teach some very painful lessons about marriage. All the people interviewed knew they had made a mistake or, more likely, several big, gut-wrenching mistakes. Some hadn't tried hard enough to make their marriages work and admitted as much, though most believed they had done all they could given their own limitations, the limitations of their partner, the constraints of the marriage they had, and the foundation on which it was built. Whether theirs was a case of immaturity, inconstancy, irresponsibility, or intractability, all, in retrospect, could recognize their own marital missteps.

Most people felt they'd put a great deal of effort and emotion into their marriages and that it took at least twice that to get out. Every single person thought his marriage and divorce had been one of the most, if not *the* most, formative experiences of his lifetime. All believed they had learned and perhaps even benefited from the experience. "I'm a different person now," they explained. "I don't even recognize who I was then." "I can't imagine who I'd be if that hadn't happened." "I never would have had the marriage I have today if it wasn't for my first." Charlotte, at twenty-nine, says, "I felt older than most other people when I got divorced. I still feel that way—like there's a permanent age gap between me and everyone else my age."

A remarkable lack of blame lurks in the wake of these starter marriages. With time, most people readily conceded wrongs on their own part as well as that of their partner. Rather than assign blame about divorce, we might be better served by examining what happened in these marriages and why.

After all, starter marriages do not signify a lifetime failure of marriage; indeed, a starter marriage can teach the lessons necessary to succeed in the next marriage. And with rare exception, everyone interviewed emphatically wanted to marry again— for a lifetime. Considering that 81 percent of divorced and separated Americans continue to believe marriage should be a lifelong commitment—a greater proportion than the general population—their optimism shouldn't surprise.[1] "As nasty as the entire experience was in many ways, somehow it didn't keep me from wanting to get married again," Sam explains. "I haven't lost faith in the institution itself."

Regrets

Some of the reasons why ex–young marrieds decide to divorce may sound superficial, immature, or weak, and oftentimes they are—they reflect marriages that were frequently superficial, immature, or weak. If the reasons to divorce sound wrong, it's usually because the marriage itself was never right in the first place.

The majority of people interviewed considered their big mistake not divorce but when, how, and to whom they got married. And while everyone valued the lessons they learned, not everyone accepted the price they had to pay. "I definitely regret having been married," says Juliet. "I wish I could take it all away. I try to think of it as a learning experience, but all the things I'm going through now in terms of learning about myself, I really should have learned on my own before I got married. If I hadn't gotten married, I would have learned these life lessons in my twenties, with time and experience—*not* with a failed marriage." James also believes that he would have grown on his own, without divorce pushing him along. "Divorce had never even come into my mind. I still feel tainted by it, having to say I'm divorced at such a young age. It's getting easier with time, but I still don't like the fact that I carry this stigma of divorce."

Many people felt remorse over how they had approached marriage in the first place. "If I could do it all over," James says, "I wouldn't have gotten married. I guess I do regret being married. I regret that I chose to marry the person I did." Starter marriagees' conceptions of marriage tend to fall into three categories: those who know what they *don't* want from marriage (generally what their parents had or what they themselves experienced in a previous relationship); those who have a perfect, idealized vision of what kind of marriage they want; and those who don't have a clue and often haven't thought about it at all. Whatever the case, many, even those with happily married parents, think they'll innovate or improve on the institution of marriage. "I thought that we were going to be like this great new marriage of the 1990s," said one twenty-seven-year-old New Yorker. "We were going to show people what it was like to be married. We'd be totally devoted to each other and yet still part of this hip, young scene. We were going to carve a new niche." Even people who think their married lives will be "untraditional" stick to most of the traditional conventions. "I thought we would have this downtown, artistic lifestyle," says Joel. "We would eventually move into a big loft space and I wouldn't wear a suit. But I'd still have the responsibilities of a husband. I would be faithful to my wife and support her in every possible way in the life we would share together."

Gen Xers, particularly men, often see marriage as a voyage of perpetual exploration and self-discovery. "When I imagined our marriage I thought we'd be traveling, having adventures," says Sam, the thirty-year-old Internet producer. When he married at twenty-six, he says, "I never envisioned us being stationary. I thought there would be all this exploring and growing together. I envisioned it as very liberating; I would finally be with this person who I wanted to see the world with." Max had a similar vision of marital bliss: "I guess I thought we'd always be like college students in a way. We'd have a lot of fun, vacations, trips, adventures."

Too many young people dive into marriage without having given any thought at all to what it entails. This third group tends to include the youngest, least experienced, and most impulsive. "I don't think I really thought about what marriage meant," Amy recalls. "He just said, 'Let's get married,' and we got the license and did it. It wasn't until about six months after that I even started to think about what marriage meant. And I realized then—and still think now—that marriage is not something to be entered into lightly. But at that point I was trapped. There was no way I was just going to quit my marriage. I wasn't going to be the kind of person that people point to and say, 'Oh, she just jumped into marriage and it lasted only two months.' I was also a practicing Catholic. I had made my vows, and it was against my religion to get a divorce even if I'd entered into marriage quickly."

Many young marrieds get engaged after only knowing each other for a short time. Amy eloped her freshman year with a man she had dated for two months. Lucy moved in with her boyfriend after two weeks, and they got engaged within six months; by age twenty-five they were married. Rushing into marriage allows couples to get caught up in idyllic, romantic scenarios, without experiencing their relationship over the long term. Bethany, who married her husband at twenty-three after three months of dating, remembers, "He asked me to marry him two weeks after we started dating. I was so unbelievably happy, just giddy and euphoric. I couldn't believe that I was engaged. I was overwhelmed and dumbstruck. We'd just look at each other and say, 'We're so happy, it's gross.' We were so tickled about it."

"I was really young and I didn't know myself at all," says Charlotte, who married at twenty-two, "I guess I thought we would be different from my parents, but I didn't think much beyond the wedding. I just did it. . . . I was young and everything like getting a house and having a kid just seemed so far away. I really didn't think about the long term. It was a whimsical decision." She remembers her divorced mother-in-law cautioned them at the time, saying, "'I hope you two are not just playing house.' At first I didn't understand what she meant. But I definitely learned later on."

Many were fairly inexperienced with relationships before marrying. "He was my first serious boyfriend," Elizabeth says of her husband, whom she met her freshman year at Harvard and dated for four years before becoming engaged. "I had never even been in an adult relationship before. I didn't have a sense of what I liked or didn't like in a relationship, or in a boyfriend. I think an older, more experienced person would have been more confident about making such a decision. But when you don't have any other comparison point, and if you're really analytical like I am, it just eats away at you. I finally remember making this decision: I'm not sure if I love him, but I know he's an extraordinary person and therefore I'd rather make the decision to get married, recognizing that on the romance, love, and affection side of things I didn't have a true partnership but that he had so many other dimensions that I didn't want to risk never meeting anyone else who measured up. That was a twenty-three-year-old thinking."

Some ex–young marrieds attribute their decision to wed as a reaction to prior relationships. One woman explained that she married because "I wanted someone safe who wouldn't hurt me. I'd been in enough relationships, and I didn't want to take any chances. . . . And I figured, I had done pretty well with this guy, why waste my time looking around for someone else when most guys were just jerks?" It's one thing to have a rebound relationship, quite another, a rebound marriage. "I think my decision to marry was a reactionary response to bad relationships I'd had before," says Amy. "One ended up being physically abusive and he raped me. I thought I would never meet someone who was actually nice to me. Even though there was never any big sexual attraction with my husband, he was really nice to me. When he said, 'Let's get married,' I was like, 'Okay, let's!' "

Often those who could talk endlessly about plans they had made for their wedding drew a blank when it came to planning their marriage. "I felt like the whole wedding industry was such a racket because they sell you on this fantasy of the wedding day but they don't give you a clue what to do the next morning," Bethany complains. "I didn't know what was expected of me."

The problem with starter marriages is rarely the wedding itself. Most people claimed their weddings were everything they imagined they would be. In fact, for a number of people the wedding day was the most positive memory they could recall from their marriages. Nonetheless, though most thought their actual weddings had fulfilled their fantasies, almost everyone had different plans for the second time around. And they looked back on their wedding day with at least some form of regret.

Those with the biggest regrets were at extremes of the wedding spectrum—couples who had eloped and people who had mammoth weddings. The elopers often felt their weddings didn't carry enough weight or meaning; the "event" itself didn't represent the enormity of marriage. For the opposite reason, those who had huge, extravagant affairs felt equally disappointed. Their weddings had been all about *other* people; they weren't personal, they didn't focus on the significance of the marriage or the married couple themselves. "My wedding wasn't really meaningful on a spiritual or religious level," Max, married at twenty-six for all of eighteen months, says. "I wish it had been. I wish I had even known the minister."

Clara's wedding was one of the most elaborate of the season. "I got so caught up in planning the wedding and everything that went into orchestrating this huge event. Much more so than in thinking about the reality of the marriage. We were actually having a lot of problems at the time, and I even called off the event at one point because of these underlying issues. But you get so caught up in the fact that everyone is counting on this wedding and all this money has been spent that it becomes very hard to call it off. I was nervous, but I suppressed it. Chalked it up to wedding jitters." George's eight-month engagement was also fraught with conflict and doubt. "But all the arguments could be rationalized away as the stress of the engagement period. And then the gravitational forces got so strong that it became, like, 'Well, we can't back down now.' We would just continue crossing hurdles, as each down payment was made. Her family would be out of this sum of money, then my family would be out of that amount of money. I remember one time saying in the heat of the moment, 'I can't do this!' But I didn't seriously in cold blood put on the table the idea of calling the wedding off."

"The whole wedding planning had taken on a life of its own, and we were afraid to take on the real issues in our relationship," Helena explains. "When I look back now, I see that there were these enormous red flags that I wonder how we could not have seen. My dad had sent us a copy of the Pre-Cana questionnaire [the premarital education program required for marriage within the Catholic church], and my husband agreed to take it with me. There were about a hundred questions. We were driving in the car, and I remember that by the time we got to the fifth question, we were in such a huge fight that I threw the questionnaire out the window. That's how we dealt with things."

Many people regretted allowing themselves to ignore their better judgment, write off their reservations, succumb to the pressure. Let the wedding march begin—*you* can't *call off the wedding now; everyone is depending on you; they've all reserved the date. We were looking forward to a weekend on the Vineyard. They've already sent in the deposit. . . . Think about how much money has been spent.* The dangerous implication is that if you can just survive the wedding, the marriage will be easy.

And compared with the stress, panic, and obsession over the wedding day, becoming married actually does seem kind of easy. "It all seemed to happen so fast." "Suddenly I realized I was married." "I don't know how we got away with it," newlyweds mused once the wedding cake was cut, the flowers tossed, the rice swept away. "What just happened?" several wondered as they lounged about their honeymoon suites. Many people felt more like they had *wed*, rather than gotten *married*. One woman recalled, "I have this journal entry from the first day of my honeymoon where I wrote, 'Oh my God. It's one thing to plan a wedding day, but this is for life. What did I just do?' I had this feeling like I had planned and executed this huge party, and whereas normally you clean up and move on to the next thing, I was now permanently stuck in this situation."

Whether people had known each other for a long time and even lived together or whether they'd practically just met, whether they were running toward marriage or running away from something else, whether they planned a big wedding or chose to elope, many starter marriage veterans felt serious doubts before the wedding day. "I kept a journal at the time, and I look back and saw that I'd written, 'I have a pain in my stomach, is this butterflies or am I doing something wrong?'" Lucy recalls. "I kept trying to cover up those feelings. The day before the wedding I was very nervous because I took marriage so seriously. I wanted it to last forever. I wondered if I should call it off but then figured it was just cold feet."

"Planning the whole wedding was very stressful," Max remembers, "but at the time I thought that that was what engagement was like—stressful. It's your first time, you don't know what to expect. I thought it was natural." Juliet also had a troubled engagement period. "We took a marriage class, 'Making Marriage Work,' with the University of Judaism, which was my idea," she recalls. "The class had ten other couples and was taught by a rabbi and a therapist. I don't know now that it worked. I look back and I realize I had so many things to deal with. I talked the talk but I don't think I really *did* anything." One thirty-year-old man explained, "I always had doubts about our relationship, but I decided the day I proposed that I shouldn't wait for somebody perfect who doesn't exist. We have a good relationship and she really wants to get married. And I thought she was right, I was being needlessly cautious. It wasn't so much a decision to do it as it was a decision not to *not* do it."

Engagement somehow makes the wedding seem inevitable, as if once the engagement ring is slipped on the bride's finger, the bond is irreversibly sealed. You've bought your wedding. Isabel confesses she "tried to make believe there weren't problems—but there were." And like many couples, she felt that once she was engaged, the marriage was a fait accompli, no matter how bad the relationship got. "After you're engaged, you think you can't back out," she recalls. "I didn't want to be embarrassed or ashamed. In retrospect it seems so ridiculous that I was afraid to acknowledge what was wrong and have the courage to end it before it really began."

Knowing they could have avoided their divorce by avoiding their marriage in the first place often compounded feelings of remorse. Noelle, a thirty-four-year-old sales executive from New Jersey, says, "I knew I made the wrong decision right after I walked out of Town Hall. I had very mixed feelings about my now husband. But he was a habit. It just seemed so right. I thought it was the thing to do." Robert says, "The second after we got married, I knew I had made a terrible, terrible mistake. I was like, 'What the hell did I just do?' But I couldn't say, 'Wait! Stop, I made a mistake.' I felt like I had made a commitment and I couldn't get out of it."

Zoë also felt unsure immediately after her wedding. "I felt both more secure and less secure. I was like, 'What if I made a mistake here?' It's not like you can just break up. And I think I started realizing after I got married that maybe I had done this a little too quickly. I hadn't been nervous about getting married, but I was *really* nervous once I was." Helena goes so far as to admit, "I think that before we got married, I might have known there was a chance things might not work out. I remember reassuring myself, you know, if things don't work out, there's always an out. Which is terrible! It worries me that people getting married would consciously realize that they have an out. But being honest with myself, that's what part of me thought. Even though I believed that marriage was forever."

Those who didn't realize their mistakes right after the wedding day learned their lessons rather quickly: a number of interviewees knew shortly after their nuptials their marriages wouldn't last. "I could have said six months after the wedding, 'No, this is *not* right,' and everybody could have gone on with their lives," Amy says. "It would have been the easier road. And it would have saved [my husband] a lot of heartbreak." It doesn't take long for people to realize their married days are numbered. "At first I didn't change my name because I was in school," Lucy remembers. "But within six months, I knew the marriage wouldn't work out so I decided not to change it." Call it the six-month itch. One divorcée suggested that rather than make divorce more difficult we should create a six-months annulment period instead.

Many wish that some sort of preventative steps had been taken. Why didn't anyone warn them? How could it have been so easy, happened so fast? "I don't think I had any basis of knowledge or experience with which to make that kind of decision," Amy says. "Neither of us was old enough. We made the decision the same way people say, 'Let's go to the beach this weekend.' The sheer ease with which we jumped into it, like it was just something fun to do, reflected how unprepared we were. But nobody questioned it. Nobody ever asked, 'Have you told your parents?' I wish there had been more checks and balances. Not from a legal point of view, but from the people around us."

In the absence of such stopgap measures, people often created their own: neglecting to change their names after they'd declared their intention to do so, avoiding the merging of finances, or holding on excessively to their independence. One man never changed his permanent address from his parents' house to the home he shared with his new bride. Sophia's husband lost his wedding ring three times during their two-year marriage. Women with new names didn't bother to update their driver's licenses or passports. One woman explains, "I didn't change my name because I think subconsciously I wasn't committed to the marriage. I didn't want to permanently change my identity. I was in total denial at the time, but I had a gut feeling that it was the wrong decision. The second time I got married, I changed my name *before* the wedding. I knew it was right immediately." Max recalls, "I didn't really want my wife to change her name when we got married. I think in the back of my mind I knew it wouldn't last. I think that six months in, I realized that I wasn't going to live the rest of my life like this."

Often people regret behavior or events associated with their marriage. "I feel like I lost a part of myself," Lucy says. "Like I lost respect for myself for a while by getting married and then putting up with things that happened while I was married. I went against my own intuition." Kate felt a different sense of loss. "I gave of myself with total abandon," she says softly. "And I did so with the understanding that I was sharing it with someone with whom I was bonded forever. When he left me, I felt like he had made off with stolen goods. If I had known he would leave, I never would have given away my deepest thoughts and emotions the way I did. I feel like he has no right to that part of me anymore—but I can't take myself back. He's out there, walking around with my memories, my hurts, my desires, my personal history, and that will always leave me feeling vulnerable."

Several people, particularly those who had initiated their divorce, often mourned having hurt others—their spouses, their in-laws, their families. For Elizabeth, "My biggest regret is that I had to put someone else through this. I caused sadness to someone who didn't deserve it . . . and that it affected my parents, who are so incredibly concerned for my welfare." Jodie also regretted hurting her family. "If I could erase that, I wouldn't care about any of the pain it caused me. They really took my husband in as a son. They loved him very much, so all the betrayals he did to me were done to them too."

But the overwhelming majority of starter marriage veterans interviewed claimed that despite their regrets, on the whole their starter marriage experience had been a valuable—in some ways, even positive—experience. They learned something, recognized bad habits, or reaped some kind of emotional reward that helped them to look back on the marriage without regret and sometimes even with fondness. Once he knew his marriage wasn't working, George says he "tried to minimize the damage and get out. It was extremely sad but also extremely liberating and important and necessary. I can't say that I really regret the marriage, and I can't say that I regret the divorce." Michael agrees: "I cherish the experience. For a long time I looked at it as a failure. But now I see that it was great to have had such a relationship. I learned so much about myself and about who I am in a relationship. And that's incredibly valuable to me." Elizabeth says simply, "It was the greatest learning experience of my life."

Recovery

A marriage can fail in many different ways; it can be a failure of will, a failure of love, a failure of respect. Sometimes it's a matter of failed fantasies. Dealing with divorce requires a difficult process of self-examination and introspection. "I went in as just a kid and I left as a woman," Bethany explains. "It was a crucial experience, both the good and the bad. If I hadn't gotten divorced, I would never have gone into therapy. Right now, I'm the happiest I've ever been."

Kate's husband left abruptly one morning and told her he was never coming back. "I completely shut down for about two days," she recalls. "I don't think I've ever cried that hard. I was amazed at the way the tears kept flowing. I felt so dried-up and bereft that I thought I would just shrivel up and blow away. But then I woke up the third morning with this sense of resolve. I was like, 'Okay, I've got to take care of me now, because that's all there is. There's no more Us. I have to stop thinking about him and about what he's done to me because I'm the only one who's going to take care of me now.' And I felt this incredible determination to show myself that I could do it."

About ten days after his wife asked him for a divorce, Sam

says, "I had a complete emotional breakdown. I had come home and she was out and had left a note saying not to fiddle with the TV because she was recording something. And I'm thinking, my life is falling apart and she's worried about some show she's taping on the VCR! I sat on the floor and cried and screamed for hours. I felt completely lost. . . . But I woke up the next morning and I was still alive. I had the sense that I had gotten as low as I could get, and I knew that it would all be better after that—and it has been."

While the end of a marriage marks a failure, the individuals involved are not. Divorcés are neither flawed material nor second-hand goods. As Sam says, "It isn't what happens, it's how you deal with it. I used to bemoan my lot in life. I'd think, 'Oh, I'm so miserable—nobody's going to want to be with me.' Every little flash of adversity would cripple me with self-loathing and fear, but after my divorce I realized that it's *how* you deal with those things that end up shaping you and determining whether or not you're a success as a person. When we talk about the effects of divorce on society, we need to consider *not* the skyrocketing numbers of divorces but rather how the people involved dealt with those breakups and live the rest of their lives."

Many young divorcés were surprised by how deeply divorce affected them. Jodie had never been particularly bothered by the idea of divorce, though she thought she'd never have one herself. "I always thought that it made better sense to divorce than to stay together unhappily. I didn't think it was some terrible thing. But I felt much differently once I was divorced myself. I thought divorced people just moved on with their lives, but I had no concept of how emotionally painful it is. I thought it would be a relief, but I was just constantly in pain—even though I knew it was the right thing. I suddenly realized that I was a divorced person and that had never occurred to me. The first time I had to check the 'divorced' box I got very upset that I couldn't go back to checking 'single.' . . . I thought it made me look like I was a person who made bad choices in life."

Many believe they'll never recover—the mere idea of getting over a divorce feels like a negation of the meaningfulness of marriage. "I guess I don't want to get over my marriage, really," Kate admits. "I mean, if I could just 'get over it,' what the hell did my marriage mean in the first place? It seemed so belittling, so diminishing of what I had thought was a lifelong vow. Who can take me seriously if I don't take my marriage seriously myself? I couldn't take myself seriously if I were to discard it that way, like it was some bad job or a friendship gone sour. What meaning is there to such a solemn endeavor if you're supposed to forget about it like a bad date?" Even after starting therapy and beginning to put her life back together, Kate balks at the notion of completely "recovering" from divorce. "I think a lot of the psychobabble is superficial," she says. "It's really just a way of rationalizing our failures. It's like, 'Feel blue? Pop a Prozac. Got divorced? Curl up with some magazines and take care of yourself.' A bubble bath doesn't cure heartache or erase your mistakes. The very idea is depressing. Sometimes when I feel too much like I've gotten over it I force myself to think about what happened. I don't care what everyone else thinks or what the dominant view is. In my own mind, I wouldn't think of myself as a good person unless I constantly held on to the profundity of what went wrong."

For Robert, coming to terms with his divorce took almost six years, mostly because he tried to ignore it at first. "It was a long process. I ended up moving to New York from California because I felt the need to move on and really start my life again." He adds, "I don't think I will ever really be one hundred percent over it. There will always be this little piece. It's always there." Several months after the interview, Robert got engaged again.

In the end, whether their recovery process was slow or immediate, everyone was overwhelmingly positive about the way they came out of the experience. Olivia's divorce enabled her to get her life back on track. "After the divorce, I felt much worse than I ever thought I would. It affected me very deeply. I decided not to date for a year because I just wanted to focus on myself and figure out who I was. I met a new group of friends who didn't dwell on what had happened, and I ended up having some of the best years of my life, just being with myself and doing what I wanted to do. I started mountain biking and running and lost all the weight I put on during my miserable marriage. I started to like myself again."

Sam went into therapy after his divorce and found that "it was wonderful to talk about myself for forty-five minutes without constantly worrying about this other person. I realized that I had completely suppressed myself, just sublimated my entire self during those couple of years. Once I was on my own, I began to pursue things that were really important to me. I like myself now, who I've become."

Realizations

Many say their starter marriage forced them to grow up. Get some perspective. To recognize areas they needed to work on. Seven years after her divorce Zoë says, "I'm at a point now where I know who I am and what I want. I take good care of my family and myself, and I know where I want to be. If somebody comes into my life that wants to be a part of those things and I want to be part of his life in a similar way, that's great. . . . I know there are certain things that I have to do; otherwise I'll feel like my life is incomplete. But I don't need a man anymore to get that validation. I have a good sense of what my place is in the world, and I'm happy with who I am now—as a result of all the struggling and thought processes that came out of my marriage and divorce."

After his divorce, James went into therapy for five months and embarked on a health kick. "I wanted to be able to look in the mirror every day and smile at myself." Now he says, "I feel a lot more emotionally grounded, not only with other people but with myself. I pay more attention to what other people are saying and to what they mean. I've become a lot more perceptive. And I feel like once I explain to people what happened in my marriage and how I've handled it afterward, it almost looks like I'm the better for it." After Amy left her husband, she lost thirty-five pounds gained during her marriage, stopped drinking, and quit her two-pack-a-day cigarette habit. "I'm glad I got married. I grew up. I learned so much about myself. For all the misgivings I had and how hard the marriage was for me and how much I wanted out of it, looking back I wouldn't change a thing."

Perhaps the most crucial lesson, the one that many young divorcés cite as a pivotal step toward recovery, is the knowledge that much of the loss they mourned was merely a potential. Something they hadn't *really* lost at all. Divorce does not, after all, mean the loss of everlasting love and happiness, of the delightful, healthy family of four, of prosperity and social well-being for years to come, the fulfillment of the American dream. All divorce means is the loss of a marriage, and probably a bad marriage at that. The rest is merely a hope and mostly a fantasy, the assorted benefits we imagine marriage magically entitles us to and inevitably provides. But everything else, alas, is *not* included. Even couples in lifelong marriages suffer through unexpected illness and infertility, job loss and birth defects, financial woes and fights over who emptied the dishwasher last.

Divorce does not mean we've lost our lease on life or ruined our chances for happiness or destroyed our family. Once people realized that they hadn't lost out permanently on the kids and the dog and the grandparenting—*because they never had them to begin with*—their loss felt smaller or at least more manageable. For many ex–young marrieds, divorce forces them to abandon their personal quest for perfection. To relinquish their sense of total control. You can't will your way to the ideal husband, the lovely home, an enviable social life, and charming children. Nor can you take for granted that all will work out wondrously once you tie the knot. And you certainly cannot take for granted that "It could never happen to me"; divorce happens to the unsuspecting. Understanding that life just doesn't follow a logical plan is an essential part of maturation, and while many people learn that lesson through an unexpected death, a tragic accident, or a health crisis, divorce is an equally effective lesson.

For many of the overachievers and go-getters who paraded into marriage, that lesson is often a bombshell. Divorce teaches a humbling lesson about getting and working for what you want. "My mother says that after I divorced I was humbler, less insufferable," Melissa confesses. "It made me feel less entitled. I no longer thought I was so special." Jodie explains, "I'm not as infallible as I thought. I've had to learn to look at myself through someone else's eyes in order to figure out how he saw me and how he thought I made him unhappy."

People discovered not only their inability to control their lives completely but the human incapacity to control other human beings as well. For those with troubled spouses, depressed wives, or abusive mates from dysfunctional families, that lesson was learned through a considerable amount of pain. You can't make your wife overcome her eating disorder, control your husband's violent temper, get your wife's career on track, separate your husband's identity from that of his parents, or cure his alcoholism. You can't force a spouse to love you, respect you, or stay married to you. You cannot create a good marriage on your own, no matter how good a person you are, no matter how many A's you got in school, no matter how smart or attractive or successful or willing or loving you may be.

Starter marriages teach people a lot about adult relationships. Because they married young, it often took these spouses time and perspective to understand that their particular marriage wasn't necessarily the way it's "supposed" to be. "For me, getting out of my marriage was a rejection of all my fears and an affirmation that somebody with whom I have a real affinity will come along," says George, who got engaged seven months after the interview. "I actually think that one of the best things to prepare oneself for marriage is to be divorced."

Everyone who had sought divorce or arrived at it by mutual decision, and even many of those who had gotten divorced against their will, reported feeling liberated, focused, and ultimately bettered by divorce. They moved, sold their house, quit their job, took a long vacation, broke bad habits, rethought their life. Jodie felt like her divorce provided a kind of rebirth. "I went to Petra on vacation for a week and had this epiphany. I like to say that I climbed to the top of this mountain and found myself. I felt completely refreshed and renewed and free, and when I got back home, the [divorce] papers were sitting there in the mail. I felt like, I'm really done with it now. I can start my life over. I got a tattoo of a butterfly to commemorate it, because it felt like I had undergone a metamorphosis."

Clara says, "I felt really down for a long time. I had to remind myself of all the positive things in my life. In the end, the marriage and divorce was probably the most empowering thing of my whole life because it forced me to look at myself and acknowledge areas where I needed to grow. But also to accept things that are part of who I am and that I'm not going to try to change because someone would eventually love precisely those things. It felt so good to finally have some control over my own life, to just be at peace with who I was. Not that you *should* get married and divorced, but when I look at my friends, I feel like I am so much more in touch with myself and my needs than most other people."

In a strange way, having been married—even with divorce the result—endows many with a new confidence. For some, marriage rid them of the insecurity that led them there in the first place. "When my marriage ended a lot of my friends were talking about wanting to get married, and I kind of felt like, 'Yeah, I did that. I got that out of the way,' " Helena says. "Now what I really want is a healthy relationship. And as whacked as it is, I felt like I had already achieved something because someone had once wanted to marry me." For others, confidence came from having weathered the challenge. "I'm proud of what I did because it was the hardest thing I ever had to do," Lucy says. "It was the bravest thing I ever did. And I'm glad I got out when I did instead of waiting ten years when it would have been a lot worse."

Young divorcés are enormously relieved to have learned their lessons sooner rather than later. As Helena, divorced at twenty-nine, says, "I felt like I still had time to figure things out. And I could learn how to do things better the next time around. So I felt like getting divorced young was more of an advantage than a disadvantage."

Divorcé Dating

Divorce can seem like a distinct disadvantage when one begins dating again. It's hard to present yourself to a potential partner when you still feel wounded by the last. Even when you're ready, dating as a young divorcé has its own dilemmas. For example, if your Friday-night companion doesn't know your official marital status, when do you "come out of the closet"? "I have a really hard time telling men that I'm interested in," Juliet explains. "I wonder, do I owe him an explanation? Am I obligated to tell him that I'm divorced? I hate it when people set me up with men and tell them beforehand that I'm divorced." Others prefer that their dates know in advance. "That way I know they won't run off immediately when they find out," one divorcé says. "It means I don't feel like I'm forced right away into either evading or explaining."

Many divorcés feel branded with the D word, and most don't want to spend a first date going over the details that would explain or justify their divorce. "I think some women are no longer opportunities for me," James concedes. "Maybe they don't want to be with someone who's been married. If people take it at face value, they might think I'm not motivated or that I didn't give my marriage a chance. I feel like if they only took the chance to know me, they might think differently." Clara found herself divorced at age twenty-four. "I worried a lot about the stigma. It was hard figuring out when I was dating someone when to tell him I was divorced, because they didn't expect it at all. And the entire thing was so strange. I mean, people had dated their ex-boyfriends longer than I was ever with my ex-husband." One woman was filling out a form for an online personals website when she realized, "I was supposed to check 'divorced.' And I'm like, 'Divorced?' I'd rather say I 'was married.' But DIVORCED. A divorcée is like an older woman who drinks iced coffee and shops at Bendel's. It's like a forty-year-old real estate broker or something. I still thought of myself as practically a teenager."

Other people can form snap judgments or jump to conclusions. "I dated a guy whose mother didn't like me because I was divorced, and that really hurt me," Elizabeth says. "I felt like she was judging me and making assumptions, and I try not to do that with other people. It also made me kind of angry because I thought of all the single women out there who are in many ways a lot worse for her son to date than me. It was very painful." Many people find that even after they recover from their divorce, society and circumstance keeps throwing it back in their faces. "I had this new job, and though I changed my name before I started, the company got it wrong," Elizabeth recalls. "So I had to change my name three weeks into the job, and everyone was coming up and congratulating me on getting married. And I was like, 'Actually, the opposite.'"

"When you're trying to make new friends and you talk about

your past, it inevitably comes up," Amy explains. "It's like this big gap between them and me. It's like, 'Oh, *she* was married, *she's* divorced.' Especially single people; they put a big gap between you and them." Young divorcés encounter the inevitable flip in social circumstance. Only a few years ago one was "the married friend," often the first or only person in the crowd to have tied the knot. Less than five years later many find themselves again unique among their peers, but for the opposite reason. Elizabeth says, "I work on a team with three other women who are all married, and I definitely feel like the odd one out. We had a golf outing last week, and they all brought their spouses. I went by myself. I would much prefer to be married."

A few people, particularly those over thirty-two, confess to jealousy because they know their friends' more mature marriages are more likely to last a lifetime than theirs ever were. Many feel isolated or out-of-sync. One thirty-four-year-old woman says, "I just did not feel my age when I got divorced. It did not feel like my life. And what made it really hard is that both my brother and sister had recently married and both of them were expecting their first child while I was going through my divorce. What was happening in their lives was what I wanted to happen in my life—and it wasn't."

A number of people almost welcomed the occasion when someone else in their circle got divorced. As George says: "I was the first one in and the first one out. As bad as it sounds, it was something of a relief to me when some of my other friends got divorced so that I wasn't the only one." Charlotte was also the first of her friends to divorce. "I felt like I had this bad social karma," she says. "I thought I was going to be an outcast. I didn't think that people would want to be around someone who was divorced. Especially someone who was twenty-four and divorced."

If they didn't feel social pressure to marry the first time around (either because they were unusually young to be marrying or had parents who disapproved), quite a few say they feel it now. Those with live-in mates feel a strong social nudge to take the next step, while the completely unattached feel increasingly anxious as they climb toward thirty and beyond. "Now that more people are getting married, it's gotten harder to have a social life," Jodie laments. "Married people spend so much time with other married people that when I'm with them, I feel like the token single friend." Back on the dating scene, Jodie is acutely aware of the pressure to marry. "Even if the pressure isn't really there, everybody feels like it is, and so it *becomes* there."

Remarriage

Everyone would like to believe in one marriage per lifetime. Michael describes his biggest regret as "the loss of that dream." Charlotte, on the verge of remarrying, says wistfully, "I wish it were the first time."

But getting divorced can actually strengthen one's belief in marriage. "As nasty as the entire experience was in many ways," Sam says, "it somehow doesn't keep me from wanting to be married again. I lost faith in the marriage, but not in the institution of marriage itself." James, thirty, says he definitely wants to remarry. "I don't think the divorce has scared me off at all," he explains. "In fact, it probably increased my desire to start a new relationship, because I'm so much more prepared now."

"People are shocked when I congratulate them on their marriage and appear genuinely happy for them," Kate notes. "It's as if they're afraid that I don't like marriage anymore or they think I'm bitter. But nothing can be further from the truth. I'm really sad that my marriage ended. I liked being married. But just because this one marriage failed—and it happened to be mine—doesn't mean that I don't think marriage is a wonderful, joyous thing. I don't want my former bridesmaids to be afraid of asking me to participate in their weddings."

To hold on to one's deeply held beliefs after they've been directly challenged by personal experience means those convictions must be strong. After all, most young marrieds are enthusiastic supporters of the institution to begin with, and even if their own first marriage don't work out, those fundamental values don't change. Indeed, remarriage rates are higher for women who divorced under age twenty-five than they are for those over, and 54 percent of all women remarry within five years of their first divorce. Many people leave unhappy marriages precisely *because* they believe that marriage can be much better than what they're experiencing. Charlotte divorced because she knew she wanted a marriage in which she could "actually be friends with my husband, be spiritually in-sync and plan for a family." Now engaged at twenty-nine, she says, "I'm much more realistic. I have a grip on what a good marriage can be. I know what being a wife is and what it is to be part of a team. I'm marrying my best friend—who I'm also attracted to—and he shares the same ideas and wants to follow the same life path with me."

Given their ongoing belief in marriage, starter marriage survivors find the most important questions on their minds are, will I marry again? When will I be ready? And what will I do differently? If you do remarry, figuring out how to "position" one's first marriage is difficult. How can I tell my new spouse that marriage is forever? How can she have any faith in me? How can I? Then there's the question of what to tell the children. If you want to teach them that a marriage is a lifelong commitment, it may be difficult to explain Daddy's past. Do you teach them that a marriage is ideally forever—but not necessarily so in practice? Instilling in a child the confidence that her family is secure and her parents' marriage lasting is difficult when experience shows otherwise. Do you explain that your first marriage was "just" a starter marriage— "Don't worry, darling, this one is the *real* thing"?

Remarriage used to be uncommon, unseemly, and even disparaged, and certain religions still consider remarriage a sin.* In the past, most remarriages took place only after one was widowed. As late as the 1920s, more people remarried following a spouse's death than following a divorce. By 1978, 87 percent of all brides and 89 percent of grooms who remarried were divorced (as opposed to widowed).[3] Today almost half of American weddings in-

---

* According to one strict Christian reading of the Bible, marriage is not only a love commitment but also one that joins two bodies of flesh into one, creating a bond of kinship. While one can dissolve the love relationship through a legal divorce (which is usually permissible under certain extreme circumstances like adultery, incest, or physical abuse), one cannot destroy the bond of flesh. Therefore, remarriage is viewed as a form of adultery.

clude at least one spouse entering a union for the second, third, or fourth time.[4] Most divorcés remarry quickly—about half of all remarriages take place within three years of divorce.[5] Five out of six men and three out of four women remarry within four years.[6]

Remarriage is also becoming more socially acceptable. Wedding planners tactfully refer to such affairs as "encore marriages." The eternally optimistic *Bride's* magazine recently added a section devoted to remarriage, and in 1999 twice married Beth Reed Ramirez started a new quarterly magazine, *Bride Again,* which now boasts over half a million readers.[7] Second weddings are often quite different from firsts. "The first time I got married it was this huge, costly affair," says Clara. "The second time was so much better—and it cost half as much. It had a completely different feeling because it was about us, not about other people and all these traditions that you're supposed to follow. It was much smaller and more personal. We walked down the aisle together."

Divorcés like to remarry. In fact, they marry at a higher rate than the general population. Seventy-five percent of divorcés end up retying the knot.[8] "I had really positive ideas about marriage," explains Clara, "and that didn't change. Even after my divorce, I never was turned off to the idea of marriage. I just had a better understanding of myself and what I needed and how I had to grow before I got married again."

While almost every single person interviewed wanted to marry again, some expressed trepidation about the idea. "I was so afraid of dating again," says Bethany. "I was alone for fourteen months afterward. I felt like I was such a mess, it wasn't fair to impose myself on other people. I didn't know if I would be capable of loving someone again or if someone would ever love me. I felt like I must have been pretty unlovable if somebody could just walk out on me like that. . . . It took a while to get over those feelings."

"When I decided to leave my marriage, I remember thinking, 'There's a big chance that you will never meet someone else and you will be single for the rest of your life, can you deal with that?' " Elizabeth recalls. "And I could, even though the idea was very sad to me." While many divorcés fear they'll never meet the right person, others lose faith in their own judgment. "I don't trust myself as much in relationships anymore," Max says. "I'm unsure about everything. I don't know if this is the right person, I don't know if I really love them. I ask myself a lot more questions than I did the first time around—which I think is a good thing." Jodie, recently divorced, feels the same way. "It makes me nervous. Even if I do get married, I don't know if I could wear a ring again. Taking my ring off was the hardest thing I've ever done in my life. I was so aware of what was happening emotionally and how it physically made me feel because I constantly felt the absence of a ring on my hand. I honestly don't know if I could put myself through the possibility of divorce again."

Whereas many people feel that their first marriages were entered into hastily, young divorcés seem far less likely to jump a second time without giving it serious thought. The majority of young divorcés are convinced that they are now much better equipped for marriage. "In some respects, I feel like I have a better shot at a successful marriage if I do get married again than people who have never been married," says Elizabeth.

Historically, the odds that divorcés remarry are good but the odds of succeeding in a second marriage less so. Remarriages fail at a higher rate than first marriages—60 percent risk of failure versus 45 percent the first time. In fact, the more often you marry, the less likely your marriage is to succeed.

However, it remains to be seen if those odds apply to starter marriages. While studies have shown that second marriages end in divorce more frequently than first ones, these statistics were compiled on earlier generations, who as we've seen were living in a different social climate.[9] Those remarriages often took place after marriages involving children. Alimony, custody issues, and stepparenting add burdens that make them inherently less stable. Starter marriage divorcés have relatively little of the complicated baggage that many previous first marriages included.

Those who have subsequently remarried (so far, slightly less than one third of those interviewed) point to fundamental differences in their second marriages. All of them contend that these unions are infinitely happier, more mature, more stable—and in some cases, already longer-lasting. Several remarrieds have become parents and expected to raise their children in their intact families. Most feel they never would have made it into their new marriage if it hadn't been for their first. "I consider myself very lucky in life," said one twenty-nine-year-old man interviewed a month before his remarriage. "I feel like I got a second chance ... and I don't think I could have fully appreciated my current fiancée unless I had gone through what I had gone through. I believe in fate. I believe in going through life's lessons. And I've gotten a lot clearer and more focused. I certainly know now what *not* to do."

Marriage That's Worth a Lifetime

Everyone who has been through marriage once knows they don't want to go *through* a marriage again—they want to stay *inside* it for life. But how can we be sure that we won't leap out of a second marriage the same way we did with our first?

Those who have remarried cite several keys to establishing strong remarriages, lessons attributed to their starter marriages. The first step is getting a grip on the concept of marriage itself. Most experts agree that much of a marriage's success depends on the ways in which both spouses conceptualize their marriage. Not only should both individuals have a clear understanding of what marriage is, what marriage means to them, and what's necessary to create that kind of marriage, but those ideas should be the same or very similar. Robert says that neither he nor his wife took their marriage seriously enough. "We were just like, 'Okay, let's have a relationship built on absolutely nothing other than a physical relationship and the fact that we're both Latin.' It was built on the most shaky foundation you can imagine." He decided to divorce because "it wasn't working and it never would work. We were too different, we weren't in love, and we didn't have any foundation whatsoever. No mutual goals, no vision of the future, no idea about the marriage; everything was wrong. I can't even begin to point to where things went wrong because things were never right. There was no basis for the marriage itself."

Yasmin, a liberal Palestinian-American, knew her marriage was done for when it became clear that she and her husband didn't even hold to the same concept of marriage. "I wanted this shared life of deep meaning ... a truly egalitarian marriage, and I asked him if he wanted to do the work necessary to attain that," she explains. "But he just said, 'Well, why can't we have a Bob and Liddy Dole marriage? They have separate lives, they go off and do their own things, and then they come home to have dinner together once a week.' And I just looked at him and was like, 'You're calling on a white, Republican, middle-aged couple as a model?' "

A good marriage is also about sharing a certain sensibility. And in order to find your like, you've got to know yourself. Marriage is something that should only be undertaken after a process of self-discovery. Before you've shaped your own identity, you're liable to either hold on desperately to the few aspects of it that do exist or submerge yourself entirely in the identity of your spouse. Either way spells disaster for a marriage. How can one give of oneself if one doesn't even know what that self has to offer? Sam notes, "I always thought that marriage would fundamentally change who we were as people. I was convinced that simply by being married, we'd be drawn in together and we'd develop this singular essence, when in fact marriage exaggerates any gap that's already there. It solidifies the individuals and where they were heading before they got married. If you happen to be heading in the same direction, great. But if not, there's very little chance of that happening once you're married."

This is the best case against marrying young—or more specifically, marrying before you've reached a certain level of maturity and stability. The idea of growing together sounds lovely, and while it can and does occur within marriage to a degree, when two people are barely formed themselves, they are liable to grow in very different directions. Some may argue that the older one gets, the more fixed one becomes in one's own ways and the less likely to compromise, but the reality is that growth and maturity are precisely what enable people to become more generous and adaptable.

The Balance Between Intimacy and Independence

The constant struggle in almost all marriages lies in maintaining one's own identity while achieving some kind of deep intimacy. Most of us expect both too much intimacy from the other and too much independence for ourselves. Basically, we expect too much.

Part of the solution is to stop aiming for some fantasy state of absolute integration. It doesn't make sense for one's partner to become a complete extension of oneself. As Barbara Ehrenreich writes, "Only in marriage do we kiss common sense good-bye and expect that every single human need can be met by a single all-too-human being."[10] Or as Michele Weiner-Davis, author of *Divorce Busters,* says, "The mental health profession has done a great disservice by telling people they'll find their soul mates. There is no such thing. In a long-term, happy marriage, people learn to negotiate their differences, work around them, or live with them."[11]

Most happy older couples exude a sense of contented, or perhaps resigned, separateness. "He's off doing his golf thing," she'll say cheerfully. "She's in there with the computer—God knows what she does with that machine all day," he'll report with a shrug. One thing that so-called traditional marriages often got right is understanding the need for a healthy separation of spheres between spouses. The difference in a modern marriage is that those lines need not be drawn according to gender.

At the same time, you can veer too far in the other direction. Researchers at the University of Washington have found that between newlyweds, frequent use of unifying words such as "us" and "we" and a significant amount of interaction in each other's daily lives are signs of long-term marital stability. Writer Nancy Mairs says of her own marriage, "What I might have thought of, in good aging-hippy [*sic*] fashion, as 'giving him space,' letting him 'do his own thing,' strikes me now as a failure of love. Respecting another's freedom does not require cutting him loose and letting him drift; the lines of love connecting us one to another are stays, not shackles."[12]

In a way, marriage poses a catch-22: if you're an independent and individuated adult, it sounds like you cannot sustain a successful marriage. But if it's only through the suppression of the self that one can be truly happy in marriage, then who wants it? Although the balance between self and sacrifice can be hazy and dangerous, a third alternative does exist. It *is* possible to fully share oneself in love without losing any of that self. In *Flux*, Peggy Orenstein found that the happiest marriages "described relationships that were a balance of independence and interdependence, that were rich with intimacy and a sense of play."[13] At its best, a marriage can be both free and grounded.

Ideally—Realistically—Equal

Much ado is made over whether "egalitarian" marriage is better than the traditional form of marriage, based on 1950s gender roles. The answer, unequivocally, is yes.

The reason lies in the meaning of "egalitarian." Proponents of "traditional" marriage argue that modern marriage is inherently unhappy and unstable because it insists on what its critics deem "precise equality," "total equality," or "perfect parity." But that is not what egalitarian marriage is about. Egalitarian or peer marriage does not mean equality nickeled-and-dimed onto some kind of scorecard. It doesn't mean men and women should be mathematically apportioned the same precise roles—any more than it means they should adopt assigned roles according to gender.

Most Americans today define marriage as a relationship between equals, understanding that freeing both men and women from restrictive roles improves marriage and makes it stronger. The majority of happy marriages are based on a division of labor that has little to do with gender and more to do with the abilities and interests of the individuals involved. And while indisputable inherent differences exist between the sexes, despite what radical evolutionary biologists tell us, we are not genetically predestined to rigid retro roles. Beyond the obvious basics (e.g., men are not going to be breast-feeding anytime soon) and in spite of our inherent and learned differences, both partners can share most functions within marriage.

Rigidity in either direction—prescribed gender roles or total parity—is what truly hampers a marriage. George and his wife had very different ideas about their roles. "My wife was more into the idea of staying home with the kids than I was. I bought into the notion that we would do it jointly and that there would be a balance with our careers. But I thought that if she didn't have a career, there would be a fundamental imbalance that would make her resentful. I also thought that it would be harder for me to relate to her if she were at home all day." In hindsight, he says, "I think she was more healthy about the whole thing than I was. She couldn't understand why I was so vehemently opposed to the idea. . . . It was a bit offensive that I wouldn't accept her choice whatever it was, I have to say now. It was a bit selfish."

An egalitarian marriage is one in which both spouses can choose what works best for them—individually and as partners. It means that not only is a woman not assumed to be the one who stays at home to care for the kids but that if she's able and willing, she can choose to do so. In turn, it means that a man can take a sabbatical or care for the children and expect that his wife will temporarily assume more of the financial burden. Noelle contrasts her first marriage with her second in terms of equality and balance. "With my first husband, I was always his strength. I was always a support system for him. I felt like I was his mother and I constantly had to take care of him in a motherly way. At the time I felt like it was God's plan that I took care of him. I did everything. But I wanted a partner in marriage, not a child. With my husband now, we're equal."

The best marriages seem to be ones in which responsibilities are shared because each partner cares enough about the other person not to want him to shoulder too much of the burden, not because that partner is so preoccupied with ending up carrying the bulk of the load herself. Rather than being obsessed with our own expected contributions and what our partner takes for granted, we could focus on what we can do, what jobs we do best, and what our spouse appreciates our having done. Giving to each other often has nothing to do with rights or assumptions or control but has everything to do with caring. It feels *good* to care for your wife when she's sick. It's *generous* to buy your husband those running shorts you know he needs but has been too busy to get himself. It's *kind* to be understanding of your partner's particular weaknesses, shortcomings, forgetfulness, or mistakes every once in a while. Every kind of giving needn't be considered a form of "giving up."

Lisa Krueger wrote the film *Committed* to act as a "potent rebuke to the self-centeredness, the cynicism, and the rampant Slick Willie–ism of our times." She intended the lead character, Joline, to exemplify strength of character. "The fact is that the character is really adhering to her vows in the most forthright, selfless, but not self-diminishing and, I think, actually, self-empowering, way," Krueger explains. "It takes so much strength to stay in it. We're so oriented toward getting what we need, we've lost track of giving, which is the real power."[14] "I know 'it's better to give than receive' is one of the oldest notions in the world," she comments. "But I feel like we've relegated that idea to the furthest back burner. We're very intent on getting what we deserve, getting what's ours. I see the pendulum swinging the other way. Because this endless getting, getting, getting is an empty goal."[15]

Krueger was disappointed by the reactions of many women to the film. "It breaks my heart that women in these preview groups were so violently offended by this lead character because they thought that she was demeaning herself by giving anything to a man. And yet I *knew* that would happen and I thought I was being really diligent to show that she's not just doing it for a man, she's doing it for herself—because that's the only thing people can relate to anymore. Showing people that generosity could be self-serving was the only way they'd accept it. Everyone is so worried about being used and taken advantage of and not getting what's their right, that it's difficult to show what a great gift it is to be loyal and giving and to have faith."

Marriage isn't meant to be tracked like some kind of running tab. Ideally in marriage one partner is meant to care equally, if not more, for his partner's well-being than for his own. And if this is true, it simply works better to assume that things will even out in the end than to bicker about petty imbalances along the way. If one can depend on one's spouse for the little things, it more naturally follows that one can depend on that spouse for the larger ones—to make the effort, to work things out, to stick around no matter what. Human beings were never meant to function on a purely individualistic basis; we are fundamentally social creatures. We not only desire the company of others—we need it, and we actually serve ourselves in the process of both needing other people and giving of ourselves.

Opportunity and Obligation

The other side of egalitarian marriage is a sense of mutual obligation. Modern marriage is by no means easy. When both spouses
work and have full, independent lives, there's obviously a great
deal of stress to deal with and overcome. Sometimes doing the
laundry for the sixth week in a row is not a wife's idea of an egalitarian arrangement or the generous thing to do, it's a pain in the
ass. But life's annoyances don't automatically cease because you've
got a shiny wedding ring around your finger.

   If anything, marriage adds a lot of new annoyances and incon-
veniences. "I don't think that my husband ever understood that the
marriage commitment meant that there was a certain obligation—
and that that wasn't necessarily a negative thing," one thirty-four-
year-old divorcée explained. "He thought that having to let me
know what he was doing was an obligation and that I was demanding that he ask permission. He resented me for it. But the
reality is that I thought that by virtue of courtesy and respect and
the acknowledgment of our bond he would want to check in with
me. I thought that was part of our commitment, but he didn't expect that at all. He saw it as a burden, that I was being demanding
and needy and overly expectant. He simply did not realize that
marriage does, after all, require certain things of both partners."

   Undoubtedly, a happy marriage, wherein both partners are
equipped with a strong sense of dedication, can be a frequent joy
and comfort. But even the best marriage has its downside. When
marriage is viewed strictly as a source of happiness and fulfillment
without an understanding of duty and responsibility, issues and
hardships—which arise no matter how good the marriage—
are more unexpected and more difficult to handle. Our positive
expectations are extremely high, while our expectations of the
negative side of marriage are naïvely, dangerously low.

   Marriage isn't all romance and ribbon-tied gifts. It's not something fun that you can simply acquire or buy or mine for benefits.
Marriage is about bringing together two individuals to build, producing something new through hard work, whether it be a sense
of the marriage as an entity unto itself or eventually through the
formation of a family. And because marriage doesn't elevate you to

some higher plane of existence (no matter what the fairy-tale marriage culture says), the responsibilities that you had in your previous life don't go away—they get bigger. Marriage is a tremendous responsibility; it's a duty and an obligation—both to your partner and to yourself. And it's in understanding this aspect of marriage that couples ready themselves to bring children into their families and raise them in an atmosphere of familial support and mutual reassurance.

One of the ways in which marriages derive strength over time is by the very fact that through dedication and obligation they endure. Sticking to a marriage through its rough spots ultimately strengthens the bonds of its participants in the same way that overcoming adversity or tragedy often creates or strengthens bonds between people, as a couple and as a family. Therein lies the opportunity. By the very act of being committed, the commitment itself is forged.

Expectations of Marriage

Perhaps it's time for us to lower our expectations—and raise them at the same time. We need to stop expecting the unrealistic of our spouses and our marriages, and start asking for and accepting responsibility from ourselves and from society. For one thing, we ought to stop treating our marriages like protected little fortresses. The Us Against the World attitude doesn't give marriage very good odds. Marriages are a fundamental unit of society; as such, they are meant to support and be supported by a network of family, friends, and community. Alexis de Tocqueville noted that in order for America's individualistic society to sustain itself, certain communitarian institutions like marriage and family must be supported as well. Amy observes, "I think in a lot of ways, marriage is not just a personal thing. I look at other people's marriages that have worked, and they all have extensive social circles outside the marriage. It helps to have a social network, both individually and as a couple. As much as people like to think of themselves as independent, they need that public affirmation."

As Steve Roberts writes in *From This Day Forward,* "Healthy marriages need those kinds of relationships and connections—as role models and advice givers and shoulders to cry on—as we've learned over and over through the years. Marriage is hard enough, and doing it in isolation without those support systems makes it much more difficult. . . . One of the key elements of keeping a marriage together is the community. The people who see you as a couple. The people who expect you to stay married, who reinforce the importance of marriage."[16] Barbara Ehrenreich proposes, "Now maybe it's time to cut the spouse some slack and put more of our demands on the rest of the human environment—in other words, to rebuild the ancient and honorable notion of community. How about friends for some of those long talky dinners? Extended family to help with the kids? Clever neighbors to turn to when the basement floods? . . . Not that husbands—and wives—shouldn't try to excel on all these fronts. But clearly, if marriage is to survive as an institution, they need reinforcements."[17]

The values of duty and obligation toward institutions like marriage have declined and weakened in American society. This is not an isolated phenomenon but the expression of a deeper shift in our common psyche and culture. Collectively, people today feel less of a sense of obligation toward their families, toward their spouses or partners, toward their communities, and toward social ties of all kinds. We live in the era of disconnect.

The impact of this failed community on marriage is twofold: first, the lack of support for single people and for people who seek alternative arrangements to marriage sends people who probably shouldn't be marrying into a state of unstable matrimony. And second, once they are married, the community fails to support them within that marriage, instead subtly and not so subtly hinting that marriage should be happy and self-sufficient on its own. To suggest otherwise is seen as undermining the very institution of marriage itself—and that's doing marriage a great disservice.

Chapter 10

The Politics of Marriage

AMY REALIZED SHE WAS A LESBIAN ABOUT THREE YEARS into her marriage. For a long time she suppressed her sexuality because she was Catholic, married, and committed to her husband. She told herself she was bisexual and stuck by her vows. It wasn't until she met a woman with whom she fell in love that she was able to reconcile herself with her sexuality and ask her husband for a divorce. "I was so unhappy I finally told him, 'You deserve to be with someone who can be physically in love with you. It's not fair, you deserve so much more.'

"It was my self-discovery and my decision to call off the marriage," she explains. "If I were not a lesbian, I would still be married."

Amy's parents were very conservative, and she feared telling them about her decision. "Finally I just called them up and said, 'I have good news and bad news. The bad news is, I'm getting a divorce. The good news is, I'm a lesbian.' I think I just needed to get it all out." With help from a lesbian counselor, she and her parents were able to reconcile and reaffirm their relationship.

Now twenty-five and living with her girlfriend, Amy says, "I'm so happy in this relationship. I wouldn't be who I am today without my marriage and divorce. And maybe [my current partner] wouldn't love the person who I would have been otherwise." Amy is a firm proponent of gay marriage. "Marriage should be open to people no matter what their sexuality," she says. "It's not fair that a certain set of laws only applies to a certain set of people. It's hard to even visit your partner in the hospital when you're not married." As long as married people get certain benefits, Amy believes, marriage will unfortunately be made into a political issue. Though as far as she's concerned, "I'm married to my partner in my heart. I don't get any privileges for that except being happy. And that's the way marriage should be for everybody."

"Sometimes when we're having a bad day, we'll kind of joke about it. We'll say, 'Oh, let's get married and have children! Let's let everybody know that we're together permanently.' We want that social recognition. We don't want people to think that we're just lovers or just roommates. We want to be socially accepted as a permanent union. Especially before we have children. The first time, I got married for all the wrong reasons. This time around I would marry for my children and my family."

Amy attributes the current focus on marriage to the debate over gay unions: "I think people are taking marriage a bit more seriously now," she says. "With same-sex marriage in the news, I think the general population is starting to look at the institution of marriage itself for the first time in a long time, and deciding that it needs to be taken more seriously."

Marriage has become a major political issue in America, as policy wonks, pundits, and lobbyists all try to impose their definition of marriage and their demarcation of who should marry on the rest of the country. From the Defense of Marriage Act to the Marriage Penalty Relief Act, marriage is increasingly becoming a matter of political rhetoric and governmental policy. Marriage has always been a social and a public issue, but whether marriage and politics mix is another question. And why should *you* care if marriage has become politicized? Why should that mean anything regarding *your* engagement, *your* marriage, *your* divorce, *your* remarriage?

While it's true that few people plan their own lives in accordance with political arguments or public policy analyses, the impact of the politicization of marriage is changing the face of marriage in America. These issues are not only being argued, they are being acted upon—with a host of implications for how we lead our personal lives. This means laws that determine who can marry, who can divorce, and how we go about doing so. It means money, making its impact in terms of tax breaks, marriage subsidies, and divorce-lawyer fees.

The effects of politicization on the institution of marriage deserve to be examined by everyone who cares deeply about marriage in whatever forms it may take. Because in addition to the cultural pressure, the social pressure, and the self-imposed pressure, people are becoming aware of a *political* pressure to marry as well. And we're being painstakingly pushed in directions that we, and our marriages, shouldn't necessarily go. Politicians and policy makers may be homing in on "the marriage issue"—but not always in the most helpful way. Current concerns include falling marriage rates, the decline of courtship and "traditional" marriage, the rising age of those entering marriage, and the desanctification of marriage as an institution. Not enough people are marrying, so we'd better offer bigger rewards. Tax bonuses. Child credits. In the 2000 electoral campaign, Al Gore's tax package focused on "working families" with nary a penny for the single, widowed, or cohabitating.

The bottom line of most marriage policy hinges on stemming the supposed decline in marriage. The "pro-marriage" forces are far less concerned with unsuccessful early marriages than they are in herding the young into marriage. Rather than address the issue of why young marriages tend to fail and urging people to wait for marriage, they are encouraging young people, particularly women, to marry as soon as possible. *Get married,* they urge, though they don't tell us why. *Stay married,* they argue, but they don't explain how.

The Fuss Over Matrimony

Why has marriage become a political issue? What *is* it about marriage that gets people so worked up? In her essay "For Better and

Worse," Lynn Darling notes, "There's something profoundly threatening to our nervous age about the idea that marriage itself isn't working, as if without it we would have tossed out the last lifeboat. Having exchanged the extended family, the neighborhood bowling league, the two-party system, and the church social for the anonymous camaraderie of the gym and for Prozac's hearty slap on the back, we are down to a nation of two. The state of marriage has become the barometer for measuring the culture's decline, the porousness of its moral fiber."[1] Mulling over marriage policy has become a national pastime. According to one guide to future trends, "After the 'Me' decade" and "given society's growing concerns over the erosion of family values, it's no surprise that a Marriage-Preservation Movement is cropping up."[2] It's as if we've got to fix marriage because marriage is going to fix all our problems.

At the Population Association of America's annual conference in 1999, sociologist Linda J. Waite delivered a much ballyhooed paper entitled "Does Marriage Matter?" which was greeted by a flurry of excitable newspaper reports and attention from the punditry. *Marriage is good for you!* Dr. Waite discovered, and a host of statistics prove it. Though her findings seem rather commonsensical (among her earth-shattering discoveries were that compared with singles, married people have more sex, more money, longer lives, and happier children), the fact that she was able to provide "scientific proof " elicited whoops of joy from the marriage police, who used it to justify a bevy of policies. Opposed to welfare for unwed mothers? Here's proof that you're right—children born to and raised by married parents are happier and better off financially. In favor of sexual-abstinence education? Here's all the more reason—married people have more fulfilling sexual lives than their loveless single counterparts. Marriage statistics can be used as heavy artillery in political debate.

The most remarkable thing about Dr. Waite's report is that it met with such intense approval and attention, even though much of what she says is long established, obvious, and noncontroversial. As far back as 1858, British public-health statistician William Farr reported that married people outlive singles, and ever since then a host of researchers have been uncovering the whys and

wherefores of this kind of data, seeking comfort in its safe conclusions.[3] The public has traditionally welcomed such reports as
proof of their own deeply held convictions. Nonetheless, as Katha
Pollitt said of Waite's report, "She writes as if the nation were
teeming with anti-marriage zealots, women (naturally) who 'see
the traditional family, balanced on the monogamous couple, as
fundamentally incompatible with women's well-being.' "[4]

Yet it's hard to find any particularly new or dangerous threat to
marriage these days or to locate these crowds of women bent on
matrimony's destruction. The fact is that Americans *agree* that
marriage is a good thing, and they aspire to it. The marriage rate is
bounding along at a healthy clip. In 1994, 91 percent of women
were married at least once by age forty-five, only a small drop from
94 percent in 1960—before the supposedly massive decline in
marriage began.[5] The plain fact is, Americans love matrimony.
And those who put forth any argument generally do so *not* in an
effort to oppose those who marry but to point out the injustice of
making marriage the *only* choice. Many so-called opponents of
marriage have simply voiced the opinion that alternatives should
get equal treatment in a culture that extols marriage above all
other lifestyles.

Marriage is happy and marriage is big.

The Marriage Crisis

But not according to some people.

- "Marriage is in decline," laments Barbara Dafoe Whitehead of
  the National Marriage Project.[6]

- "The institution of marriage appears to be dying," warns James
  Dobson on his Focus on the Family website.

- "Not only is marriage in danger of disappearing, but though we
  do not fully recognize it yet, it already has," charges Maggie Gallagher of the Institute for American Values.[7] "The law no longer
  permits men and women to make permanent commitments to

each other. Marriage did not collapse from its own weight. It was ruthlessly dismantled, piece by piece, under the influence of those who (though they do not say it and may not realize it) believed that the abolition of marriage was necessary to advance human freedom."

If you could listen to a tape recording of American history, you'd hear an incessant background wail about the death of marriage. It seems that marriage has *always* been in crisis, that the imminent failure of marriage has forever troubled American society. In 1608 minister Robert Abbot bemoaned the "lamentable ruptures and divisions betwixt husband and wife everywhere to be seene amongst us." In 1915, at the height of the progressive era, William E. Carson wrote *The Marriage Revolt: A Study of Marriage and Divorce,* in which marriage woes were likened to "a national disease." Throughout the 1920s social critics despaired, convinced that "modern marriage" was fated to failure. A 1928 book *The Marriage Crisis* worried that marriage had simply become the means to sexual pleasure. The following year, Ira S. Wile and Mary Day Winn wrote *Marriage in the Modern Manner,* in which they complained that marriage in America needed "saving." Historian Nancy Cott's 2001 study of marriage in America, *Public Vows,* and Marilyn Yalon's *A History of the Wife* both provide ample evidence that marriage has always been an unstable institution. We just have more statistics and public polls nowadays to prove it.

But according to the self-appointed marriage police, marriage, the bedrock of social stability and cultural cohesiveness, is *really* in trouble now. A frantic sense of urgency permeates the current arguments. Listen to the cultural scolds as they bemoan the lack of monogamy among young adults. Hear them wail that cohabitation is on the rise. They're shocked by the levels of premarital sex. They're scared that people are marrying later. They're furious at working women for destroying traditional marriage. They're appalled at gay marriage for "denigrating" the basic tenets and purposes of the institution. What they consider normal marriage is long dead and gone.

Look at the numbers, they cry. The 2000 Census shows that only 23.5 percent of U.S. households consist of a married couple with children (compared with 45 percent in the early 1970s). In 1998, 32 percent of all households were unmarried people with no children—more than double the percentage in 1972.[8] Alarmists wave these figures as signs of a decaying society.

Yet such statistics can be misleading. Fewer households of married couples are also an indication of an aging society. Many households are headed by widows and older couples who choose to cohabitate. In 1998, 370,000 of the 4.2 million cohabitating couples were among people between the ages of forty-five and sixty-four. A significant number of couples over sixty-five also choose to live together (as opposed to marry),[9] a far cry from the stereotypical slacker kids shacking up in defiance of traditional values. Couples of all ages are choosing to live together monogamously, though most eventually intend to marry. And they're encouraged to do so on all sides.

The Marriage Movement

A new movement is on the rise, one that likes to think of itself as a major social cause. In June 2000, more than one hundred policy analysts, marriage researchers, clergy, judges, lawyers, marriage counselors, and sociologists issued a thirty-five-page document, "The Marriage Movement: A Statement of Principles," at the Coalition for Marriage, Family and Couples Education conference. According to David Blankenhorn of the Institute for American Values (which cosponsored the conference along with the Religion, Culture, and Family Project of the University of Chicago's Divinity School), the movement "is growing significantly. There's a growing sense of enthusiasm and commitment to social change, a blossoming of programs,"[10] aimed at resanctifying marriage and discouraging divorce.

A wide variety of organizations are taking part. Marriage Savers is a church-based group that aims to organize premarital counseling and marriage-mentoring programs at the grassroots level. Founder Mike McManus plans to mobilize two million married couples working as mentor couples in three hundred thousand churches in order to slash the divorce rate in half by the year

2010.[11] Now with branches in more than one hundred communities nationwide, they claim to have reduced divorce rates in cities like El Paso, Texas, by 63 percent and in Kansas City, Kansas, by 33 percent over the past three years.[12]

In 1997 the National Marriage Project at Rutgers University was founded as a nonpartisan, nonsectarian, interdisciplinary organization devoted to "revitalizing marriage." Among its activities is to "investigate and report on younger adults' attitudes toward marriage" and "examine the popular media's portrait of marriage." The Alliance for Marriage calls itself "a nonpartisan research and education organization dedicated to promoting marriage and addressing the epidemic of fatherless families in the United States." AFM exists to educate the public, the media, elected officials, and civil society leaders on the benefits of marriage for children, adults, and society. Its website describes reforms designed to "strengthen the institution of marriage and restore a culture of married fatherhood in American society."

At the Institute for American Values a research-and-advocacy division called the Marriage Project is headed by Maggie Gallagher, author of *The Abolition of Marriage: How We Destroy Lasting Love.* Like many of these organizations, the institute favors heavier involvement of the government in marital affairs. According to Gallagher, marriage is an appropriate area for government involvement, because it's an economic agreement as much as a romantic commitment. Like private property, she contends, though not created by government, marriage must be offered government protection for its maintenance.

Judging from the way things are going these days, Gallagher has little to worry about in terms of laissez-faire marriage. On the contrary, marriage has provoked a host of political activity. Over the last few years several states have passed bills creating incentives for betrothed couples to receive premarital education. In Florida, high school students are now required to take marriage classes, and the state recently announced a "sale" on marriage licenses, slashing the $88.50 fee to $32.50.[13] Across America, a number of states are launching their own marriage plans. In Arizona, one million dollars was set aside in 2000 to develop community-based marital-skills courses. In Kansas Senator Sam Brownback sponsored a marriage summit. In 1999 the governor of Arkansas, Mike Huckabee, sponsored a conference on marriage education and counseling after declaring a "state of marital emergency" and calling for a 50 percent reduction in the divorce rate. Huckabee also advocates a tax credit for couples who enroll in marriage class. Oklahoma governor Frank Keating is trying to reduce the state's divorce rate by 30 percent[14] by instituting a ten-million-dollar "marriage initiative" program to do marriage research and train people to teach marriage classes at welfare, health department, and agricultural extension offices.[15] Covenant-marriage laws were passed in Arizona and Louisiana (measures have been introduced in numerous other states and thus far rejected in twenty), allowing couples to choose a stricter form of religious marriage in which no-fault divorce laws don't apply (though only 2 to 3 percent of couples to date have elected this option). Florida recently mandated a three-day waiting period for weddings. (Strange that we can pass waiting-period laws for new marriages but not for the purchase of guns.)

Another "pro-marriage" position is repeal of the so-called marriage-penalty tax, which supposedly has dewy-eyed lovers avoiding vows to evade higher taxes. In reality, most current tax policies are wildly favorable to married couples,* with assorted marriage bonuses—dependent exemptions, education credits, earned income tax exemptions, tax brackets based on marital status, and child care credits—exceeding the so-called marriage penalty by roughly four billion dollars.[16] Nonetheless, the rallying cries have successfully reverberated in Congress from right to left, with many Democrats joining the crusade for the impoverished spouses-to-be. The bill's passage in 2001 proves that nobody wants to take a political stand against wedded bliss.

Much of marriage reform is mixed up with the nation's welfare policy. The Coalition for Marriage, Family and Couples Education advocates using "leftover" welfare funds to finance pro-

---

*Many arguments for gay marriage are indeed based on the range of economic, legal, and social benefits accorded to married couples and denied to their homosexual counterparts.

marriage programs. Utah established a Governor's Commission on Marriage, and Wisconsin has created the country's first public office of Marriage Counselor, a state employee whose job will be to work with clergy in establishing the requirements for church-based weddings. The program uses funds from the 1996 Welfare Reform Act, which conveniently included a vague provision allowing allocations for policies that "strengthen families."* Republicans cheered as a triumphant headline in *The New York Times* blared, "Changes in Welfare Bring Improvements for Families," over an article describing a study of welfare in Minnesota that claimed welfare reform had increased marriage rates by 50 percent and improved marital stability. In 2001 the conservative Heritage Institute urged the Bush administration to create an "Office of Marriage Initiatives" that would "make all federal social programs more marriage friendly" and find ways to lower divorce rates, particularly among welfare recipients.[17]

Making marriage into a tax and welfare issue offers a weirdly modern take on the more medieval marriages of the past. Historically, a bride was exchanged for a dowry and a husband took a wife off her parents' payroll. Today vows are paid off by a tax-reduction package. Reducing matrimony to a matter to be regulated via tax codes and economic incentives is not only out-of-sync with modernity, but it robs marriage of deeper meaning. Yet pro-marriage policy makers still want to up the ante. One proposal suggests that couples create a "marriage commitment fund" in which a percentage of their income is set aside annually to serve them in old age if they remain married. If the couple divorces, the fund is redistributed to their children. Even Gertrude Himmelfarb, a conservative historian and social critic who advocates policies to penalize the unmarried, concedes that like premarital agreements, such a proposal is "so calculating and materialistic as to create an initial skepticism about the marriage itself and ultimately to undermine the moral, to say nothing of the spiritual or romantic, meaning of marriage."[18]

---

*Part of this plan was eventually deemed unconstitutional by a Wisconsin federal judge.

A Return to Courtship

According to the marriage police, the problem with marriage begins with problematic premarital behavior. They argue that our departure from traditional gender roles has destroyed the rituals of dating and courtship. Contemporary social structures are not steering people efficiently toward marriage and are instead promoting serial monogamy, premarital sex, and cohabitation. In September 2000 the Institute for American Values issued a paper, "The Experts' Story of Courtship," to understand and address the issue.

A return to courtship would eradicate premarital sex, eliminate meaningless flings, and promote the end goal of matrimony, our current champions of chastity exclaim, as if in dusting off a discarded pebble they've uncovered a brand-new gem. Their argument is, after all, hardly new; conservatives like George Gilder (who views woman as the civilizer of the male beast) have been advocating a return to "traditional" courtship rules for a long time. Courtship advocate Leon Kass and his wife, Amy, stalwartly teach a course at the University of Chicago to promote the practice of traditional courtship rituals and morality: "Classical courtship begins by holding back sexual desire, and uses desire's energy to inspire conduct that will demonstrate devotion and gain devotion. . . . Courtship enables a couple to develop habits of the heart. Dependability. Fidelity . . . those are the goods of courtship if it has marriage as its end." In a 1997 essay "The End of Courtship," Kass asks plaintively, "Is there perhaps some nascent young feminist out there who would like to make her name great and who will seize the golden opportunity for advancing the truest interest of women (and men and children) by raising (again) the radical banner 'Not until you marry me'? And, while I'm dreaming, why not also, 'Not without my parents' blessings'?"[19]

True, when a long-married, sixtysomething professor makes the point, it doesn't have the same resonance as when eagerly outlined by an attractive twentysomething female. Enter Wendy Shalit. In *A Return to Modesty: Rediscovering the Lost Virtue,* the twenty-three-year-old author argues that women should return to the modest comportment of an earlier era, which would force ("inspire") men to conform to the strictures of courtship rituals and steer virginal women to marital bliss. Several freshly minted female voices like Mona Charen, Jennifer Grossman, Maggie Gallagher, and Danielle Crittenden are also leading this charge. Most of their arguments come down to the old wives' warning, "Why buy the cow if you can get the milk for free?"

Danielle Crittenden, former editor of the conservative *Women's Quarterly,* claims that "women are hurt most by the absence of these rules" because courtship rituals "protected a larger sexual order, one that ushered men and women into marriage at a younger age and kept them there by clamping down on extramarital temptations."[20] Maggie Gallagher agrees that marriage does the trick by "civilizing the erotic drives of men."[21] In the eyes of these abstinence aficionados, men seem to value women for sex alone. According to this reductive biological formula, a woman's intelligence, sense of humor, values, and talents provide little incentive to marry her. (Makes you wonder who the real "man haters" are.) "Ironically, when it comes to their roles within the family," journalist Jennifer Pozner notes, "feminists have much greater faith in men's potential as attentive husbands, dedicated fathers and loving partners than do many conservative women."[22]

For courtship fans who wax poetic about crinoline skirts and purloined letters, everything about romance seems to be biologically determined, rather an unromantic view of things when you get down to it. And when it's not biological determinism, it's a free-market ideology that guides our longing to love. ("It's very tough, in the aftermath of the sexual revolution," Crittenden explains, "to find men willing to marry and take on the responsibilities of family when there's a big supply of single women out there willing to sleep with them without demanding commitment.")[23] Yet reducing marriage to a neat little function of either biological determinism or cold-blooded capitalism is an insulting point of view that demeans both women and men.

Such black-and-white visions of marriage require a victim and a villain, an innocent party and a condemned culprit. The courtship contingent, ever ready, places the fault squarely with women. The charges generally run like this: women, and specifically feminists, set the ball rolling inexorably downhill by demanding economic and sexual freedom, both of which compromised femininity and negated the importance of masculinity. As Melinda Ledden Sidak of the conservative Independent Women's Forum explains, "Women, the traditional enforcers of sexual morality, abandoned their posts in the 1960s and 1970s under the onslaught of the sexual revolution. It never has been men who took the lead in enforcing the sexual code. Left to their own devices, men apparently are programmed to prefer sex with as many women as possible. It has been the special province of women to civilize men and to ensure a stable and secure economic and social position for themselves and their offspring by guarding fiercely the sanctity of marriage."[24]

Due to woman's "promiscuity," man no longer has any reason to respect her or treat her well. Instead he succumbs to his basest instincts, sleeping with her and rejecting the consequences, refusing to marry or cheating on her when he does, and eventually divorcing her guiltlessly to seek out younger prey. Clearly marriage cannot survive without premarital virginity, chaste womanhood, chivalrous maleness, a return to traditional gender roles within marriage, and the public vilification of every alternative. In short, marriage cannot exist without every advance of the women's movement systematically reversed.

Because according to many "pro-marriage" arguments, the women's movement bears a large responsibility—if not the primary responsibility—for the "collapse" of marriage in America. "The denigration of marriage—the famous nuclear family—was feminism's greatest failure," accused a 1998 editorial in *The Wall Street Journal*.[25]

The Rush Limbaughs and Phyllis Schlaflys like to hone in on the fringes of academic radical feminism and exaggerate these images further with incendiary language about "femi-Nazis," and naturally, the media latches on to the specter of such visually exciting extremists. Together they've managed to convince a generation of young people that feminism is all about bra-burning lesbian lunatics who hate men, scorn most women, and live lonely, ideologically driven existences punctuated by hairy-legged marches and protest signage.

It's shocking that such silliness persists. These characterizations, often politically motivated, oversimplify and distort the feminist legacy. First of all, the antimarriage, antimotherhood sentiment was always restricted to a small circle of radical feminists and mostly for a brief period of time. Though the women's movement was long established in America, it wasn't until the 1960s that feminism even became affiliated with the anti–double M's, with radicals like Kate Millett and Shulamith Firestone claiming the family as the source of women's oppression and urging women to abandon child rearing, and the radical group WITCH calling marriage "a dehumanizing institution—legal whoredom for women."

Bewitching or bewildering as this imagery may be, one must remember just how widely disputed these ideas were even at the time—often by other feminists. Such voices do not embody the breadth and diversity of feminism any more than Montana militia groups represent the political thought of the right. Just as all Republicans (or Democrats) don't ascribe to every other Republican (or Democratic) political agenda, each and every feminist adherent doesn't dictate every feminist woman's beliefs. Most feminists, like most women, not only support marriage and motherhood, they actively seek ways to promote and preserve them.

What most feminists *do* object to is a government mandate for a rigidly defined family structure predicated on male heads of household and stay-at-home wives—and not because it promotes marriage but because it constrains it. Mainstream organizations like the National Organization for Women have always argued that strengthening women by giving them ways to achieve their goals outside of marriages strengthens the marital bond. The idea of liberalizing the workplace doesn't mean that a woman *must* work if she has the money and desire not to—that would be just as oppressive as the assumption that she must be a housewife. So while most feminists argue that other choices should be allowed (and certainly not stigmatized), it's equally acceptable for women to choose to be stay-at-home moms.

The fact is, from the inception of the women's movement its most driving issue wasn't voting rights or abortion rights or the ERA—it was the rights of wives and mothers. In the nineteenth century, issues surrounding motherhood and marriage were central to the women's movement. As proud mother Elizabeth Cady Stanton put it, "Maternity is an added power and development of some of the most tender sentiments of the human heart and *not* a limitation." Women's groups fought hard to pass Married Women's Property Acts enabling women to retain their own property and wages after marriage (before, a woman's worth was automatically ceded to her husband). And in the 1980s women legally won the right to own their bodies after they married; with the passage of the laws against marital rape, it was no longer assumed that a wife's body was the property of her husband.

Today's so-called postfeminist era actually marks a return to some of early feminism's roots: marriage and children. Gloria Steinem's public statement following her own wedding attests to these eternal concerns. "I've worked many years to make marriage more equal.... I hope this proves what feminists have always said—that feminism is about the ability to choose what's right at each time of our lives."[26]

Feminism has been attacked for its premise that women can "have it all"—a futile promise falsely ascribed to the movement as an easy way to discredit it.* But Steinem, like most women, has always concurred that we can't have it all (at least not all at the same time). Something's got to give—there's no such thing as full independence on all fronts, or independence at any cost. Both men and women have to make choices, whether that means choosing not to marry, choosing not to work, or choosing not to have children; at certain times, sacrifices must be made. What's important is for both men and women to have the ability to make that choice instead of having it dictated by the state or a rigid society.

Unfortunately, this kind of flexibility and equality seem to threaten those whose marriage prescriptions rest on more "traditional" arrangements. For the courtship crowd, the destruction of marriage not only is women's fault, but the onus is on women to change. If she stopped giving sex so freely, refused to work, and demanded that men marry and pay her keep, men would follow, marriage would be fixed, and society would return to normal.

---

*If anything, the idea of "having it all" was a concept promoted by the advertising community in the 1980s to hit women on all fronts—as working consumers, earning consumers, and housekeeping consumers.

Unfortunately (or fortunately), the courtship ideal isn't "normal" at all—and never was. In their half-complete historical sketches, fans paint courtship as the natural, original, traditional way of the world. Yet courtship is more fairy-tale fiction than established institution, largely a cultural invention of the Victorian era and the 1950s. As Cathy Young points out in *Ceasefire! Why Women and Men Must Join Forces to Achieve True Equality:*

> This vision of male-female relations is strangely ahistorical, ascribing universality to twentieth-century courtship patterns: the woman withholds sexual favors until she has roped the man into "commitment." For most of history, men were hardly in a position to press for sex, since they were rarely alone with unmarried women. The bride and groom might never meet before the wedding; even in the West, unchaperoned dates are a modern phenomenon. Among peasants and the urban poor, the sexes mingled far more freely—and premarital sex was common. If a girl got in trouble, it was less her civilizing influence than that of her kinsmen's fists that harnessed the culprit into marriage.[27]

An important concession: even if their historical analysis is faulty, parts of the courtship contingent's diagnosis are undeniably true. Most young people find themselves highly dissatisfied with the current dating scene. A sort of mass insecurity pervades the process, with its muddied expectations and desires, practices and ends. Casual sex is dangerous and emotionally debilitating. It's hard to meet people—or at least meet the right people. (No wonder once people find someone they don't want to let them go. No wonder many people seem to marry out of fear of not finding "someone better.") There's a reason that *The Rules* sold more than two million copies.

Many of the old-fashioned customs and rituals involved in traditional dating are indeed conducive to serious romance. As sociologist Andrew Cherlin notes, "We have lost the ability to slow down the process of becoming intimate and choosing a partner. We have lost the assistance of parents and elders in the community, who were sometimes helpful and sometimes not. . . . Courtship was about waiting until you were sure."[28]

Yet courtship need not rely on the reductive roles that its proponents see as essential to—and perhaps the real point of—

courtship. A return to courtship need not translate into female submission and required stay-at-home motherhood, patriarchal authority and promise-keeper manhood. The structure provided by the invitation, the dinner date, the follow-up phone call, and the path toward monogamy is a comfort to many young people who feel lost in the mire of group dates, hookups, and messy friendships. Minus its political insinuations, the courtship proposal might be welcomed in some quarters with a wink and a semi-ironic smile.

COURTSHIP PROPOSAL: Women should eschew premarital sex and cohabitation.

REAL AGENDA: Women should revert to traditional gender roles (divinely ordered and biologically determined). They must be chaste or they'll end up brutalized, starved, unloved, and unhappy. According to Wendy Shalit, "Our mothers tell us we shouldn't want to give up all the hard-won 'gains' they have bequeathed to us, and we think, what gains? Sexual harassment, date rape, stalking, eating disorders, all these dreary hook-ups?"[29]

Marry Now

Another popular marriage proposal is very straightforward: more people must marry—the sooner, the better. This argument rides on two basic premises: a practical one focusing on the dearth of marriage opportunities in one's thirties and an emotional one that equates delayed marriage with doomed marriage.

The practical premise runs like this. Women place a primacy on career when they graduate from school. Instead of focusing on marriage early, they wait until it's too late, severely limiting or reducing their chances of finding a marriage-worthy mate. As Barbara Dafoe Whitehead warns, "The career strategy now favored by well-educated young women, in part to establish their own economic viability as a cushion against the likelihood of an eventual divorce, exacts a maddening cost of its own: it makes it less likely that they will marry in the first place."[30]

The emotional case for early marriage is that the longer you

wait to marry, the more people you sleep with, the more failed relationships you have, the more rejections you endure, the more
emotionally degraded and jaded you become—the less likely you
are to find a mate. And if such a hardened independent woman
manages to find a husband, she'll be so embittered, distrustful,
anxious, and self-obsessed that she'll doubtless fail at lifelong matrimony.

In her book *What Our Mothers Didn't Tell Us: Why Happiness
Eludes the Modern Woman,* Danielle Crittenden trots out both
theories. The problem with marriage, Crittenden declares, is that
"if women don't settle down at the same time as their friends, if we
insist on our right to lead sexually unconstrained lives into our
thirties and beyond, then we have to accept that there will be consequences to the long-term stability of *all* marriages, and even to
our own ability to marry."[31] Twentysomething females mistakenly
cherish their financial and sexual freedom above the obligations of
marital commitment. Instead of embarking on a career after college they should marry in their early twenties at the height of their
sexual powers (naturally, being accomplished, experienced, and
cultivated with age do not count as "attractive" enough features to
interest the opposite sex), and stay at home during their twenties
in order to raise children. Failure to adopt this plan has disastrous
consequences. Crittenden intones ominously, "By waiting and
waiting and waiting to commit to someone, our capacity for love
shrinks and withers."[32] Supposedly if one marries at a younger age,
this progression of events and subsequent personality developments could be avoided entirely. Instead, one would meld at an
early age with one's spouse, never developing the quirks, passions,
idiosyncrasies, habits, and convictions that could hamper a har-
monious union.

Yet it's unclear why men should marry younger or how young
men could support such a family on the single salary of his presumably low-level job. Nor is it apparent why or how men and
women should make such a pivotal decision just out of college,
when most have no idea what they want to do with their lives.
"That's ridiculous," says Elizabeth, a twenty-nine-year-old conservative Republican. "You're not old enough or mature enough at
that age to even know what a lifelong commitment is."

Furthermore, young women are no less eager than men to explore their independence or interests outside the home. As for women's careers, Crittenden breezily suggests that if they decide to work—and that's only if they're unusually ambitious—they do so after the children have "toddled off to school." Yet there's little incentive on the part of employers to hire such a person, someone who has spent the past seven years removed from developments in her chosen field, her college education long dormant, her work experience nonexistent. What kind of positions would these women be ready for? What jobs would potential employers care to offer, and for what kind of pay? It's difficult to believe that such a setup is even financially manageable. Furthermore, as the Centers for Disease Control and Prevention notes, "recent evidence suggests that the increasing economic independence of women may actually increase the probability of marriage because earnings and employment may make either partner an attractive potential spouse."[33]

There's absolutely no proof that it pays to marry young. In fact, all evidence points to the contrary. According to sociologist Larry Bumpass, "The inverse relationship between age at marriage and the likelihood of marital disruption is among the strongest and most consistently documented in the literature."[34] Bumpass handily refutes recent efforts to prove a risk to women marrying over the age of thirty.[35] Those who marry early tend to agree with him. Marriage researcher Barry Sinrod explains that in a poll of newlywed couples, "nearly all of those who said they regretted marrying were women in their early 20s."[36] Tom Smith of the University of Chicago's National Opinion Research Center has found that "women who marry in their early 20s are much more likely to be divorced within five years than those who wait."[37] Even the National Marriage Project concedes that there is no proof of greater success for marriages in the earlier twenties compared with those beginning in the late twenties and thirties. They conclude that a higher median age of marriage appears to have "a strongly positive effect" on the institution as a whole.[38] According to Stephanie Coontz, "Women who marry for the first time at age 30 or more have exceptionally low divorce rates."[39]

One wonders why Crittenden would argue that women in their early twenties are ready to marry when she herself acknowledges that "traits that are forgivable in a twenty-year-old—the constant wondering about who you are and who you will be, the readiness to chuck one thing, or person, for another and move on"[40]—are tendencies certainly not conducive to a long-lasting union. As one reader complained in an online chat with the author, "I'm not sure why you advocate marrying early and having children right away. I'm thirty-six years old. I'm not even remotely the same person I was at twenty-six—my goals, tastes, and profession are radically different now than they were ten years ago. Back then I was interested in musicians. Now I'm a little more sensible. I know for a fact that any marriage I would have entered into at that age would have dissolved long ago. God forbid I had had children as well!"[41]

The early-marriage advocates contend that if you marry young, you'll grow together. What they don't tell you is that growing older often means growing apart. "If we had been older and more mature, maybe I wouldn't have gotten married or it could have worked," says Clara. "But we were so young that by the time we developed our careers, we were going in completely different directions." Noelle, who remarried at thirty-three after her first marriage at twenty-one, balks at the idea of early marriage: "I'm living proof that when you get married young, you don't grow together. You grow up." An active Republican, she argues for marrying at a later age. "I had no right to get married that young," she says. "I had no idea who I was. I had no idea who he was. . . . Nobody at twenty-one knows how to get married. You have no idea. Getting remarried at thirty-three was a much smarter decision."

MARRY NOW PROPOSAL: Women should abandon their career ambitions for early marriage, wedding after college and having children right away before they're too old to run after them on the playground. Mothers should stay at home and only join the workforce (if they so desire) after their children reach school age. Otherwise, they'll end up thirty, single, and miserable, or if they do marry, they'll be too old and "independent" to make it last.

REAL AGENDA: The women's movement and big government doom women to loneliness and failure. (Crittenden: "The more pervasive the state grows, the scarcer decent, reliable men seem to become.")[42] Women should cede power in the marketplace to men. Families can afford to live on one income, and any governmental policy that suggests otherwise should be eradicated. And while we're at it, easing the tax burden would encourage the desired return to traditional, one-income families.

The Pedestal Proposal

The marriage police charge modern culture and the welfare state with denigrating marriage—and believe the government needs to do something about it. Maggie Gallagher says, "In almost every measure of human progress, the collapse of marriage drags down the fortunes of men, women, and especially children," and that we live in a "post-marital" culture marred by "declining health, declining fortune, declining physical safety, declining psychological security, declining education, and declining job attainment."[43] She and other social critics like Gertrude Himmelfarb and William J. Bennett agree that new laws are necessary to revive the institution of marriage, elevating it through social, economic, and legal incentives.

The idea behind these laws is based on two strangely contradictory lines of thought. The first is that the government has overstepped its boundaries by creating programs (such as welfare) that replace the private functions of marriage and family with various apparatuses of the state. The second line of thought is that new governmental programs enforcing these private institutions and promoting two-parent families (such as "marriage penalty" tax relief) are necessary. Stranger still that the small-government conservatives who back them see little conflict between the two.

The absence of stable marriages and intact families has led social conservatives, who fear that an increased reliance of women and children on the state displaces the role of men as breadwinners and providers, into an alliance with fiscal conservatives, who argue that the "decline in marriage" causes an increase in governmental expenditure. Barbara Dafoe Whitehead argues in her essay "Dan Quayle Was Right" that the erosion of marriage and the family "may lead to greater dependency on the resources of the state."[44] In *The Decline of Males,* anthropologist Lionel Tiger suggests that instead of being married to men, women today become married to the state welfare agency, a state of affairs he terms "bu-reaugomy." (This scheme apparently doesn't leave men in a very good position either. Tiger apocalyptically warns, "The male of the future is likely to be confused. Many will be undereducated and unable to assume a fatherly role. And the large number of mothers without husbands *will turn countless men into outlaws, not in-laws.*" [emphasis added])[45]

In other words, lower marriage rates mean bigger government. Increase the number of marriages, and government will become leaner and more efficient. Failure to do so will lead to social chaos and economic collapse.

For the marriage police, marriage is a zero-sum game. You sim-ply cannot say that marriage is a good thing unless alternatives are simultaneously seen as bad, and as they see it, the government supports other lifestyles over marriage. According to Gallagher, "Over the past thirty years, American family law has been rewrit-ten to dilute both the rights and obligations of marriage, while at the same time placing other relationships, from adulterous liaisons to homosexual partnerships, on a legal par with marriage in some respects. To put it another way, by expanding the definition of marriage to the point of meaninglessness, courts are gradually re-defining marriage out of existence."[46] Thus policies designed to strengthen "traditional" marriage usually entail denouncing other lifestyles. In order to make marriage privileged and desirable, eco-nomic and legal benefits must be awarded to married couples to the exclusion of all others.

Advocates of resanctifying marriage urge that other lifestyles not only be denied equal rights and benefits, but that they be stig-matized. If you want to revive marriage, you've got to come down hard on divorce, single motherhood, welfare, and the like. This "pro-marriage" stance is used to justify tax policies, anti–gay-rights legislation, and discriminatory insurance and housing policies. It seeks to eradicate any program designed to ease the burdens of single mothers, domestic partners, stepfamilies, and other "nontra-ditional" family structures. Many proposals to sanctify marriage are in fact efforts to dismantle an assortment of government pro-grams that accommodate alternatives. Their fear of "social engi-neering" makes the marriage police wary of any policy that seeks to support a lifestyle that might not otherwise survive under pure free-market economics. They argue against subsidies to single parents for fear of creating a nation of state-sanctioned and regulated unmarried families. Thus the "fight for" marriage becomes linked to everything from the war against communism to the death of welfare.

Much of this line of thinking comes out of a stark cold-war perspective. A strong sense of family is seen as a bulwark against the communal lifestyle of communism, with the family and the state poised in a permanent, adversarial relationship. According to this strict dichotomy, responsibility allocated to the state is removed from the family and vice versa, so that any aid to the family deprives it of its customary obligations, responsibilities, and functions and undermines its usefulness. To trust the state in any way is to *distrust* the family, and vice versa. Historian Elaine Tyler May notes the convoluted nature of this reasoning: "In the decade since the end of the cold war, right-wing politicians have called for a return to 'family values' of the early cold war years, blaming a wide range of social problems not on communist infiltrators, but on feminists, unwed mothers, 'welfare queens' and 'deadbeat dads.' Domestic containment is a relic of the past, but the family has landed in the middle of the American political background."[47] Yet those who argue so strongly for sanctifying marriage seem themselves to have very little faith in the institution. If marriage is the bedrock of a healthy society, then surely it's strong enough to function without an assortment of economic props holding it up. The pro-marriage forces seem to lack confidence in their own product. What's so great about marriage if you've got to give it a big ad campaign and marketing budget? Surely it is a desirable enough lifestyle that people will readily choose it over other alternatives, regardless of whether those other alternatives are penalized and downgraded.

Even if one agrees with the premise of resanctifying marriage, measures for carrying it out are problematic, with unintended consequences or implications. Take the new covenant-marriage laws. The message they send is that for regular marriages, divorce is perfectly excusable and even to be expected. Exalting one kind of marriage while scorning another does nothing for the institution as a whole (an argument that can also be made in favor of gay marriage).

There's also the question of whether marriage should or even need be put on a pedestal in the first place. After all, we seem to have pretty lofty ideals of marriage already. Our problem is not in idealizing marriage but in viewing it realistically and being able to cope with that demanding reality in order to reap marriage's realistic rewards.

PEDESTAL PROPOSAL: We need to resanctify marriage, making it more desirable, more beneficial, and more enduring.

REAL AGENDA: The state's duty is to legislate morality, legitimizing certain lifestyle choices while delegitimizing others, and traditional marriage is the only kind that works. Marriage should be "restored" through the creation of favorable social and economic incentives. In order to achieve these measures, married people should form their own "political class," lobbying and voting according to a pro-marriage agenda. This agenda entails publicly judging and denigrating alternative lifestyles, stripping them of any state support or social sanction. Discrimination on the part of landlords and employers in favor of married couples over those cohabitating should be reinstituted. Legal incentives should be awarded only to heterosexual marriages; premarital sex and unwed motherhood should be socially and economically condemned. Furthermore, we should restigmatize illegitimacy so that children of married parents are favored over those of the unwed.

Marriage Is <u>Not</u> a Political Position

Marriage is clearly considered a useful tool for making a larger political point. Everyone—liberals, conservatives, family-values activists, right-wingers, feminists, gays, children—cares about marriage, so when the M word is mentioned, all ears are cocked. But marriage itself is often merely a convenient symbol used to justify a range of posturing, grassroots proposals, and legislation. The marriage issue is distorted by the constant urge to nail a culprit—it's the fault of feminists, liberals, socialists, government, taxes. As it does to many moral issues, the politicization of marriage creates false dichotomies, forcing people into black-and-white positions on inherently gray issues. Ethical problems are not so easily conveyed through political rhetoric, nor are they readily solved through the political process, as is evidenced by the debate over abortion. In the highly charged world of abortion politics, pro-choice defenders are forced into formulating antiseptic, ultrascientific definitions of the miraculous potential of a human fetus. And antichoice crusaders find themselves in positions that hinder doctors and insist that women bring even rapists' fetuses to term. Nobody should be forced into an extremist stance on such an individualistic, highly personal decision. In the end, public moralizing should not and cannot replace personal judgment.

With marriage, the threat is just as strong and the implications equally disturbing. If you argue that divorce can be a good thing, you're labeled an antifamily hedonist. If you endorse the institution of marriage, you're considered a Christian Coalition moralist. It has become impossible to defend the rights of alternative lifestyles while still championing the virtues of traditional ones. Political proposals on marriage, with their polar swings between radicalism and reaction, reveal a near-total indifference to the reality of most Americans' lives. These prescriptions ignore that marriage is a personal choice and that it's one of several choices. And sometimes—gasp!—it's *not* the right choice for two particular people at a given point in time. Perhaps some women will find that premarital virginity or the early-motherhood model works for them. But these options won't work for everyone, and to recommend them as remedies to be swallowed indiscriminately is unduly restrictive. One can make other choices without condemning the institution of marriage to obsolescence.

In today's politicized atmosphere, divorced conservatives are made to feel guilty, happily married liberals to feel defensive. Conservative radio host Dennis Prager has claimed that "Democrats are saying to single women: you don't need to get married. You can marry the government—the government will be your husband."[48] But the desire to marry is a personal decision, not a political position. Liberals hardly think to themselves, "Well, the state could provide me with better loving support than I could get from a wife," any more than conservatives think, "Uh-oh, according to my political beliefs, I should get married soon! Don't want to be over thirty and single—that's the *liberal* lifestyle."

Making marriage into a political issue underestimates the complexities of human emotion. Regardless of one's political leanings or affiliations, marriage is at base a personal contract between two people who love each other. It is not something people enter into to improve their tax returns or carve a position on social issues. To politicize the decision to marry is to belittle it in the most simplistic way.

Another consequence of the politicization of marriage is that fundamentally centrist ideals have been corralled into the province of the right. The majority of Americans believe in marriage and family, but only conservatives seem to actively defend them. By grabbing hold of "the marriage issue," the right positions itself in line with mainstream America, even when many of its "pro-marriage" positions go much further—advocating male-headed families, discouraging women from working, et cetera—than most Americans are comfortable with. Because of this weighted agenda, it's become impossible to advocate marriage without implying a reactionary social agenda. It seems that one can't champion the values of duty, commitment, and responsibility and their inherent involvement in marriage without being pigeonholed as a right-winger. Yet obviously, liberals care for their spouses and family; they marry and value the institution of marriage to the same extent as conservatives. Commitment to a man doesn't take away from a woman's power, nor does it compromise commitment to oneself. The same is true for gays and lesbians, no less adept at "to have and to hold" than their heterosexual counterparts. Ties to others strengthen *all* of us as human beings.

Marriage is a centrist, humanist position—if it can be considered a "position" at all. None of the men or women interviewed wanted to return to retro roles, and those who had those kinds of marriages got out. In both ideological outlook and day-to-day reality, most couples work out some kind of exchange of rights and responsibilities based on their individual personalities, their respective strengths and weaknesses, and their interests. Not according to their political predilection.

Obviously marriage brings with it a wide range of economic,

cultural, and social implications. But rather than use marriage as a shield to cover up or obfuscate other serious issues like welfare reform, tax policy, and equality in the workplace, those issues warrant discussion on their own merits—and marriage is best left out of the equation. Ironically, one of the best arguments against politicizing marriage has been made by one of its most ardent advocates. "As more people of all political persuasions become concerned about the effect of the collapse of marriage," Maggie Gallagher writes, "reform proposals have begun to circulate. Almost without exception the proposed solutions are timid, abstract, inhuman, afraid of or unaware of the need to confront or engage the power of eros. A few might be minor improvements, but most are simply irrelevant and many would make matters worse."[49] Once marriage becomes the subject of a political debate it becomes privy to a host of underlying agendas. And clearly many of the current fixations—chastity, retro roles, early marriage, discriminatory tax policy—do nothing to benefit young marrieds and may very well harm them. They do nothing to prevent starter marriages— nor to understand and learn from their legacy. Ex–young marrieds are appalled by the politicization of marriage and by the messages its proponents send. "I think it's a great thing to publicly encourage marriage," says Joel, who describes himself as a centrist. "And people should have a better idea of what marriage requires, as long as it doesn't become too politicized. I mean, you don't want to start controlling who can get married and who can have children. If some government were allowed to deem a couple unworthy of marriage, that would be insane."

When it comes to marriage politics, no matter which side of the debate "wins," marriage is usually the besides-the-point loser. Political arguments surrounding marriage lead to a rush of judgment about other people's lives that inevitably ends up in confrontation, hatred, and usually, in the end, hypocrisy.

Marriage Is a Public Concern

Nowadays, the idea that "the personal is political" has come to mean that private choices determine public morality. Private choices are not your own business, but the state's. In other words, your choices are dictated by what you're required to do, not by what you want or ought to do given your individual circumstances.

Some will argue that because marriage begets family and family is the primary socializing agent in our society, marriage is an inherently political issue. This is mistaking a *public* issue for a political one. We should not confuse a societal concern with one that warrants campaign speeches, legislation, and taxation schemes. Clearly marriage cannot be entirely taken out of its social or historical context; our very understanding of marriage stems in part from our culture and our society. But marriage can be studied and discussed by sociologists, psychologists, and historians without being oversimplified and underanalyzed by pundits, pollsters, and politicos. "Marriage is a much more powerful force than politics," Laurel says. "The divorce rate is changing the face of our society, and we need to look at the repercussions of those changes and work within it, without expecting everyone to adhere to the same kind of traditional marriage. We need to find a way to work as a society in this new context."

It is not up to the government to uphold the sanctity of marriage. While everyone should be concerned about the general welfare of society and attempt to lead their personal lives in line with the type of society in which they'd like to live, the idea that our legislators will decide what kind of personal lives determine a desirable society is anathema to most Americans. Granted the marriage ceremony itself is coordinated by the state, but marriage continues as a nongovernmental enterprise long after the wedding day.

If we want to ensure the sanctity of marriage, we can do so through our own emotional and moral convictions—as individuals, through our relationships, and within the expanded network of our families and communities. The high incidence of starter marriages is important to us as a society, but rather than calling for political judgments and policy adjustments, people who have had starter marriages hope for personal exploration and public discourse.

Conclusion

Marriage in the New Millennium

Robert: "Marriage should be a community issue."

ROBERT GOT MARRIED WHEN HE WAS TWENTY-FOUR TO A woman he had dated for three months. "The second after we were married, I knew I had made a terrible, terrible mistake," he says. They were divorced within two years.

Robert's expectations of what one can get from marriage decreased at the same time that his understanding of what one must give to a marriage expanded. "I think it's a shame that as a collective, we don't know what it means anymore to make a commitment," he says. "My grandparents remained married until they died. Even my parents are still married. But we don't have any idea what it takes. . . . Our generation was told as kids that we could be anything we wanted. But the downside is that that doesn't teach you to have responsibility for anything other than yourself.

"Each successive generation gets smarter but, at the same time, more and more removed from the core beliefs of their tribe—and I think that's a problem," Robert says. "We're too damn smart for our own good. We think we know everything, and we don't see the value of our past and the communities we come from. I'm very much to the left, and I still believe that strongly.

"Marriage is not what it used to be," he laments. "Now it's just like a legal contract. Before, marriages took place within the community, and when the community takes an active interest and when the process helps further the needs of the community, the relationship is going to be stronger. But in our modern society we're so removed from our families and our base that we don't have that community, that foundation to fall back on. If marriages had that foundation in the community and that sense of roots and connections, they would be infinitely stronger."

In Robert's eyes, marriage has become degraded because people don't take it seriously enough anymore. "Marriage is way too easy to come by. It's harder to get a driver's license. It's so easy for people to jump into it without thinking about what they're doing." Robert believes everybody should be made to take a marriage class. "People are no longer taught about marriage. . . . The Pre-Cana is a good idea, though I think marriage classes should be taught by people who have been married for a long time. You learn from experience."

❧

Starter marriages could become the standard. Our marriages today are shorter and less stable. We divorce frequently and do so faster than ever before. And because we're living to an increasingly old age, a lifelong marriage has to last a whole lot longer. In 1900 the average life span was forty-seven years; today it's seventy-six.

We've got lots more marrying time. With the advent of puberty at an ever-younger age on the one end and with Viagra and "treatable" menopause extending sexual activity on the other, our sexual lives are lasting longer. People could begin marrying even younger as the age at the onset of adolescence lowers and premarital dating takes place over a longer time span. This means entirely new things for marriage, which once lasted fifteen or twenty years before a spouse's death marked its end.

Given the new biology, both natural and pharmacologically induced, marriage at twenty-five can mean a sixty-year active commitment. With almost twice the time to be adults, should we insist on an entire lifetime of marriage—especially when active parenting only absorbs about twenty years? Or perhaps, given changing biological and social realities, a series of two, three, possibly even four marriages might make more sense. A 2000 report in *Newsweek*, "Feeling the 50-Year Itch," notes that "seniors aren't waiting around for death do them part." Though most states don't track divorce rate by age, Maryland found that the divorce rate among men over sixty-five has risen by 11 percent in the last twenty years.[1] Could marriage for life be dead?

Multiple predictions of twenty-first-century marriage support the claim that the future will bring a series of marriages per person. Back in the 1970s, Alvin Toffler predicted in *Future Shock* that rapid change would bring about "temporary marriages"—different relationships for each stage in life. A 1996 report by the World Future Society foresees "serial marriages" as the wave of the future: "Almost surely there will continue to be people who have three, four, or five spouses, without any intervening widowhood."[2] In 1999, Barbara Ehrenreich predicted that in the twenty-first century "there will be renewable marriages, which get reevaluated every five to seven years after which they can be revised, recelebrated or dissolved with no, or at least fewer, hard feelings."[3] Writer Lynn Darling suggests, "Instead of getting married for life, men and women (in whatever combination suits their sexual orientation) should sign up for a seven-year hitch. If, at the end of those seven years, they want to reenlist for another seven, they may do so. But after that, the marriage is over. Those who wish to stay together after that may live in what used to be called sin."[4]

Sociologists call this "conjugal succession"; most people refer to it as serial monogamy, and many think it's inevitable. The book *Next: Trends for the Near Future* predicts, "Among the results of our diminished attention span will be the growth of serial life partners. . . . Already many Baby Boomers are admitting that the institution of marriage doesn't work for most people their age":[5]

> In an era in which people entering the workforce are likely to have five or six careers over a span of five or more decades, we'd be naïve to assume that one's shifting needs will be met by a

single life partner. Given the unprecedented rate of change in our world, people now live multiple "life spans." And the recently announced breakthroughs in cellular research suggest that one's "productive" years might soon extend far beyond what the average person experienced during the 20th century. Will second, third, and even fourth families become increasingly common? Will movement from one "life" to the next be prepared for and celebrated?[6]

Futurist Sandy Burchsted estimates that people may eventually marry an average of four times over the course of a lifetime. According to Burchsted, within the next one hundred years marriage will come to be seen as a "conscious, evolutionary process" that begins with the "icebreaker marriage." Icebreaker marriages (basically starter marriages) last no longer than five years, during which time couples learn to live with a partner and divorce without stigma "once disillusionment sets in." The second marriage is the "parenting marriage," which lasts fifteen to twenty years and ends when the children are grown up and gone. This is followed by the "self-marriage," in which one seeks self-actualization without the burden of raising a family. Finally, there's the "soulmate connection" marriage for the twilight years, which is an equal partnership of spirituality and marital bliss.[7] "The truth is that Americans are nuts about the institution," Peter Godwin writes in *The New York Times,* "so much so that, unlike their parents and grandparents, they enter into it three, four, five times, or more."[8]

But to marry repeatedly is to fit old patterns into a new social and biological reality. Rather than repeat ourselves at regular intervals, we could instead stretch out our life decisions to accommodate our life spans. We could delay our decisions about what we want to do with our lives, whom we want to marry, and what kind of families we want to build until our thirties, rather than make such decisions in our twenties, with the expectation that we'll make new decisions in five years' time. Our lives could be adjusted accordingly. For example, it may make more sense to delay our marriages until our thirties but *not* delay childbirth within the marriage, serving within the first year or so one of the main functions of marriage and solidifying its foundation. This would put us more in line with the stable families of yesteryear, as well as with the economic and biological realities of today. Call it the new traditionalism.

The New Traditional Marriage

It's not true, as Pat Robertson claimed during the 1992 election campaign, that "a socialist, antifamily political movement that encourages women to leave their husbands, kill their children, practice witchcraft, destroy capitalism and become lesbians" is taking over the country. Nor is it true that the Clintons' Monica mess indicated some kind of death to the family ideal. In a 2000 Roper poll, "protecting the family" ranked number one among fifty-seven values that Americans hold dear. Diane Sollee, director of the Coalition for Marriage, Family and Couples Education, is optimistic. "I think that what's going to happen in the next millennium is a marriage renaissance," she predicted at a 1999 conference on family policy.[9] In a 2000 poll a majority of Americans said that "as society continues to progress" marriage will become a *more* desirable option for young couples.[10] And 50 percent of Americans say they're optimistic about the institutions of marriage and family, up from 41 percent in 1995.[11]

Other positive signs support the security of our matrimonial future. According to the U.S. Census, two-parent families have started to "stabilize in the 1990s" and the divorce rate is dropping: from 5 per 1,000 in 1985 to 4.3 percent in 1997.[12] A 1996 article in *The New York Times,* "Traditional Family Stabilized in the 90s, Study Suggests," cites a report issued by the Population Reference Bureau* that claims that with the divorce rate declining, the number of two-parent households increasing, and the decrease in births to unwed mothers, the major changes in the family structure are probably passed. Even the generally pessimistic National Marriage Project talks about a new "familism" that has emerged in

---

*A private, nonprofit organization that uses Census Bureau data and other sources to paint demographic portraits of the United States.

recent years. Many believe that a process of "renorming" is taking hold, with a commitment to marriage on the rebound. In a lecture given to the Beverly LaHaye Institute's 2000 forum, "Marriage in the New Millennium," social theorist Francis Fukuyama cited anecdotal evidence pointing to women's return to the home in what he described as "well-to-do, professional, middle-class families," and a change in the postfeminist cultural biases opposing such choices. The causes behind these changes are certainly open to debate, but evidence suggests that we are in the throes of what historian Ann Douglas has called a "retro quiver."

The factors leading Gen X to marriage are even stronger for the next generation. *American Demographics* notes a "trend of early coupling" among Gen Yers and predicts that the ascent of Generation Y will yield a "second coming of family values."[13] Today's teenagers are zipping forward at a faster rate than ever. According to one major study, 17 percent of seventh- and eighth-graders have had intercourse; other studies place the percentage even higher.[14] In other ways, rapid change has marked this new generation. Today's teens live increasingly in fractured families. Eleven percent of children are born to unmarried, cohabitating parents,[15] and one of every four children growing up in the 1990s will have been raised at least part-time in a stepfamily.[16] They may be even more eager than Gen X to fix up families of their own.

Generation Y or the Echo Boomers—those supposedly bratty, degenerate kids brought up by Baby Boomers—are actually much more conservative than their parents. In a 1999 poll of college freshmen, the market research firm Louis Harris found that the majority (85 percent) cite clear differences between their own values and lifestyle and those of Mom and Dad. They trust their grandparents over their parents. According to the poll, honesty and integrity are the attributes they hold most important, and they strongly value community, cooperation, and loyalty as well. And they very much want to get married. In 1998, 72 percent of high school senior boys and 81 percent of girls said that having a good marriage and family life is "extremely important."[18] Ninety-six percent of those polled plan to marry, at an average age of twenty-six. Ninety-one percent hope to have children—on average, three.[19] A 2000 *Newsweek* study of teens concluded, "As a group, today's teens are also infused with an optimism not seen among kids in decades."[20]

Young people today, even after they divorce, clearly subscribe to family values. According to Joel, "The term 'family values' has gotten this stigma attached to it because of the hypocritical ways in which it's been used to denigrate realistic situations like the divorced family or the single-parent family. But for me, it's about creating an emotionally supportive environment within the family. It's about a constant education for both parents and children. I can't wait to teach my kid stuff, to tell him what I've learned, and to give him guidance." In many ways, starter-marriagee views are wiser and more sophisticated than those of the aging family-values moralists—they seem to understand implicitly that the idea of family has always been a fluid one, much like marriage, and to rigidly promote one recent variation is both ahistorical and unnatural. "I think the people who have appropriated that term don't know what family values actually mean," says Jodie, a liberal Democrat. "For me, it's about loving and caring for the people you consider your family, whoever they are."

The young divorcés interviewed all believe that their starter marriages led them beyond abstract ideals to the realities of family values. Clara, a politically active Republican, says, "It's a term that in many people's minds conjures up antigay, right-wing groups that teach hate and not acceptance. But for me it's about the Golden Rule, treating people as you want them to treat you. Loving and respecting others. If more people thought that, it would change the way people treat one another." For Zoë, "Family values mean you only have one family so you better love them as best as you can while you have them. Love your children with everything you have."

While some critics may bemoan the fact that only 2 percent of Americans define family values as being about the nuclear family (an invention that's actually so recent demographers have trouble tracking it before 1940),[21] is it really so bad that fully 90 percent of American women define family values as being about "relationships, loving, and taking care of one another"? Or that 88 percent of women today believe they are responsible for taking care of their families?[22] If conservatives are so bent on weaning a supposedly dependent populace off governmental support, they might celebrate the fact that the majority of Americans profess to want to take care of themselves. Such caring need not be restricted to narrowly defined nuclear families.

It may not be family itself that is at risk so much as certain narrow conceptions of the family. A 1999 poll found that 93 percent of Gen Xers, 89 percent of Boomers, and 86 percent of Matures agreed with the statement "Being a 'traditional' family is not about having a stay-at-home mom, it's about having a family built on love and strong moral values." Seventy-six percent of those surveyed believed that a single-parent household is "just as much a family as one with two parents."[23]

Today families can be seen as growing closer, reaffirming the intergenerational bonds that were so strong in the earlier half of the nineteenth century. According to a March 2000 article in *The New York Times,* intergenerational ties are strengthening in America: it's "as if increasing individualism had reinforced the value of kinship." More people living alone, children returning to the nest after college, and stronger relationships between adult children and parents have all served to strengthen families, albeit in a somewhat roundabout way.

This is in line with how many demographers describe the modern family. Instead of being tightly knit nuclear bubbles, today's families are larger and freer. They are apt to include communities and churches, grandparents and aunts, stepparents and stepsiblings. Instead of an emphasis on blood and obligation, the focus is on choice and caring. Steven Nock, a sociologist at the University of Virginia, says that in some ways today's marriages are more traditional even than those of the 1950s. He compares today's dual-income egalitarian couples to their nineteenth-century counterparts, who, in a more agrarian society, worked equally at home and in the field. According to Nock, today's marriage is "a very traditional model that's emerging. It's one where there's an interdependency that holds people together in those inevitable hard times."[24]

This new vision of marriage and the family frightens those wedded to a more formal interpretation. Some warn that the transition from a prescriptive to a voluntary conception of family weakens the bonds of kinship. Social critic Gertrude Himmelfarb contends that as "people move in and out of families at will," friends will gain equal ground with blood relatives, and obligations will be voluntarized rather than taken as givens. "This is the meaning of divorce, serial marriages, cohabitation, single-parentage, and 'alternative lifestyles,' " she explains. "The 'family of choice' is defined not by ties of blood, marriage, or adoption, but by varieties of relationships and habitations among 'autonomous,' 'consensual' adults and their offspring."[25] Such dire warnings overstate both the reality and the potential threat of these new kinds of relationships. Rather than releasing the family from its traditional obligations, this new version in many ways extends and reinforces them. Many aspects of this "new" family actually recall the small-town-based families of an earlier era. A network of people supporting the family is infinitely stronger than a weak smattering of nuclear bubbles, each indifferent to the needs and concerns of the bubble next door. Besides, the cold war is over, free-market capitalism reigns, and there is no longer any serious threat (if indeed there ever was) that strengthened community ties will lead to communism.

The way in which we view social changes today will be very different from the way we look back on them twenty years from now. Time and again, we have seen a social phenomenon derided and decried by its contemporaries only to have later generations cite it as a positive development. For example, what many see today as the epitome of family values, the rise of the 1950s nuclear family, was in its day viewed as a social disaster. Contemporary conservatives thought that women marrying younger and leaving the family home early to start their own families meant the demise of the "traditional" family, which was then thought of as intergenerational and extended. Little nuclear families sprouting Jimmys and Sallys meant that the younger generation was abandoning the older one. Furthermore, in the 1950s nearly half of women were marrying in their teens, which we now know is dangerous for long-term marital stability.[26] So when we look back at the reality, in terms of family values, even the exalted 1950s weren't all that.

It's easy to conclude that the starter-marriage trend bodes ill for the state of marriage. After all, we're getting married, screwing it up, and divorcing—a practice that certainly isn't strengthening our sense of trust, family, or commitment. But though starter marriages seem like a grim prospect, there is also an upside. For one thing, if people are going to divorce, better to do so after a brief marriage in which no children suffer the consequences. Our parents' generation and the Baby Boomers often tore families apart before embarking on second marriages. When you contrast our first marriages with those of our parents, the picture doesn't look quite so bleak. Maybe we're getting our earlier, naïve, more unstable marriages out of the way before it really matters—or at least before it negatively impacts our children. Perhaps we'll learn from our early marital mistakes and bring our children into new, more stable second marriages. Perhaps our second marriages, unburdened by the complexities of stepparenting, will be more successful than those of the previous generation. "When I went into my first marriage, I went in expecting to succeed where my parents failed," Ben says. "I pretty much failed miserably, but at least I did it without involving kids. By getting a divorce when I did, I became a hero because I saved our future kids from what would have been an agonizing experience. We were headed for a surefire divorce, which would have been a terrible thing for children. I may have made one mistake, but I avoided another."

George thinks starter marriages draw undeserved criticism. "I have to say, I'm a bit of an optimist. If there is a surge in starter marriages, I don't think that's necessarily a negative thing. Many fewer people are trapped in unhappy marriages, and people are figuring it out before they have kids, rather than after."

The Future of Starter Marriages

But while starter marriages shouldn't be demonized nor their participants cast as social pariahs, they shouldn't be entered into willingly or celebrated and certainly they should not be encouraged. No young divorcé would wish a starter marriage on anyone. He might wish the education that such an experience gave him, but certainly not the terrible pain it entails. "My sister is only twenty-seven, and I just cringe at the idea that she's married so young," says Juliet. "I wouldn't want my worst enemy to have to go through a divorce—never."

Clara agrees. "It seems like there are so many people my age who are divorced. It's amazing how many people I meet who've been through a similar thing. But I'm hoping that it's starting to go back the other way. I would hope that at this point, enough people have seen what happens with these impulsive marriages and become more cautious. That they think things through. I know that my twenty-three-year-old brother is a lot more wary now that he's seen firsthand what can happen."

If we don't know how to get married appropriately or stay married once we do, perhaps our culture and society are failing to teach us. "This generation has so much anxiety about marriage, says Les Parrot, director of Seattle Pacific University's Center for Relational Development. "Marriage changes you and you change together, and you need skills to do that. Skills that society is failing to impart."[27] For one thing, we are collectively guilty of perpetuating unrealistic ideas about marriage. Marriage is held up as an ideological linchpin on which we hang all of our hopes, ideas, opinions, and policies. One man who married at twenty-five confessed, "I didn't know what to expect. The culture portrays marriage unrealistically, like everything is going to be perfect all the time. So when it wasn't—and it definitely was not—I wasn't prepared."

There's practically a taboo against badmouthing the institution. "When it came to marriage, I thought much more romantically than practically," Laurel explains. "A lot of it is due to our marriage-happy culture rather than to my own family experiences, because my family background dictated that I should be a lot more wary. . . . I had a pretty naïve idea about marriage—I thought that you meet this one person who you have a lot in common with and you have a similar background and you just fall in love and that was that. I didn't see marriage as something that required constant effort and energy." As Barbara Ehrenreich writes, "We lurch from marriage to marriage, doomed to perpetual disappointment. . . . In short, we wrecked the institution of marriage by expecting too much of it. We loved it to death. Our expectations are way too high."[28] "American culture portrays marriage as this huge fantasy, big love-in, happily-ever-after, everything-will-be-fine-once-you're-married solution to everything," Yasmin says with a sigh. "And even knowing that, and despite myself, I really bought into the whole fantasy."

Rather than romanticizing marriage for the purpose of cinematic happy endings, bridal-registry sales, and inflated marriage rates, we need to be franker about what marriage can and cannot offer. According to David Olsen, who studies marriage and divorce patterns at the University of Minnesota, a major factor for marital success is realistic expectations.[29] To create an image of matrimony that defies reality most of the time sets people up for major disappointment. And disappointing people about marriage is no way to encourage or enhance it.

To portray marriage realistically is by no means to denigrate or discourage it. Instead, it would enable people to understand what's involved before entering into it, and increase their chances for success if they do. Decreasing the divorce rate would do much more to enhance marriage's reputation than shuffling more young people into a situation in which they're liable to fail.

We have to decide what's more important—higher marriage rates or higher rates of successful marriage. In other words, do we want to promote marriage (happy or not) or promote good marriages? Rather than insist that young people rush to marry at the "appropriate" age, we should care more that they enjoy long-term marriages.

Starter marriages *can* be avoided. Almost everyone interviewed warmed to the idea of marriage education, though they disagreed about the effectiveness of formal proposals. Many felt they simply ought to have learned more about marriage growing up. Barbara Dafoe Whitehead argues that the surge of divorce in the 1970s robbed parents of their role as the likely messengers. "There has been a nearly total breakdown in the capacity to transmit a usable body of thought and practice on marriage to the next generation," Whitehead contends. "The cultural infrastructure that once existed to guide and instruct young adults in marriage has collapsed. Today's young adults are slouching toward marriage in a profound state of cluelessness about its requirements and rewards."[30]

Perhaps our parents, embarrassed by or ashamed of their own unhappy marriages or divorces, feel they're in no position to guide their children, when in fact the opposite is true. Children of divorce could be learning from their parents' divorces, not just suffering through them. Teaching one's children about marriage is not simply offering an example of its success but also exposing and explaining its risks and failures. Parents who seek to protect their children end up hurting them by hiding the harsher realities of marriage. If twentysomethings heard an explanation of why their parents' marriage ended or understood the troubles they endured, they might not get married without adequate foresight and preparation.

All the divorcés interviewed said that their parents gave them no direction about marriage beyond telling them upon their engagement that "as long as you're happy" they supported it. This is a fine sentiment, as far at is goes, but it's not enough to equip one with the ability to choose whom to marry and when. Yet most parents keep mum until it's too late. Voicing misgivings or warnings at the point of engagement is a decidedly bad move; the matrimonially inclined usually view such last-minute entreaties as an assault either on their integrity or an affront to their intended. The decision to marry, just like the decision to choose one's friends and career, should be up to the adult child, who should be equipped long before that with the resources to make that decision wisely. Making friends and career choices can be done on a trial-and-error basis; marriage cannot.

Yet parents should not be held solely responsible. One place to educate about marriage is through religious institutions, many of which provide some form of marriage preparation as part of the wedding process. Juliet paid for her sister's marriage class at the University of Judaism. Laurel's second marriage took place within the Catholic church, which, she believes, made a huge difference. "We didn't actually go through the entire Pre-Cana process," she admits. "But we did learn a lot about it. I really admire the Catholic church's way of dealing with people getting married. It affords people a greater opportunity to avoid a bad marriage. It shows that marriage is far less about magic than love. Their approach is actually really pragmatic, focusing on the practical elements of marriage. It's a very responsible education. You would have to believe in the church's conception of marriage, though—that the purpose of marriage is procreation—and if you don't believe in those old-fashioned definitions of marriage, it wouldn't work for you. Maybe they could get rid of some of those traditional elements."

Religion-based premarital education isn't for everyone. "My husband's parents had us go to this fundamentalist Christian marriage-training thing," Olivia says. "The pastor was completely biased. He had these very traditional ideas about roles within the marriage. It didn't even last that long, only forty minutes or so. There may have been a few valid points, but mostly he just wanted to be sure that I was 'serving' my husband and prepared to submit. So I just wrote most of it off." Noelle, raised Catholic, says, "The idea of the Pre-Cana is great, but I don't know how much you learn—you need to talk to someone with experience, and Father John isn't going to know." Religion-based marriage education also doesn't work when spouses are from different religious back-grounds or have secular ideas about marriage based on emotional, humanistic, legal, or philosophical grounds or a combination thereof.

A number of secular programs have sprung up in recent years, offering a mix of premarital compatibility testing, marriage edu-cation, conflict-resolution classes, and preventative therapy for nervous newlyweds. Some people advocate the adoption of early-intervention programs and marriage-education plans along the lines of a public health campaign. They believe that couples con-templating marriage should be urged or even required to formally learn the skills, attitudes, and values required for sustaining mar-riage. In 1999 the Smart Marriages movement organized a confer-ence of counselors, psychologists, educators, journalists, and policy makers to rally around marriage education. One program for high schoolers, the Preserving Marriages Project, was begun by a di-vorce lawyer; today it boasts a membership of more than three thousand divorce lawyers.

Naturally, the government is getting involved. The Coalition for Marriage, Family and Couples Education in Washington urges legislators and educators to consider programs that instruct stu-dents on the importance of marriage and on how to ensure suc-cessful marriages of their own. In 1997 the coalition attracted six hundred "marriage movement leaders" to its annual conference; by 1999 that number had doubled. Florida has become the first state to require that "marriage skills" be taught in special courses to ninth- and tenth-graders in all public and private schools. Students can now bring home marriage worksheets along with their geometry textbooks. Several states are considering similar legislation.

Many divorcés wondered why such a matter would be appropriate for high school. Others preferred the idea of a college course taught by a series of visiting professors, including religious leaders, married couples, marriage counselors, and, interesting, divorced couples (no better way to learn than through failure), and many thought that marriage education should be taught not only by older, wiser parties but also by their peers. "I'm a big believer in peer education," says Amy. "You need to hear people from your own background, your own culture, your own age talk to you about their experiences with marriage and divorce, so that you can relate."

Perhaps in a society of new traditional families, an expanded network of friends and relatives will take the lead in explaining both the joys of a good marriage and the trials of any marriage. We'll all help expose the sadness and frustrations, rather than hide the details out of shame or fear of ruining our children's sense of romance and desire for marriage.

The Best Marriage "Prescription"

It's past time to recognize that the days of universally prescribed lifelong marriage beginning in one's early twenties are largely over. That fleeting era of the 1950s depended on a society and an economy that no longer exists, for better or for worse, and many marriages that took place within it *were* for worse and are better off over. Not only is that kind of marriage not always the right choice, it is certainly no longer the only choice. Though raising children within a marriage is my personal preference, allowing others to pursue different lifestyles by no means threatens my own.

In order to ensure that a wide range of choices—including marriage—remain available and supported, we might consider certain changes. We could celebrate delayed marriage rather than discourage it. By encouraging people to marry young and in a hurry, we are in fact bringing about the demise of the very institution we fear undermining. Our promulgation of single disaster tales exacerbates this. The idea that there aren't any good men around once a woman hits her early thirties is absurd, and what's more, it's insulting to both sexes. Men are waiting to marry even longer than women, and there's nothing particularly wrong with them either. Why consider youth a better quality in a husband than caution and maturity?

While the negative effects of divorce on children have recently been heavily documented by writers like Judith Wallerstein (*The Unexpected Legacy of Divorce*), one overlooked positive result is that adult children of divorce often delay marriage or cohabitate until a later age. Wallerstein condemns this as a sign of trauma rather than praising it as an indication of lessons learned. We might be better served by fully accepting cohabitation, rather than being threatened by it. Largely due to the active antagonism of a loud minority, cohabitation hasn't enjoyed the proud public-service campaign that marriage has. Cohabitation doesn't get adorable advertisements, bulky magazines devoted to its rituals, or admiring odes. Nor do live-in partners get the same economic bonus packages that legislators rush to bestow upon their married counterparts. No wonder married people are richer and healthier and more stable. No wonder "real" marriage as an ideal still comes out on top and that some trial-marriage couples find themselves heading toward marriage even when they're not sure if it's the best idea.

The marriage-police dogs should stop barking at "living in sin" and instead roll over with glee. Most of these allegedly debauched couples are taking the precaution of confirming their compatibility. They want to see if they can get along on a daily basis, whether their faithfulness will hold, and whether their partner will change over time. They want to make sure that if they make the leap to matrimony, they won't divorce. Those who continue to hail the hallowed marriages of the fifties, many of which were shotgun weddings, aimed at avoiding societal condemnation of premarital sex, abortion, and illegitimacy, might think to laud this more thoughtful approach to marriage. Better to take commitment seriously than to cling to it or jump into it out of fear.

As a society, we might best be served by upholding marriage as a desirable, if difficult, lifestyle choice—one that in its ideal conception supports children and creates a cohesive society. "I think the most positive thing that has come out of my divorce is how it's affected my family in certain ways," says Kate. "My sister and her boyfriend were hurtling quickly toward engagement. They'd been dancing sweetly at my wedding, and the murmurs of 'Look who's next' put a lot of pressure on them, even though they'd only been together for a few months. Now I think she's realized how slowly and carefully she should take things. I also have a brother whose wife is going through a hard time right now. My mother has kind of swept in as a support system for both of them, and I think the feeling is, we don't want another divorce in the family. And it's all too easy for that to happen when you don't pay attention to a couple's happiness and watch out for potential trouble spots. I feel like my family has really come together in a way."

It's true that starter marriages teach their participants valuable lessons. It's also true that starter marriage veterans may be better prepared for subsequent marriage than most people are for their first. But I don't believe we should all be having starter marriages. The right marriage can and ideally ought to be a lifelong endeavor. One may argue that starter marriages are inevitable, but they don't have to be.

At root of the starter-marriage phenomenon is a conflict between our cultural conception of marriage, which has not changed, and the society surrounding it, which has. We continue to configure marriage in precisely the same way we did fifty years ago, even though almost none of the factors shaping marriage then still apply. We are no longer required to enter into marriage for financial security, yet an endless barrage of articles tell us that if we marry, we'll be financially better off. We are no longer required to marry for sexual fulfillment, yet streams of data are publicized to show us that married couples indeed have better sex. We are no longer required to enter marriage for our personal fulfillment, and yet we constantly see books and articles that tell us married people are happier and more satisfied with their station in life than singles. We are urged from all sides to marry fast and to beware of the consequences if we don't. What's truly shocking is *not* that we are marrying older or less but that we continue to marry at a remarkably high rate and at a relatively young age. Both men and women's opportunities have expanded, yet we act as if the only sensible path to follow is straight down the wedding aisle. Given our lack of information, role models, and community support, given the complications of our lives, our long life spans, and the demands of two-career couples, the marriage rate is astoundingly high. By most measures, it would seem that marriage should be in a steep decline. Starter marriages may be a sign that all is not happily ever after.

Some will argue that the way to "fix" this problem is to pull us back to marriage's original meaning, to force society to adhere to its "traditional" definition. This is neither wise nor pragmatic, and given the shifting definitions of marriage, the very premise is a fallacy. People's lifestyles and their ideas about how they want to live have fundamentally changed; a stricter definition of marriage won't alter that. We're redefining marriage because our lives have changed dramatically. Rather than tug ourselves back to an older definition, we ought to move forward to better survive within the new one.

Though marriage should not be a one-size-fits-all proposition, we can make it a more workable possibility. And that means approaching it differently, not with regulations and rhetoric, but with thoughtfulness and commitment, both on a personal level and as a society. We can take responsibility for our own marriages as well as create communities that sustain marriages and are sustained by them. Because if we abdicate personal responsibility for marital success, politicians are all too ready to jump in and do the job for us—in ways that may not best serve our individual needs.

Perhaps we do require a kind of moral renewal, though not the one so dogmatically promoted in certain quarters. Today society is marred by an increasingly strict line between "us" and "them," where "we" no longer have any obligation toward other members of society. People care more about their own tax returns than they do about the health of their communities. Rather than fight for marriage bonuses, married couples could devote themselves to the communities that support the institution of marriage in the first place. Why expect from and depend on marriage to provide our sole support? If we want to recapture social stability, lasting marriages, and fifties-style centrality of family, rather than focusing on the reactionary social differences that marred those relationships, we could foster the kind of social capital, trust, and confidence in public institutions that allowed that stability to thrive.

Starter marriages are painful, but they certainly do not signal the end of marriage. The best marriage policy would be for each of us, individually, to approach marriage with a better understanding of what it requires, and how we can make it a happy, successful, and long-lasting choice. Those of us who once were wed can learn from our starter marriages. And all of us who choose matrimony can learn how to marry realistically, consciously, and conscientiously. We can support our friends and family in their own quests for and struggles with marriage, no matter how it's defined. And when marriage doesn't end up being a lifelong choice, we can try to understand why not and what that means for us individually and as a society. Then pass on those lessons to everyone else.

Acknowledgments

When I first decided to write this book, I breezily declared that it would include "over fifty interviews with starter marriage veterans from around the country." Then I realized, "Uh-oh, now I've got to find them." So my first thanks go to all the friends, family, and colleagues who whipped out their address books and worked their Palm Pilots, sending me well over eighty contacts from as far-flung as Idaho to a subway ride away on West Eighty-first Street. Which leads me to my next and greatest acknowledgment of all. To the men and women who devoted hours of their time to submit to personal and often painful questioning, I cannot begin to express my gratitude. Often, after our conversations, an interviewee would ask, "So, did I do okay? I don't know if I had any insight to add— was that helpful?" My invariable response was, "You have no idea how helpful you are." Quite simply, this book could not have been written without them. I cannot thank you all enough.

I would like to thank the people who instructed, encouraged, and inspired me: Jim Morone at Brown University; Steve Cohen, my first "real" boss, and everyone at Scholastic; and Edmund Fawcett, Tony Thomas, Fiammetta Rocco, Steve King, and the incredible staff I've worked with at *The Economist*. I would like to thank my agent Andrew Blauner, who steadfastly stuck to this client since I wandered back from Thailand seven years ago, and Joann Miller at Basic Books, who introduced me to him in the first place. I want to thank Kate Niedzwiecki, who acquired my book and edited it brilliantly; Bruce Tracy, who shepherded it through the process; and Judy Sternlight, who carried it to its final stage with grace, energy, and insight. Many thanks to Brian McLendon, Carol Schneider, and everyone else at Villard.

Thanks to Kathleen Gerson at NYU, Andrew J. Cherlin at Johns Hopkins, and Larry Bumpass at the University of Wisconsin for responding to my questions by phone and e-mail. And to Lisa Krueger and Peggy Orenstein for adding their own words of wisdom.

I want to thank especially the brilliant Vanessa Mobley at Basic Books, who helped hone a tentative idea into a train of thought into a book proposal and beyond—and was a wonderful friend throughout. Huge gratitude to my cherished friend Mindy Lewis—I can't wait for your turn. Carol Tichler provided a psychotherapist's wise perspective in reading my manuscript, and my mother offered her editorial genius; both deserve a mighty thanks for slogging through an early draft and providing crucial input. Ericka Eisen Tullis did the same, and deserves gratitude not only for that but also for her unparalleled friendship of twenty-three years. The unrelated but sister-in-writing Annie Murphy Paul for all her help through the intermittent First Book Group. The fabulous Pauline O'Connor gave a much-appreciated boost with her probing questions and encouragement. Alysia Abbott was an incredibly good friend to me—I look forward to reading her first book. Victoria Camelio has also been wonderful—I want to thank her and wish her and Mike the best that marriage can be. My personal thanks also to Lydia Randolph, Kirsten Osur, Emily McCarthy, Jennifer Sigall, Suzanne Immerman, Amy Plattsmier, Jason Gonsky, Greg Sorensen, Charlotte and Amer Siddiqui, Becky Wolsk, Sara Federlein, ma Maman Francaise et tous les Mathieus du Crepy-en-Valois et la Rue Rambuteau. Thanks to my Mom, Dad and Carol, Roger and Brian, Nick, Erik, and Debbie. And to all the other friends, colleagues, and family members who supported me through a difficult year and helped me turn lemons into lemonade.

Notes

INTRODUCTION: SAYING "I DO" IS EASY TO DO

1. Roper Reports, 1997.

2. Roper Reports, 1998.

3. U.S. Bureau of the Census, current population survey, March 2000.

4. Maggie Gallagher, "Marriage-Saving: A Movement for Matrimony," *National Review,* 8 November 1999, p. 38.

5. 1999 *Yankelovich Monitor,* Table 140.

6. American Dialogue/TBWA Chiat/Day "Talking Beauty" poll, July 1995.

7. Peggy Orenstein, *Flux: Women on Sex, Work, Love, Kids, and Life in a Half-Changed World* (New York: Doubleday, 2000), p. 31.

8. Blum & Weprin Associates, *New York Times Magazine* poll, March 2000.

9. "Time to Repaint the Gen X Portrait," *Yankelovich Monitor,* 12 October 1998.

10. 2000 Roper Reports 00-1, Q.63X.

11. 1999 *Yankelovich Monitor,* Table 165 (54 percent).

12. Jackie Calmes, "Americans Retain Puritan Attitudes on Matters of Sex," *Wall Street Journal,* 5 March 1998, p. A12.

13. Roper Reports 1998, 98-6, Q-79, How Acceptable Find Each of Listed Behaviors.

14. General Social Survey, University of Chicago.

15. Roper Reports, 1999, 99-7, Table 4.

16. Gallup poll, 1999.

17. Helene Stapinski, "Y Not Love?" *American Demographics,* February 1999.

18. *Yankelovich Monitor,* 29 March 1999.

19. Ibid.

20. U.S. Bureau of the Census, *Current Population Reports,* Series P20-514, "Marital Status and Living Arrangements" (Washington, D.C.: U.S. Government Printing Office), March 1998 Update.

21. Sarah Bernard, "Early to Wed," *New York,* 16 June 1997, p. 38.

22. Katherine Davis, "I'm Not Sick, I'm Just in Love," *Newsweek,* 24 July 1995, p. 12.

23. Francine Prose, "Why Confidence Soars After Marriage," *Redbook,* February 1999, p. 84.

24. *Yankelovich Monitor,* 1999, Tables 159 and 160.

25. Megan Fitzmorris McCafferty, "When Should You Marry," *Cosmopolitan,* August 1999, p. 238.

26. Marcia Mogelonsky, "The Rocky Road to Adulthood," *American Demographics* 18 (May 1996), p. 26.

27. Matthew D. Bramlett and William D. Mosher, "First Marriage Dissolution, Divorce and Remarriage: United States," advance data, 31 May 2001, Centers for Disease Control and Prevention.

28. U.S. Bureau of the Census, "Marital Status," March 1998 Update.

29. Openletters.net, January 2001.

30. Katha Pollitt, "The Solipsisters," *New York Times Book Review,* 18 April 1999.

CHAPTER 1: GETTING STARTED ON A STARTER MARRIAGE

1. "National Vital Statistics Report," Vol. 49, No. 1, 17 April 2001, National Center for Health Statistics.

2. Francine Russo, "Just Married, Just Split Up," *Self,* April 1996, p. 110.

3. U.S. Bureau of the Census, *Current Population Reports,* Series P20-514, "Marital Status and Living Arrangements" (Washington, D.C.: U.S. Government Printing Office), March 1998 Update.

4. Barbara Dafoe Whitehead and David Popenoe, "The State of Our Union 2001," The National Marriage Project, 2001.

5. William Mattox, Jr., "Could This Be True Love? Test It with Courtship, Not Cohabitation," *USA Today,* 10 February 2000, p. 15A.

6. The Marriage Project, Rutgers University, "The State of Our Unions Project," 1999.

7. Janice Shaw Crouse, Beverly LaHaye Institute. "The State of Marriage in Twentieth Century America: Implications for the Next Millennium," 2000.

8. U.S. Bureau of the Census, "Marital Status," March 1998 Update.

9. Sara Terry, "The Unexpected Consequences of 'Living Together,'" *Christian Science Monitor,* 10 April 2000, p. 1.

10. Karen S. Peterson, "Changing the Shape of the American Family," *USA Today,* 18 April 2000, p. 1D.

11. Larry L. Bumpass and James A. Sweet, "National Estimates of Cohabi-

tation: Cohort Levels and Union Stability," NSFH working paper no. 2 (June 1989), published in *Family in America New Research,* September 1989.

12. Larry Bumpass and James Sweet, "National Estimates of Cohabitation," *Demography* 24, no. 4 (1989): pp. 615–25.

13. "Cosmo's Guide to Getting Engaged," *Cosmopolitan,* June 2000, p. 258.

CHAPTER 2: GENERATION WE: THE ME GENERATION REBELLION

1. Emily Jenkins, "Bridal Fantasies," Salon.com, 27 November 2000.

2. J. Walker Smith and Ann Clurman, *Rocking the Ages: The Yankelovich Report on Generational Marketing* (New York: HarperBusiness, 1997), p. 10.

3. " 'M' Is for Mother, Not Marriage," *American Demographics,* May 2000, p. 7.

4. Michael Kammen, *In the Past Lane: Historical Perspectives on American Culture* (New York: Oxford University Press, 1997), p. ix.

5. Cokie Roberts and Steven R. Roberts, *From This Day Forward* (New York: William Morrow, 2000), p. 286.

6. Teresa Castro Martin and Larry L. Bumpass, "Recent Trends in Marital Disruption," *Demography* 26, no. 1 (February 1989), p. 37.

7. E. J. Graff, *What Is Marriage For?* (Boston: Beacon Press, 1999), p. 240.

8. Elaine Tyler May, *Homeward Bound: American Families in the Cold War Era,* rev. ed. (New York: Basic Books, 1999), p. 14.

9. Stephanie Coontz, *The Way We Really Are: Coming to Terms with America's Changing Families* (New York: Basic Books, 1997).

10. Andrew J. Cherlin, *Marriage, Divorce, Remarriage: Social Trends in the United States* (Cambridge: Harvard University Press, 1981), p. 24.

11. " 'M' Is for Mother," p. 7.

12. Susan Faludi, *Backlash: The Undeclared War Against American Women* (New York: Crown, 1991), p. 54.

13. Coontz, *The Way We Really Are.*

14. Ibid.

15. Myriam Miedzian and Alisa Malinovich, *Generations: A Century of Women Speak About Their Lives* (New York: Atlantic Monthly Press, 1997), pp. 270–71.

16. Cheryl Russell, "The Rorschach Test," *American Demographics,* January 1997, p. 10.

17. Robert T. Michael, et al., *Sex in America: A Definitive Survey* (Boston: Little, Brown, 1994), p. 105.

18. Miedzian and Malinovich, *Generations,* p. 286.

19. Cherlin, *Marriage, Divorce, Remarriage,* p. 6.

20. Roberts and Roberts, *From This Day Forward,* p. 286.

21. Barbara Dafoe Whitehead, "Dan Quayle Was Right," *Atlantic Monthly,* April 1993, p. 47.

22. Ibid.

23. Coontz, *The Way We Really Are,* p. 31.

24. "By the Numbers: The State of Divorce," *Time,* 25 September 2000, p. 74.

25. U.S. Bureau of the Census, *Current Population Reports,* Series P20-297, "Number, Timing, and Duration of Marriages and Divorces in the United States: June 1975" (Washington, D.C.: U.S. Government Printing Office, 1976).

26. U.S. Bureau of the Census, *Current Population Reports,* Series P23-107, "Families Maintained by Female Householders" (Washington, D.C.: U.S. Government Printing Office, 1980).

27. Whitehead, "Dan Quayle Was Right," p. 47.

28. Margot Hornblower, "Great Xpectations," *Time,* 9 June 1997, p. 58.

29. Larissa Phillips, "Mothers Who Think," Salon.com, 16 November 1999.

30. David Popenoe and Barbara Dafoe Whitehead, "The State of Our Unions: The Social Health of Marriage in America," National Marriage Project, 1999.

31. Jennifer Lach, "The Consequences of Divorce," *American Demographics,* October 1999. Study cited is by Nicholas Wolfinger, University of Utah, "Coupling and Uncoupling: Changing Marriage Patterns and the Intergenerational Transmission of Divorce."

32. Phillips, "Mothers Who Think."

33. Wolfinger, "Coupling and Uncoupling," in Lach, "The Consequences of Divorce."

34. Stephanie Staal, *The Love They Lost: Living with the Legacy of Our Parents' Divorce* (New York: Delacorte Press, 2000), p. 186.

35. Hornblower, "Great Xpectations," p. 58.

36. Hanna Rosin, "Separation Anxiety: The Movement to Save Marriage," *New Republic,* 6 May 1996, p. 14.

37. Faludi, *Backlash,* pp. 99–104.

38. Ibid., p. 97.

39. Jenkins, "Bridal Fantasies."

40. Katie Roiphe, *Last Night in Paradise: Sex and Morals at the Century's End* (New York: Little, Brown, 1997), p. 133.

41. Staal, *The Love They Lost,* p. 28.

42. Lisa E. Phillips, "Love, American Style," *American Demographics,* February 1999, p. 56.

43. 1999 *Yankelovich Monitor,* Table 164.

44. Ibid., Table 150.

45. Marie Brenner, "Nothing Like a Dame and She's Back," *New York Times,* 26 March 2000, Style section, p. 1.

46. Alexandra Jacobs, "Love, Honor, Obey and . . . Oh, Hell!" *New York Observer,* 18 June 2001, p. 1.

47. Mary Meehan, Larry Samuel, and Vickie Abrahamson, *The Future Ain't What It Used to Be: The 40 Cultural Trends Transforming Your Job, Your Life, Your World* (New York: Riverhead, 1997), pp. 193–94.

48. Maureen Dowd, "Freud Was Way Wrong," *New York Times*, 4 June 2000, Week in Review section, p. 17.

49. Coontz, *The Way We Really Are*, p. 30.

50. Louise Bernikow, *The American Woman's Almanac* (New York: Berkley, 1997), p. 296.

51. "Generation X Revisited," *Yankelovich Monitor*, 5 April 2000.

52. U.S. Bureau of the Census, "Marital Status of Persons 15 Years and Over, by Age, Sex, Race, Hispanic Origin, Metropolitan Residence, and Region" (Washington D.C.: U.S. Government Printing Office, 1998), Table 1.

53. "Romantic Resurgence," *American Demographics*, August 1997, p. 35.

CHAPTER 3: MATRIMANIA

1. Cokie Roberts and Steven R. Roberts, *From This Day Forward* (New York: William Morrow, 2000), p. 35.

2. Linda J. Waite, "Social Science Finds: 'Marriage Matters,'" *Responsive Community* 6, no. 3 (Summer 1996), pp. 26–35.

3. Sara Terry, "The Unexpected Consequences of 'Living Together,'" *Christian Science Monitor*, 10 April 2000, p. 1.

4. Lisa E. Phillips, "Love, American Style," *American Demographics*, February 1999, p. 56.

5. "Of Wedding Bells and Bills," *New York Times*, 11 June 2000, section 3, p. 12.

6. Lois Smith Brady, "Why Marriage Is Hot Again," *Redbook*, September 1996, p. 122.

7. Margaret Mead, *Male and Female: A Study of the Sexes in a Changing World*, rev. ed. (New York: William Morrow, 1967), p. 342.

8. Peter Godwin, "Happily Ever After," *New York Times*, 25 July 1999, section 6, p. 13.

9. "Fox's Arranged Marriage Draws Viewers, Protest," Reuters, 17 February 2000.

10. Pollyreport.com survey, *Adweek*, 13 March 2000, p. 35.

11. Kathryn Harrison, "Connubial Abyss: The Mysterious Narrative of Marriage," *Harper's Magazine*, February 2000, p. 83.

12. Lesley Dormen, "Is It True Love or Marriage Panic?" *Self*, November 1999, p. 148.

13. "U.S. Marriage Is Weakening, Study Reports," *New York Times*, 4 July 1999, section 1, p. 15.

14. Francine Prose, "A Wasteland of One's Own," *New York Times Magazine*, 13 February 2000, p. 70.

15. Jennifer Frey, "Wedding Cake for the Soul," *Washington Post*, 25 October 2000, p. CO1.

16. Megan Fitzmorris McCafferty, "When Should You Marry," *Cosmopolitan*, August 1999, p. 238.

17. Barbara Dafoe Whitehead, "The Plight of the High Status Woman," *Atlantic Monthly,* December 1999, p. 120.

18. Jennifer Kornreich, "Help! Everyone's Hitched," *Cosmopolitan,* September 2000, p. 208.

19. Christina Del Valle, "Marriage Is Back: Want to Be Hip? Stay Together," *Newsday,* 21 October 1997, p. B15.

20. Leslie Yazel, "20 Questions," *Glamour,* April 2000, p. 68.

21. Ilene Rosenzweig, "A Bachelorette Fears Making a Commitment," *New York Times,* 14 February 2000, p. 4.

22. "Meet the New Housewife Wanna-Bes," *Cosmopolitan,* June 2000, p. 164.

23. "Cosmo's Guide to Getting Married," *Cosmopolitan,* May 2000, p. 257.

24. Brady, "Why Marriage Is Hot Again," p. 122.

25. Sarah Bernard, "Early to Wed," *New York,* 16 June 1997, p. 38.

26. Marcelle Karp and Debbie Stoller, *The Bust Guide to the New Girl Order* (New York: Penguin, 1999), p. xi.

27. "Marriage Mania," *Life as a Loser* by Will Leitch, Ironminds.com, 10 May 2000.

28. Andrew Sullivan, "State of the Union," *New Republic,* 8 May 2000.

29. Rick Marin, "As a Bachelor's Clock Ticks Away," *New York Times,* 14 February 2000, Style section, p. 1.

30. Barbara Ehrenreich, "Why It Might Be Worth It (to Have an Affair)," in Deborah Chasman and Catherine Jhee, eds., *Here Lies My Heart: Essays on Why We Marry, Why We Don't, and What We Find There* (Boston: Beacon Press, 1999), p. 6.

31. "Cosmo's Guide to Getting Married," *Cosmopolitan,* May 2000, p. 260.

32. Alexandra Jacobs, "The New Vows," *New York Observer,* 10 April 2000, p. 2.

33. Valli Herman-Cohen, " 'I Do' It My Way," *Los Angeles Times,* 28 January 2000. p. E1.

34. Marie Brenner, "Nothing Like a Dame and She's Back," *New York Times,* 26 March 2000, Style section, p. 1.

35. Melissa Ceria, "Melissa's Diary," *Harper's Bazaar,* May 2000, p. 168.

36. Brady, "Why Marriage Is Hot Again," p. 122.

37. "Let Them Eat Cake," *Vogue,* June 2000, p. 260.

38. Pamela Fiori, Editor's Letter, *Town and Country,* February 2001, p. 25.

39. Maria Puente, "Wedded to the Year 2000," *USA Today,* 12 June 2000, p. 1A.

40. Ibid.

41. Jennifer Evans Gardner, "The Facts and Figures," WeddingChannel.com, 22 June 2000.

42. Puente, "Wedded to the Year 2000."

43. Herman-Cohen, " 'I Do' It My Way."

44. Puente, "Wedded to the Year 2000."

45. "Of Wedding Bells and Bills."

46. Puente, "Wedded to the Year 2000."

47. Ibid.

48. "The Mail," *Us Weekly*, 27 March 2000, p. 20.

49. "Old Fashion Tradition Returns in New Century: Engagement Announcements Are New Sign of the Times," *Business Wire*, 14 February 2000.

50. Puente, "Wedded to the Year 2000."

51. Jennifer Tung, "Attack of Bridezilla: Demanding Perfection Before 'I Do,'" *New York Times*, 20 May 2001, Style section, p. 1.

52. Puente, "Wedded to the Year 2000."

53. Millie Martini Bratten, online chat with the editor of *Bride's* on USAToday.com, 6 June 2000.

54. Puente, "Wedded to the Year 2000."

55. Ibid.

56. Kimberly Stevens, "I Do . . . Take Mastercard," *Wall Street Journal*, 23 June 2000, section W, p. 1.

57. David Popenoe and Barbara Dafoe Whitehead, "Why Wed? The Next Generation Project," National Marriage Project, 2000, p. 2.

58. Felicia R. Lee, "Looking for Mr. Goodbucks," *New York Times*, 5 March 2000, City section, p. 1.

59. Felicia R. Lee, "Mr. Goodbucks, The Sequel: True Confessions," *New York Times*, 19 March 2000, City section, p. 1.

60. Ellen Flein and Sherrie Schneider, "What's Love Got to Do with It?," *New York Times*, 17 February 2000, Op-Ed.

61. Nancy Jo Sales, "Who Wants to Marry a Multimillionaire?" *Harper's Bazaar*, April 2000, p. 211.

62. Abby Ellin, "Preludes: Marriage Insurance for the Young," *New York Times*, 18 June 2000, p. B15.

63. Brady, "Why Marriage Is Hot Again."

64. Peggy Orenstein, *Flux: Women on Sex, Work, Love, Kids, and Life in a Half-Changed World* (New York: Doubleday, 2000), p. 19.

65. Pam Belluck, "States Declare War on Divorce Rates, Before Any 'I Dos,'" *New York Times*, 24 April 2000, p. A1.

66. Katie Roiphe, "The Independent Woman (and Other Lies)," *Esquire*, February 1997, p. 84.

67. Lori Leibovich, "Reversal of Fortune," *Harper's Bazaar*, August 2000, p. 192.

68. Ruth La Perla, "They Want to Marry a Millionaire," *New York Times*, 14 March 2001.

69. Ann Marlowe, "Pros and Amateurs," Salon.com, 24 February 2000.

70. Nancy Ann Jeffrey, "The New Economy Family," *Wall Street Journal*, 8 September 2000, section W, p. 1.

71. Maureen Dowd, "Rescue Me, Please!," *New York Times*, 7 June 2000, p. A31.

72. Susan Faludi, *Backlash: The Undeclared War Against American Women* (New York: Crown, 1991), pp. 82–95.

73. Louis Harris and Associates and Families and the Work Institute for the Whirlpool Foundation, 1995.

74. Ira Matathia and Marian Salzman, *Next: Trends for the Near Future* (New York: Overlook Press, 1999), p. 213.

75. Jeffrey, "The New Economy Family."

76. *Cosmopolitan*, June 2000, p. 166.

77. "Gen Xers Likely to Take Lessons from Matures," *Yankelovich Monitor Minute*, 29 March 2000.

CHAPTER 4: THE SEARCH FOR MARRIAGE

1. Charlotte Mayerson, *Goin' to the Chapel: Dreams of Love, Realities of Marriage* (New York: Basic Books, 1996), pp. 31–34.

2. Sarah Bernard, "Early to Wed," *New York,* 16 June 1997, p. 38.

3. Stephanie Coontz, *The Way We Really Are: Coming to Terms with America's Changing Families* (New York: Basic Books, 1997), p. 37.

4. Barbara Dafoe Whitehead, "The Plight of the High Status Woman," *Atlantic Monthly*, December 1999, p. 120.

5. "Generation X Revisited," *Yankelovich Monitor*, 5 April 2000.

6. U.S. Bureau of the Census, *Current Population Reports*, Series P20-514. "Marital Status and Living Arrangements" (Washington D.C.: U.S. Government Printing Office), March 1998 update. In 1960 it was 13%.

7. The Report Reports 2000 Annual Presentation, Roper Starch Worldwide.

8. Young & Rubicam's Intelligence Factory, 2000.

9. Celina Hex, "Fear of a Boy Planet," in Marcelle Karp and Debbie Stoller, eds. *The Bust Guide to the New Girl Order* (New York: Penguin, 1999), p. 134.

10. Jason Berry, "A Modest Proposal: 'Courtship'?" *Chicago Tribune Magazine*, 16 April 2000, p. 10.

11. Leon R. Kass, "The End of Courtship," *Public Interest* 126 (Winter 1997), p. 39.

12. 1999 *Yankelovich Monitor*, Table 164.

13. Katie Roiphe, *Last Night in Paradise: Sex and Morals at Century's End* (New York: Little, Brown, 1997), pp. 28–29.

14. Ibid.

15. Bernard, "Early to Wed."

16. Mildred Gilman, "Why They Can't Wait to Wed," *Parents*, November 1958, p. 46.

17. Sharon Begley, *Newsweek*, 8 May 2000, p. 52.

18. Valli Herman-Cohen, " 'I Do' It My Way," *Los Angeles Times*, 28 January 2000, p. E1.

19. Lois Smith Brady, "Why Marriage Is Hot Again," *Redbook*, September 1996, p. 122.

20. Peggy Orenstein, *Flux: Women on Sex, Work, Love, Kids, and Life in a Half-Changed World* (New York: Doubleday, 2000), pp. 30, 31.

21. Lisa McLaughlin, "Personal Time: Your Family," *Time,* September 2000, p. 82.

22. Francine Prose, "Why Confidence Soars After Marriage," *Redbook,* February 1999, p. 84.

23. Berry, "A Modest Proposal."

24. Ira Matathia and Marian Salzman, *Next: Trends for the Near Future* (New York: Overlook Press, 1999), p. 399.

25. Margorie Ingall, "Going to the Temple," in Deborah Chesman and Catherine Jhee, eds., *Here Lies My Heart: Essays on Why We Marry, Why We Don't, and What We Find There* (Boston: Beacon Press, 1999), p. 29.

26. Matathia and Salzman, *Next,* p. 290.

27. Blum & Weprin Associates, *New York Times Magazine* poll, March 2000.

28. Anna Quindlen, "Playing the Perfect Pattycake," *New York Times,* 13 April 1994, p. 21.

29. Blum & Weprin/*New York Times* poll.

30. Rosalind C. Barnett and Carol Rivers, *She Works/He Works: How Two-Income Families Are Happier, Healthier and Better Off* (San Francisco: HarperCollins, 1996), p. 6.

CHAPTER 5: WHERE STARTER MARRIAGES STUMBLE

1. Lawrence A. Kurdek, "The Nature and Predictors of the Trajectory of Change in Marital Quality for Husbands and Wives Over the First 10 Years of Marriage," *Developmental Psychology* 35, no. 5 (1999), pp. 1283–96.

2. J. K. Repel, J. G. Holmes, and M. P. Zanna, "Trust in Close Relationships," *Journal of Personality and Social Psychology* 49 (1985), pp. 95–112.

3. L. A. Kurdek and J. P. Schmitt, "Interaction of Sex Role Self-Concept with Relationship Quality and Relationship Beliefs in Married, Heterosexual Cohabitating, Gay, and Lesbian Couples," *Journal of Personality and Social Psychology* 51 (1986), pp. 365–70.

4. T. N. Bradbury, S. M. Campbell, and F. D. Fincham, "Longitudinal and Behavioral Analysis of Masculinity and Femininity in Marriage," *Journal of Personality and Social Psychology* 68 (1995), pp. 328–41.

CHAPTER 6: WHEN STARTER MARRIAGES FALL APART

1. Elizabeth Gleick, "Should This Marriage Be Saved?" *Time,* 27 February 1995, p. 51.

2. Shirley Barnes, "Keeping It Together," *Chicago Tribune,* 2 August 1998, p. 1.

3. Frank F. Furstenberg, Jr., and Andrew J. Cherlin, *Divided Families: What Happens to Children When Parents Part* (Cambridge: Harvard University Press, 1991), p. 22.

CHAPTER 7: WHY STARTER MARRIAGES FAIL

1. Lois Smith Brady, "Why Marriage Is Hot Again," *Redbook*, September 1996, p. 122.

2. Monica Davey, "Perspective: On the Record: David Popenoe, Co-Director of the National Marriage Project," *Chicago Tribune*, 1 August 1999, p. 3.

3. Julian E. Barnes, "Young-Life Crisis," *New York Times*, 25 April 1999, section 14, p. 1.

4. Arlie Russell Hochschild, "Coming of Age, Seeking an Identity," *New York Times*, 8 March 2000, p. H1.

5. Margot Hornblower, "Great Xpectations," *Time*, 9 June 1997, p. 58.

6. Teresa Castro Martin and Larry L. Bumpass, "Recent Trends in Marital Disruption," *Demography* 26, no. 1 (February 1989), p. 37.

7. Hochschild, "Coming of Age."

8. Sara Terry, "The Unexpected Consequences of 'Living Together,'" *Christian Science Monitor*, 10 April 2000, p. 1.

9. Kari Jenson Gold, "Opinion," *First Things*, November 1992, p. 9.

10. Sarah Bernard, "Early to Wed," *New York*, 16 June 1997, p. 38.

11. Alex Kuczynski, "Between the Sexes, It's World War III Out There," *New York Times*, 19 July 1998, section 9, p. 1.

12. Myriam Miedzian and Alisa Malinovich, *Generations: A Century of Women Speak About Their Lives* (New York: Atlantic Monthly Press, 1997), p. 223.

13. Megan Fitzmorris McCafferty, "When Should You Marry," *Cosmopolitan*, August 1999, p. 238.

14. Lisa E. Phillips, "Love, American Style," *American Demographics*, February 1999, p. 56.

15. David Popenoe and Barbara Dafoe Whitehead, "The State of Our Unions: The Social Health of Marriage in America," National Marriage Project, 1999.

16. David Popenoe and Barbara Dafoe Whitehead, "The State of Our Unions: The Social Health of Marriage in America," National Marriage Project, 2000. p 8.

17. Barbara Dafoe Whitehead and David Popenoe, "The State of Our Unions 2001," National Marriage Project, 2001.

18. Valli Herman-Cohen, " 'I Do' It My Way," *Los Angeles Times*, 28 January 2000, p. E1.

19. Whitehead and Popenoe, "State of Our Unions," 1999.

20. Terry, "Unexpected Consequences."

21. "Leaps of Faith," *Elle*, May 2000, p. 100.

22. Charlotte Mayerson, *Goin' to the Chapel: Dreams of Love, Realities of Marriage* (New York: Basic Books, 1996), p. 103.

23. Marcia Mogelonsky, "The Rocky Road to Adulthood," *American Demographics* 18, no. 5 (May 1996), p. 26.

CHAPTER 8: DIVORCED UNDER THIRTY

1. Mavis Hetherington, Martha Cox, and Roger Cox, "Divorced Fathers," *Psychology Today,* 1977, p. 42.

2. Hara Estroff Marano, "Divorced: Don't Even Think of Remarrying Until You Read This," *Psychology Today,* March/April 2000, p. 57.

3. Tracy L. Pipp, "Divorce Drives Young Adults Home to Get Back on Their Feet," *Detroit News,* 24 June 1996, Accent section.

4. *Statistical Abstract of the United States,* 1998, p. 111, Table 156; *Statistical Abstract of the United States,* 1972, p. 63, Table 86; *National Vital Statistics Reports,* 19 August 1998. Figure applies to divorces per married women age 15 and older.

5. Elia Kacapyr, "Population Update," *American Demographics,* October 1996.

6. Teresa Castro Martin and Larry L. Bumpass, "Recent Trends in Marital Disruption," *Demography* 26, no. 1 (February 1989), p. 37.

7. E. J. Graff, *What Is Marriage For?* (Boston: Beacon Press, 1999), p. 229.

8. Robert J. Blendon, et al. "The 60s and the 90s: Americans' Political, Moral and Religious Values Then and Now," *Brookings Review* (Spring 1999), p. 17.

9. Jackie Calmes, "Americans Retain Puritan Attitudes on Matters of Sex," *Wall Street Journal,* 5 March 1998, p. A12.

10. Hanna Rosin, "Separation Anxiety: The Movement to Save Marriage," *New Republic,* 6 May 1996, p. 14.

11. Andrew J. Cherlin, *Marriage, Divorce, Remarriage* (Cambridge: Harvard University Press, 1981), p. 49.

12. Maggie Gallagher, *The Abolition of Marriage: How We Destroy Lasting Love* (Washington, D.C.: Regnery, 1996), p. 143.

13. Barbara Dafoe Whitehead, "End No-Fault Divorce?" *First Things,* August/September 1994, pp. 24–30.

14. Melinda Ledden Sidak, "Not at My Table," *Women's Quarterly* (Fall 1997), p. 13.

15. Christina Del Valle, "Marriage Is Back: Want to Be Hip? Stay Together," *Newsweek,* 21 October 1997, p. B15.

CHAPTER 9: LESSONS FROM A STARTER MARRIAGE

1. David Blankenhorn, Steve Bayme, and Jean Bethke Elshtain, eds. *Rebuilding the Nest: A New Commitment to the American Family* (Milwaukee, Wisc.: Family Service America, 1990), pp. 97–98.

2. Matthew D. Bramlett and William D. Mosher, "First Marriage Dissolution, Divorce and Remarriage: United States," advance data, 31 May 2001, Centers for Disease Control and Prevention.

3. Andrew J. Cherlin, *Marriage, Divorce, Remarriage,* Rev. and Enl. Ed. (Cambridge: Harvard University Press, 1992), p. 27.

4. Walter Kirn and Wendy Cole, "Twice as Nice," *Time,* 19 June 2000, p. 53.

5. Cherlin, *Marriage, Divorce, Remarriage*, p. 29.

6. Dalma Heyn, *Marriage Shock: The Transformation of Women into Wives* (New York: Delta Books, 1997), p. xii.

7. Kirn and Cole, "Twice as Nice."

8. Hara Estroff Marano, "Divorced: Don't Even Think of Remarrying Until You Read This," *Psychology Today*, March/April 2000, p. 57.

9. For a good explanation about the relative instability of second marriages, see Teresa Castro Martin and Larry L. Bumpass, "Recent Trends in Marital Disruption," *Demography* 26, no. 1 (February 1989): p. 37.

10. Barbara Ehrenerich, "Why It Might Be Worth It (to Have an Affair)," in Deborah Chasman and Catherine Jhee, eds., *Here Lies My Heart: Essays on Why We Marry, Why We Don't, and What We Find There* (Boston: Beacon Press, 1999), p. 8.

11. Laura Gree, "And the Case Against," *Mirabella*, March 2000, p. 91.

12. Nancy Mairs, "Here: Grace," in Chasman and Jhee, *Here Lies My Heart*, p. 124.

13. Peggy Orenstein, *Flux: Women on Sex, Work, Love, Kids, and Life in a Half-Changed World* (New York: Doubleday, 2000), p. 101.

14. Aaron Gell, "Better Off Wed," *Mirabella*, April 2000.

15. Margy Rochlin, "A Berkeley Brat, Seeking Structure," *New York Times*, 23 April 2000, Arts and Leisure section, p. 11.

16. Cokie Roberts and Steven R. Roberts, *From This Day Forward* (New York: William Morrow, 2000), p. 35, 125.

17. Barbara Ehrenreich, "Why It Might Be Worth It," p. 8.

CHAPTER 10: THE POLITICS OF MARRIAGE

1. Lynn Darling, "For Better and Worse," in Deborah Chasman and Catherine Jhee, eds., *Here Lies My Heart: Essays on Why We Marry, Why We Don't, and What We Find There* (Boston: Beacon Press, 1999), p. 180.

2. Ira Matathia and Marian Salzman, *Next: Trends for the Near Future* (New York: Overlook Press, 1999), p. 224.

3. E. J. Graff, *What Is Marriage For?* (Boston: Beacon Press, 1999), p. 45.

4. Katha Pollitt, "Healthy, Wealthy, and Wise," in Chasman and Jhee, *Here Lies My Heart*, p. 3.

5. Frank F. Furstenberg, Jr., "The Future of Marriage," *American Demographics*, June 1996, p. 34.

6. Barbara Dafoe Whitehead, "The Plight of the High-Status Woman," *Atlantic Monthly*, December 1999, p. 120.

7. Maggie Gallagher, *The Abolition of Marriage: How We Destroy Lasting Love* (Washington D.C.: Regnery, 1996), p. 7.

8. National Opinion Research Center, 1999.

9. U.S. Bureau of the Census, *Current Population Reports*, Series P20-514, "Marital Status and Living Arrangements" (Washington D.C.: U.S. Government Printing Office), March 1998 Update.

10. Karen S. Peterson, "The Matrimony Manifesto," *USA Today*, 29 June 2000, p. 9D.

11. Maggie Gallagher, "Marriage-Saving: A Movement for Matrimony," *National Review*, 8 November 1999, p. 38.

12. Yvonne Zipp, "Wisconsin Hires A Marriage Counselor," *Christian Science Monitor*, 16 November 1999, p. 1.

13. Pam Belluck, "States Declare War on Divorce Rates, Before Any 'I Dos,' " *New York Times*, 24 April 2000, p. A1.

14. Zipp, "Wisconsin Hires a Marriage Counselor."

15. Belluck, "States Declare War."

16. William G. Gale, "Don't Toss Out the Baby with Reform," *Los Angeles Times*, 14 April 1998, p. 7.

17. Ronald G. Shafer, "Washington Wire," *Wall Street Journal*, 2 February 2001, p. A1.

18. Gertrude Himmelfarb, *One Nation, Two Cultures: A Searching Examination of American Society in the Aftermath of Our Cultural Revolution* (New York: Knopf, 2000), p. 77.

19. Leon Kass, "The End of Courtship," *Public Interest* 126 (Winter 1997): p. 63.

20. Danielle Crittenden, *What Our Mothers Didn't Tell Us* (New York: Simon & Schuster, 1999), pp. 41–42.

21. Gallagher, *Abolition of Marriage*, p. 141.

22. Jennifer Pozner, "Is Early Marriage the Best Choice for American Women?" *Insight on the News* 15, no. 7 (22 February 1999), p. 24.

23. Danielle Crittenden, "The Next Advance for Women: Early Marriage and Motherhood," *New York Post*, 8 January 1999, p. 029.

24. Melinda Ledden Sidak, "Not at My Table," *Women's Quarterly*, Fall 1997, p. 13.

25. "Teen Moms," *Wall Street Journal*, 8 May 1998, p. A14.

26. Jennifer Frey, "Feminism's Unblushing Bride," *Washington Post*, 7 September 2000, p. C1.

27. Cathy Young, *Ceasefire! Why Women and Men Must Join Forces to Achieve True Equality* (New York: Free Press, 1999), p. 253.

28. Karen S. Peterson, "Courtship Flirts with a Comeback," *USA Today*, 27 September 2000, p. 9D.

29. Wendy Shalit, *A Return to Modesty: Rediscovering the Lost Virtue* (New York: Free Press, 1999), p. 141.

30. Whitehead, "High-Status Woman."

31. Crittenden, *What Our Mothers Didn't Tell Us*, p. 42.

32. Ibid.

33. Matthew D. Bramlett and William D. Mosher, "First Marriage Dissolution, Divorce, and Remarriage: United States," advance data, 31 May 2001, Centers for Disease Control and Prevention.

34. Teresa Castro Martin and Larry L. Bumpass, "Recent Trends in Marital Disruption," *Demography* 26, no. 1 (February 1989), p. 41.

35. Ibid., p. 42.

36. Megan Fitzmorris McCafferty, "When Should You Marry," *Cosmopolitan*, August 1999, p. 238.

37. Celeste Perron, "I Was Divorced by 25," *Cosmopolitan*, March 2000, p. 260.

38. David Popenoe and Barbara Dafoe Whitehead, "The State of Our Unions: The Social Health of Marriage in America," National Marriage Project, 2000, p. 23.

39. Stephanie Coontz, *The Way We Really Are: Coming to Terms with America's Changing Families* (New York: Basic Books, 1997), p. 82.

40. Crittenden, *What Our Mothers Didn't Tell Us,* p. 74.

41. "The Perils of Modern Womanhood with Author Danielle Crittenden," WashingtonPost.com, 5 July 2000.

42. Crittenden, *What Our Mothers Didn't Tell Us,* p. 173.

43. Gallagher, *The Abolition of Marriage,* p. 31.

44. Barbara Dafoe Whitehead, "Dan Quayle Was Right," *Atlantic Monthly*, April 1993, p. 47.

45. Bryanna Hocking, "Interview with Lionel Tiger on His New Book, *The Decline of Males*," *The Guide*, January 2000.

46. Gallagher, *The Abolition of Marriage,* p. 131.

47. Elaine Tyler May, *Homeward Bound: American Families in the Cold War Era,* rev. ed., (New York: Basic Books, 1999), p. 207.

48. Fox News, 30 November 2000.

49. Gallagher, *The Abolition of Marriage,* p. 240.

CONCLUSION: MARRIAGE IN THE NEW MILLENNIUM

1. Karen Springen, "Feeling the 50-Year Itch," *Newsweek*, 4 December 2000, p. 56.

2. Joseph F. Coates, "What's Ahead for Families," World Future Society, 1996.

3. Barbara Ehrenreich, "Will Women Still Need Men?" *Time,* Visions 21 issue, 21 February 2000, p. 62.

4. Lynn Darling, "For Better and Worse," in Deborah Chasman and Catherine Jhee, eds., *Here Lies My Heart: Essays on Why We Marry, Why We Don't, and What We Find There* (Boston: Beacon Press, 1999), p. 200.

5. Ira Matathia and Marian Salzman, *Next: Trends for the Near Future* (New York: Overlook Press, 1999), p. 394.

6. Ibid., p. 396.

7. "Marriage Will Be Multiple in the New Millennium," *Insight on the News*, 13 December 1999, p. 30.

8. Peter Godwin, "Happily Ever After," *New York Times,* 25 July 1999, section 6, p. 13.

9. Cheryl Wetzstein and Matthew Katz, "Further Erosion of Marriage Is Expected After Millennium," *Insight on the News*, 1 February 1999, p. 42.

10. "Will Marriage Still Be Desirable?" Reuters/Zogby, 21 June 2000.

11. The Report Reports 2000 Annual Presentation, Roper Starch Worldwide.

12. Gerald F. Seib, "In Real America 'Character' Line Points Upward," *Wall Street Journal*, 9 September 1998, p. A24.

13. Helene Stapinski, "Y Not Love?" *American Demographics*, February 1999, p. 63.

14. Anne Jarrell, "The Face of Teenage Sex Grows Younger," *New York Times*, 2 April 2000, section 9, p. 1.

15. Eric Nagourney, "Study Finds Families Bypassing Marriage," *New York Times*, 15 February 2000, section F, p. 8.

16. Barbara Dafoe Whitehead, "Dan Quayle Was Right," *Atlantic Monthly*, April 1993, p. 47.

17. *Monitoring the Future*, University of Michigan, Senior Class 1999, 12th Form 3.

18. Monitoring the Future Surveys conducted by the Survey Research Center at the University of Michigan, 1998.

19. Matathia and Salzman, *Next*, p. 398.

20. Sharon Begley, "A World of Their Own," *Newsweek*, 8 May 2000, p. 52.

21. E. J. Graff, *What Is Marriage For?* (Boston: Beacon Press, 1999), p. 98.

22. Louis Harris and Associates and Families and the Work Institute for the Whirlpool Foundation, 1995.

23. 1999 *Yankelovich Monitor*, Table 124.

24. Sara Terry, "The Unexpected Consequences of 'Living Together,'" *Christian Science Monitor*, 10 April 2000, p. 1.

25. Gertrude Himmelfarb, *One Nation, Two Cultures: A Searching Examination of American Society in the Aftermath of Our Cultural Revolution* (New York: Knopf, 2000), p. 51.

26. Cheryl Russell, "The Rorschach Test," *American Demographics*, January 1997, p. 10.

27. Terry, "Unexpected Consequences."

28. Barbara Ehrenreich, "Why It Might Be Worth It (to Have an Affair)," in Chasman and Jhee, *Here Lies My Heart*, p. 8.

29. Francine Russo, "Can the Government Prevent Divorce?" *Atlantic Monthly*, October 1997, p. 228.

30. Barbara Dafoe Whitehead, "End No-Fault Divorce?" *First Things*, August/September 1994, pp. 24–30.

Index